INDIA TO AVALON

INDIA TO
AVALON

A MEMOIR

Cathy Whitefield

India to Avalon
Cathy Whitefield

Published by Aspect Design 2014
Malvern, Worcestershire, United Kingdom.

Designed, printed and bound by Aspect Design
89 Newtown Road, Malvern, Worcs. WR14 1PD
United Kingdom
Tel: 01684 561567
E-mail: allan@aspect-design.net
Website: www.aspect-design.net

ISBN 978-1-908832-52-8

To Patrick without whose support this
book never would have been completed.

Contents

Acknowledgments

Many thanks to Patrick for his inspiration and editing; to Ange for her proof reading and editorial help; Michel, for help with the cover; to Lisa for being such a great friend; and to all my other supportive and inspirational friends, teachers and travellers along the path.

Part One: India

Formentera, 1968

We took the afternoon ferry from Ibiza and walked along the only tarmac road on Formentera towards the village of San Francisco. We'd heard there was a bar there where hippies hung out and we'd be able to find where it was cool to sleep. At the bar we met Juan, a young, dark, curly haired Spanish guy, who said he'd walk with us to a beach where we could camp. He carried our rucksacks on his bike which he wheeled all the way, while looking appreciatively at Suzie's blond curls and slender legs.

The land was parched and rocky, dotted with twisting pines, scrubby rosemary and wild asparagus. Around the flat roofed white houses were glowing geraniums, succulent vines, cane tripods of sun baked tomatoes and purple aubergines. We took a rough track down towards the sea. The sun was setting and the air musky and dry with the scent of pine. My feet felt at home and excited on this warm sandy earth. We walked through a group of white-washed *casitas*, small one storey peasant houses, towards a little pine wood on the edge of the beach. There Juan helped us set up camp. A sleeping bag, rucksack and a few discarded clothes lay around. A sun-faded towel hung from a branch and a box of food lay beside the remains of a wood fire in a circle of stones.

'Is OK,' said Juan as we looked questioningly around, 'I know the one who lives here. English—Graham. You like him. Cool man!' We unrolled our sleeping bags and took a few belongings out of our rucksacks while Juan started to make a fire from bits of driftwood. He collected a container of water from a tap behind the *casitas* and put on a battered kettle. I ran down to the beach and walked the frilly edge of the soft sun-warmed water. The sky was beginning to turn gold and I could hardly believe that we'd landed in such a paradise after the heavy grey of London.

When I returned to camp Juan was getting bread and cheese out of his knapsack. We added travel bruised fruit, nuts and melted chocolate. My fingers were sticky, my lips salty, and this felt like the home I had always been looking for. Dusk fell like a sudden indigo cloak under the vast sky of waking stars and we dropped into awed silence. That's how it all began, the adventure which led me to India and changed my life in ways I couldn't have imagined. It was as if that island, which had been known as the island of witches, cast its magic spell on me.

The following night Graham appeared. A stocky Irish man with matted reddish hair in tatty torn off jeans, who laughed and talked to himself and anyone who would listen. He was a traveller in his thirties, a joint-rolling story teller. Juan stayed, as if he belonged with us. He sidled up to Suzie at night and she flirted with him happily through the day. This was our base camp family of four.

A few days later I saw a figure strolling along the dunes at sunset. He was tall and graceful, bare chested and wearing cotton Indian trousers. As he walked he paused and played a wooden flute, as if communicating with the sun. A mongrel dog danced at his heels. I watched him from the shelter of our pine shaded camp and my mouth went dry. He was a hundred yards away and I felt as though I knew him and loved him. 'Who's that?' I asked Graham, who was sitting with me, idly beating a Moroccan drum.

'Oh that's a German guy. Keeps himself to himself. I think he might be studying something. Lives in that little white *casita* just up there, on the edge of the dunes.'

'Is that his dog? It looks sweet.'

'Yes that's Hobbit. He attached himself to Johann as soon as he arrived— must be over three weeks now—and they always walk around together. Nice guy, not a great party goer but he plays guitar, and sings a lot of Donovan round the fire.'

'Sounds interesting,' I said lightly, looking away.

We were invited to our first Formentera party. It was full moon. Graham showed us the way across flat sheep dotted fields until we reached an ochre track that ran towards the south of the island. 'This whole place is only about ten miles long and five miles wide,' said Graham. We made our way past a group of derelict looking farmhouses surrounded by a few olive and fig trees, sweet scented in the afternoon sun. 'Very different scene from Ibiza,' he said. 'Most serious travellers seem to end up here. Lots have already been east and come for a break before going farther north or back to America. Suddenly, being twenty two and fresh from London no longer so seemed hip.

We walked into a shadowy room in the rambling stone farmhouse where the party was being held. A circle of wild looking hippies sat amidst a haze of smoke and the sweet, dark smell of hashish. I suddenly wished that I wasn't wearing my cut off white Victorian nightdress. At least I'm with Graham, I thought, and he looks pretty hip. The air was thick with sweat and drums. We sat down and I was passed a smouldering chillum. I'd smoked hash plenty of times before but never with one of these. I passed it to Graham whispering, 'How do you use this thing?'

'Watch me,' he replied. It was a conical pipe, with a small hole in the thin end at the bottom and a burning mix of tobacco and hash in the thick end at the top. He held it upright, cupping both hands round the narrow bottom, drew it up above his head, tilted his head back and inhaled deeply through the hole he made between his hands. 'Easy' he smiled thickly, pupils dilating. I followed his example and immediately started coughing. I felt as if all eyes were on me, but looking up only met blank stares or friendly looks from across the room. Suddenly the drums seemed louder and more frenetic. I inhaled again and the world flipped into a different gear. I didn't care what anyone thought any more. Girls in long cotton dresses started swaying to the beat. Soon I was up dancing with them, dissolving into an ancient tribal rhythm in that stark, shadowy room.

Half an hour later I sat down dripping with sweat. The drummers were still beating a furious rhythm while the others repeatedly passed round pipes and joints. Hardly anyone seemed to be talking, but communicating in long deep stares or sudden bursts of laughter. I sat quietly watching, not daring to start a conversation. I watched the drummers. With their long matted hair and bits of cloth draped around their loins, I felt I was looking at a group of bizarre holy men in India. I was staring at a particularly beautiful 'holy man' with blond hair and a saffron loincloth when he suddenly looked directly into my eyes and gave me a dazzling smile. I had the sensation that he was bouncing a great ball of joy over towards me. Perhaps these people have really got something special, I thought, or maybe it's just the dope. Certainly the guy with the smile had power. I'd never felt energy like that before. He must be Swedish, I thought, something about his blond good looks . . .

And I'm back there in Sweden, five years old, waiting at a country bus stop for my stepfather who doesn't arrive day after day. We have no telephone and my mother doesn't know what's happened to him. As we walk back to our wooden summer house in a sad crocodile, my mother is weeping. He's supposed to meet us there where we're holidaying by the sea.

Finally he arrives, several days late. I remember sitting on a rock, suddenly aware of my nakedness as he looks at me strangely. Then I'm in that dimly lit room with furniture covered with dust sheets and something frightening's going on. He tells me it's a secret between us. I want to run or scream but no sound comes out and my heart is beating in my ears. I'm feeling sick. I've got to get out of that five year old room.

I got up and wobbled through the bodies and gasped in the warm evening air outside. I held onto a dry stone wall as my heart began to slow down. I breathed deeply and watched the sun setting in a great display of apricot and crimson, gilding the vines which covered the veranda. Thank God I'm here in Formentera, I thought, away from all that.

I lay down on the veranda, my thin shawl under me. The sun had become a rich red orb. Drum beats washed over me. I gazed at the pattern of vines above my head, a shelter of green, patterned with dark maroon bunches of grapes, dusted with filmy white. Dusk fell fast. I drifted off until I was aware of a presence beside me. I opened my eyes slowly. It was the 'Swedish' man looking down on me.

'Hi,' he smiled. 'It's hot in there isn't it?'

'Yes. I needed a break.' I sat up. The moon was just rising. 'It's beautiful out here. I was feeling weird. That drumming gets pretty intense.'

'Yes the drumming. It'll go on all night—full moon. You just arrived?' He picked a bunch of grapes and handed me few.

'Thanks. Yes, I just arrived. I was in London couple of days ago. I've been in some crazy scenes there but not like this. I think the heat makes it all seem more . . . surreal.' My hands were wet with grape juice and sweat. How could a man be so beautiful?

'You'll get used to it.' He gave me a knowing smile and wiped his hands and face casually with the edge of his loin cloth. 'Gets dark really quickly here.' He turned and walked down the steps towards the sea. 'See you.' He flashed me that smile and strolled off in the direction of the beach. I sat looking after him in the growing dusk, the sticky grapes in my hand.

Inside again, Graham was drumming an African beat with several others. The group was smaller, and a garlicky, spicy smell wafted in from behind the house. In the darkness men were heaving lumps of wood onto a fire while several bare breasted women were kneeling and sitting cross legged on the ground cutting up vegetables by candlelight. At the edge of the fire a young man with Jimi Hendrix hair was stirring a wok. Next to it, on a metal rack supported by bricks, was a huge blackened pot bubbling with grain.

I went towards a motherly woman wearing a purple sarong. She smiled at me and I asked her if there was anything I could do. She pointed to a battered esparto grass basket on the ground near her, filled with melons, figs bananas and grapes. 'You could make a fruit salad,' she said. I didn't bother asking for a bowl, but found my way into the kitchen. It was dimly lit by a couple of oil lamps hanging from the dark-beamed, cobwebby ceiling. Pale blue patterned bowls decorated the walls. Thick sooty pots hung from butchers hooks, and stacks of chipped terracotta plates and serving bowls filled the dusty shelves.

I sat outside, chopping fruit on a scarred wooden board as the cicadas sang and dusk enfolded me. It was becoming cooler and the drumming had subsided. A young woman wearing only a man's shirt handed round plates of food. Graham came and sat with me silently as we ate. The beautiful man smiled at me from across the fire and I could hear that familiar slightly

Swedish accent my mother had. I watched the flames as we ate meditatively in small groups. I was lying on my back gazing at the indigo sky when a thin feathery looking guy appeared, asking us in a heavy American drawl if we'd like some best quality acid from California.

'My first trip on this stuff got me out of college,' he laughed. 'The next couple of trips opened my eyes and I headed for India. It's the best, really pure, takes you direct to paradise.' He laughed again. Graham looked at me questioningly. I shook my head.

'Maybe some other time. Cathy's new here and just getting used to the dope.'

'I had a couple of bad trips in London, so I'm going to be careful next time.' I smiled at the dealer, who was looking at me as if he could penetrate my soul.

'That's cool,' he said. 'Any time you wanna change your mind, Graham knows where I hang out.' He did a mock bow and sauntered over to the next group. I wanted to go home. Home being my sleeping bag in the sandy dell.

'We'll take the coastal route,' said Graham taking my hand in the dark. His feet seemed to read the bleached rocks like a goat's. The sky was huge, like a dark lapis shawl sprinkled with thousands of stars. I felt at one with these rocks glowing in the eerie blue light. I was walking on the bones of the Earth, touched by her being, my body caressed by the spirit of breezes and starlight, feeling like one of those Tibetan trance walkers who can fix their gaze on a star and travel hundreds of miles at an incredible speed, never looking at the terrain. I found myself leaping along the rocks ahead of Graham, drinking in the warm salt taste of the sea, feeling so high and free. Then I lost my footing and stumbled to the ground.

'You were going too fast,' he said pulling me up gently. I didn't try to explain. I'd always tried to go too fast for my delicate physical body.

Back in our little hollow encampment the resinous scent of pines mingled with the burnt wood smoke residue. Suzie was already there, curled up asleep with Juan by the dying embers. I snuggled into my bag near them. Graham moved his sleeping bag purposefully close, his arm reaching out to stroke my hair. 'Just friends,' I said sleepily. The shadowy, graceful image of the dark German guy I'd seen a few days before lulled me to sleep.

'OK, we'll see what's meant to be,' Graham muttered, rolling over onto his side.

I woke up in the night after dreaming about someone offering me an acid trip. I lay awake and watched the moon.

I'm nineteen and with Mike at a party in a huge house in West Hampstead. He's the only person there I know. A girl hands me a bit of pink blotting paper and we tear it in half and swallow half each. Then we sit there waiting. 'I can't feel anything much happening,' I say, taking Mike's hand.

'Don't worry, it will. This is the strongest stuff around. It just takes a while.' Everyone is sitting around expectantly, chatting, eating nuts and crisps, listening to Ray Charles on the record player. I go upstairs to have a look around the house and end up in a bedroom. Suddenly it's happening. The wallpaper is rolling around like it's corrugated, and covered with myriad drops of rainbow colour, the candlewick bedspread becomes exquisite with intricate textures and patterns. The chairs come alive, the wood moving and swirling, the floor heaving. It's like being in a Van Gogh painting. I feel elated. I see an orange, on the chest beside the bed. It takes my breath away. It shimmers like a golden sun. I sit on the bed gazing at it. I've discovered the meaning of the universe! Time no longer exists. But I need a pee. The loo is just along the corridor. I sit in there enjoying the dancing colours of the wall paper—great swirls of light rippling up and down in iridescent waves, a shimmering curtain of jewels. But suddenly the walls have decided to close in on me. Now I'm sure I'm locked in. I sit like a rabbit frozen by headlights in the middle of a dark road. I hear a thread-like voice coming from the distance calling, 'Mike I'm locked in! Mike help!' I sit there while the walls leap around me and my heart pounds. An eternity of fear. Finally I know that I have to get up. I stagger to the door. I'm surprised when the latch opens easily and I step out into the corridor. Shakily I make my way down the stairs. The lounge looks like a huge stage set with all these people in strange costumes, talking and acting, pretending to be characters who they think they are. Why are they all parodying themselves?

I find Mike sitting silently with a few others. 'Where have you been?' His voice seems distant. 'You've been gone an eternity.' He takes my hand. His hand feels warm and comforting, but alien.

'I think I'm having a bad trip. I want to go home. Please take me home.'

'How can I take you? We can't get on buses like this and it's much too far to walk. Anyhow I want to stay. Just relax, relax and listen to the music.'

I sit in a squashy armchair and listen to the most poignant music I've ever heard. Billie Holliday is singing just for me. I dissolve into the roots of soul. I know she understands all humanity's sadness and yet she can sing about it. This seems to be the key to life, to know the beauty and the suffering and to be able to continue singing. Her voice becomes my only reality. I dissolve into peace.

The breath of waves and the memory of that haunting voice lulled me back into a deep sleep and I didn't wake until eleven with the sun high, shining through the twisted pines. 'No sign of Suzie,' I said to Graham's tousled form, 'or Juan.'

'She's probably gone to Ibiza for the day. Juan's been showing her around.' Graham was pulling on his tatty shorts. 'Lets go to the Blue Bar. There's no food around here.' He seemed grumpy and impatient. Some locals had got wise to the influx of hippies and built The Blue Bar, a wooden shack perched on top of the dunes overlooking the sea. It had a makeshift cane shade outside, decorated with pieces of driftwood. 'They make a mean tortilla,' Graham told me. 'That with coffee and tostada with olive oil and tomato topping is the full breakfast menu.'

I went for a swim, enjoying the clear turquoise water and when I got to the bar Graham had already eaten. He was sitting with an empty coffee cup, reading, with his back to the sun. There were a few other bedraggled travellers sitting around another table, laughing and smoking over cups of coffee. I ordered a tortilla and cappuccino. I ate slowly, watching the calming patterns of sun dancing on the sea while Graham rolled another cigarette.

'You wanna visit some friends of mine?' he asked as he stuffed his paperback *Siddhartha* into his back pocket. 'They've lived here the last three years doing crafts. Got a sweet little daughter too.'

'Yes, I'd love to meet people who live here all the time,' I replied enthusiastically, wiping up the last of the olive oil with my remaining chunk of bread.

We walked up the path from the sea to Jacquie and Volker's place. It was a simple whitewashed stone house guarded by a couple of gnarled fig trees. They'd constructed an outdoor living and work space in a lean-to against the house, shaded by vines. Jacquie was working on an industrial sewing machine, stitching long pieces of fine soft leather. Volker was cutting what looked like moccasin shapes with a craft knife. Sky came running out to greet us, a naked blond curly haired girl of about seven with bright blue eyes.

We were sitting drinking chai, chatting and listening to a tape of Indian music when a dog bounced into the room. He looked familiar. He was followed by the German guy I'd seen walking along the shore. I felt that adrenalin rush. Volker introduced him as his friend from their university days and me as a new escapee from London. Johann took my left hand in an informal handshake.

'So you come from the heart of swinging sixties?' he said.

'Yes, I was working as a children's nanny there, but I don't like being in the city—although I went to some great concerts before I left. I love sunshine and the sea . . . That's why I came here'. I heard my own nervousness and looked around for distraction.

Johann and Volker started bantering with each other in German, while Jacquie showed Graham and me the leather bags and shoes she was making. As she put on a blackened kettle in the half partitioned room I glanced at Johann. Smooth dark shoulder length hair, fine almost sculpted features, intelligent smiling bear-brown eyes, long legged and loose limbed, wearing a white Indian shirt.

'Would you like me to show you the rest of the house?' asked Jacquie when we saw Volker start rolling a joint.

'I'll show her.' Sky skipped towards me and put out her tiny plump hand enthusiastically. I took it gratefully and she led me across the room.

'I'll be up in a minute,' said Jacquie as Sky pulled me towards the tiled stairs. I felt dazed as my bare feet touched the cool steps. A few days before I had been in London and now I was in another world, close to a man who was making my senses lurch. Sky led me into a dim room, its shutters half closed against the sun. The walls were covered with Jacquie's vibrant landscapes, the floor with old Moroccan rugs. Jacquie joined us, chatting easily, but I was distracted. I looked into her mosaic decorated mirror and saw my eyes startled and vibrantly blue against my new suntan, my dark hair wild and curly from the sea. Could he love me? I looked quickly away and tried to catch the gist of what Jacquie was saying. 'Once they get together they're like a couple of schoolboys talking secretly in the back of the class,' she said laughing apologetically as we walked down to the kitchen. I felt she was lonely for a woman friend.

'They seem really nice,' I replied hesitantly.

'Yes they're both interesting guys, creative and intelligent and don't smoke too much dope when they're together. Sometimes Volker drives me mad with his smoking.'

'Yes, smoking too much really changes people,' I replied looking around at the shelves filled with glass jars of dried beans and different herbs. 'You collect herbs then,' I said admiringly. 'I'd love to know more about the local plants.' She reached into several jars and put a few handfuls of leaves into a glass jug, where they expanded like Chinese paper flowers as she added boiling water.

'I'll teach you if you come around another day. We can go and collect wild sage and rosemary. I want to dry some more before winter.' She put five chipped ceramic beakers onto a wooden tray with the jug of tea, and we walked back into the sitting area. The men were joking about an old local man whose mule kept escaping and trying to graze in Volker and Jacqui's vegetable patch. I watched and listened, imagining living here, collecting herbs, growing vegetables and partying in the sun. Bob Dylan was droning 'All I really want to do-o is baby be friends with you,' longingly in the background as we drank herb tea sweetened with wild flower honey. Graham passed round another joint.

'I need to go now,' Graham grumbled, after we'd drunk our tea. 'I've got some work to do today.' The joint was finished and he'd begun to look restless. 'Are you coming Cathy?'

'Yes, sure,' I replied. 'It's been good to meet you all.' I reluctantly put on my sandals. Jacquie gave me kisses on both cheeks.

'Are you staying on the island for a while?' asked Volker, aware that he'd paid me little attention. 'You must come again.'

'We're going to collect herbs together.' Jacquie smiled standing beside him.

'Good. Then we will see you again soon.' He gave me a warm crinkly smile.

'Glad to meet you,' said Johann stepping forward lightly, to give me a Spanish double sided kiss. A cheek dusting kiss which lit a fire all through me.

'What's the business so suddenly?' I asked as we walked along the beach.

'Oh I do a bit of wheeling and dealing, buying and selling. I'm selling Moroccan rugs and ceramics in Alicante through a friend who lives there. I've got to catch the ferry to go and meet him. Then I've got to make a quick trip to Marrakesh. I'm glad you liked my friends. They're good people.'

'Yeah, they seem to have found a good way of living.'

'They just rent that place from the local farmer. It's really cheap here.' I had visions of myself finding a little place to rent and staying forever. 'Look at this shell.' He stooped to pick up a tiny pink shell, like a fragile jewel in his large thick hand. 'For you.' He handed it to me, giving me a deep questioning look. 'You really like that Johann don't you?' I looked out over the sea, feeling my face burning.

'I didn't think you'd noticed.'

'I don't miss much, even though I may look thick skinned.'

'He's . . . He seems so familiar. It's strange but I feel as if I've always known him,' I said, trying to soften any comparison. We walked back to the camp in silence.

Suzie was lying reading under the pine trees when we got back. Graham packed his rucksack and said good bye. 'Graham really fancies you, you know,' Suzie told me eagerly once he'd gone.

'I know, and he's a really nice guy, but I just don't fancy him. It's a shame, because he's the only man I'm really getting to know but I'm just not attracted to him.'

'Well I'm gonna be with the man I really fancy tonight. We spent the morning down in the San Francisco bar and I love the warm open way he is with everyone. We met lots of his friends.' She gave me her mischievous smile. 'There's going to be a gathering with a fire and shared food later, around that little group of houses just off the beach on the way to the road.'

She was pulling a filmy shirt over her tiny bikini. 'Juan will be there. He's so physical, not at all like my English boyfriends. He's lovely.'

'He seems pretty cool.' I was shaking sand out of my beach sarong.

'Yeah. He invited us both. You will come won't you?'

Suddenly I felt completely exhausted, a familiar exhaustion that fell over me like a blanket. 'I've got no food to share,' I said, looking around the 'kitchen'—two empty boxes, a single camping gas burner and a pile of tatty camping crocks. 'And I'm really tired.'

'Don't worry. Juan and I bought lots of veggies today. We'll make a big ratatouille together. Have a siesta and you'll feel better. Then we could go along the beach and collect some drift wood when it's a bit cooler and see how you feel after.'

It was velvety dark and smelt strongly of wood smoke as we walked through the twisting pines towards the clearing between three little white houses. We could see a blazing fire with figures silhouetted against the flames. Juan was already frying onions and garlic in a blackened frying pan. 'I make food for all,' he smiled and handed us a bag of vegetables. Suzie and I sat next to each other and started chopping. I was beginning to feel envious of how simple it had turned out for her.

'You know that guy with the dog, Johann, the one we saw when we first arrived?'

'Of course,' she smiled.

'I feel really drawn to him. We met at this couple's place today. Graham took me there. But we've hardly talked yet. I thought he might be here tonight.'

'He's lovely. He's probably up in his *casita* now. Why don't you go and invite him down?'

'Oh, I don't really know him well enough. I only met him this morning, to talk to,' I said, busying myself with chopping peppers and wishing I hadn't mentioned him.

Suzie handed Juan my chopped vegetables. 'Well it's up to you.'

After the meal the musicians got out their instruments and started playing. Johann appeared, walking into the light of the fire, carrying his flute. He gave me a quick smile, sat behind the drummers opposite and started to improvise a tune on the flute. The flames made golden patterns against the sky as we all improvised together until at last the food was ready. Joints were passed around and travellers' stories told. When he wasn't playing music Johann had a warm contained and centred energy about him, while my nervous over-sensitive nature made me feel too shy to speak. Slowly the music faded, the fire died down and I crept away to sleep.

A couple of weeks later Suzie and I cycled to a gathering in the north of the island. I hadn't seen Johann since the evening of the fire and was beginning to think that I'd invented the whole special connection thing. 'I'm sure he doesn't feel it anyway,' I confided to Suzie as we pedalled slowly up the only hill on the island. The gathering was in a converted farmhouse on a high coastal path near the lighthouse, home of some friends of Juan's.

'Where's Graham?' asked Rosa Maria, our hostess, when we introduced ourselves.

'I'm a bit worried about him,' I answered. 'He said he'd only be a week visiting Marrakesh and now it's almost two.'

'Don't worry,' she replied. 'He's always a bit unpredictable. He'll be back in his own time. Come and meet the crowd.' A group of hippies and artists were sitting in the moon shaped walled garden, which was scattered with strange sculptures and ringed with vivid red geraniums and deep purple bougainvillea. Rosa Maria passed around a tray of iced lime and slices of succulent red watermelon, followed by a series of joints. Someone put on the Beatles' 'Here Comes the Sun', and I leaned back on an old wicker chaise longue, watching wisps of cloud drift across the blue Mediterranean sky. When I came back to earth several people had stripped off, and I watched fascinated as breasts became laced with spirals and serpents and torsos started undulating with dragons and trees.

'You want a turn?' asked a dark El Greco face.

'No. I'm not good at painting, and anyway I'm too stoned. But you can paint me if you like'. He looked too interesting to refuse.

'You like to lie in shade? I am artist, so I make you look very beautiful.' I took my top off under the old carob tree and sat shyly, trying desperately not to be embarrassed by my small breasts.

'I cover you with sunflowers.' He was sitting close with a melting yellow wax stick. I sat very still as he circled each nipple with yellow and started drawing the petals coming out from the centre. I was dampening as he coloured in the petals, his curls dusting my nipples.

'Now I make the leaves and stems in green,' he was looking provocatively serious. I started laughing. He smiled uncertainly. 'You think I am funny?'

'I think you're beautiful.' I ruffled his coarse Spanish curls.

'And you are too. I have never known an English girl.' He stroked my shoulders lightly looking into my eyes. 'Let me finish these leaves and then we go to show the others.' That hot afternoon I became Sunflower Woman and my new admirer became Snake Man.

It was too late to cycle back, so Rosa Maria said we could sleep on mattresses upstairs. I crept up there around midnight, while the others were still dancing, and fell straight to sleep. I woke up to find my back being gently caressed. I pretended to be sleeping while he continued exploring the edges of my breasts until it was impossible not to roll over and let him explore further.

The next morning he had disappeared before I woke. 'Didn't Snake Man stay for breakfast?' I asked the bleary Rosa Maria.

'Who?'

'You know, the Spanish guy I was body painting with yesterday.' I felt really foolish not even knowing his real name, thinking of Johann and wishing I hadn't got carried away.

'Oh you mean Nico. No, he had to get back to his animals. He left soon after you went to bed. Nice guy, but a bit of a Casanova. I hope you didn't fall for him'.

'Not really,' I said blushing. 'I just enjoyed his company.'

Suzie and I cycled home to our camp in the early afternoon. She was bubbly, looking forward to seeing Juan again that night, but I sat on a log staring at the cold fire pit, feeling empty and burnt out. It had all been so magical but now I felt a terrible sense of loss. Then I looked up and saw Johann and his little dog strolling through the pine trees, he smiled at me and said hello and I immediately felt better.

There was something dreamlike about the following weeks, living close to the sea, sunbathing, swimming, reading and writing poetry. Poetry had always been my solace and way of expressing myself ever since I was six, when I wrote my first poem: *Dobbin is my hobby horse. He loves to run and jump. He lives in the stable behind the pump.* I had longed to live in the country and have a horse. In the transparent island light I could see my childhood more clearly. The flat on the Great North Road where I was brought up seemed like a twilight life, full of nightmares of lorries running through my bedroom and the constant fear of my strange sexual and unpredictable stepfather, Terence. Through him my innocent happy nature became overcast and frozen. He collected miniature steam engines. Every corner of our small flat was crowded with them and my mother tried to hide their ugliness with pretty Swedish drapes.

My brother Robbie and I saw our father, Harold, at weekends. By the time I was eight he was remarried and within a few years they had their two sons, my half brothers.

I'm seven years old, on my brand new bike. Harold is holding the back of the saddle, running with me as I wobble along. I get up a little speed and he lets go. I'm alone, the cool air rushing against my skin, my little legs peddling as I yell, 'I can do it! I can do it!' I wobble and fall off. But Harold is there picking me up and we're off again. This is freedom!

I'm ten. Robbie and I are spending the weekend with Harold and my stepmother in Hampstead. My half brother Oliver has just been born. As I watch him in his little cot, he gazes at me and smiles. Love explodes in my chest and I lean over and take his tiny fingers. I know then that what I want most of all when I grow up is to have a baby.

Suzie now spent most of her time with Juan in San Francisco or Ibiza and I missed her companionship. Johann, my enigmatic German, was a constant presence but always distant, walking along the beach, or around the pine woods collecting firewood. Most days I'd eat in the Blue Bar and chat with anyone who happened to be there. Often I wondered what had happened to Graham. Most evenings I would sit with friends around the fire, eating, smoking dope and making music. Johann usually appeared, always a beautiful warm but unattainable presence. He seemed to look at me in that male, appreciative way but when we spoke it was as if we were skimming the surface of hidden depths which really united us. I felt I would follow him anywhere if he asked.

Johann, October 1968

Night-Scented Jasmine

Lady of the night
Your perfume colours my dreams
Softening my scarred broken places
With the scent of tenderness
Dona de la noche
You touch me like a secret lover
Wearing a white lace mantilla
On a sky cloaked in indigo
Bringing the fragrance of stars
To my verandah
Bringing sweetness
Back
To my heart

There was a feeling of excitement in the air as another full moon party came close. I had already been here over a month! I pulled out a long patterned Indian dress, shapely though slightly crumpled from my rucksack. I tried to unravel my tangled hair and put some kohl around my eyes, hoping that Johann would really notice me tonight.

'Watch out,' Suzie muttered as we arrived. 'There's the dreaded Snake Man.' Sure enough, there was Nico pouring drinks and charming everyone around him. I watched him take a pretty girl's hand in a mock chivalrous kiss. I hurried away before he could see me. We sat down on the edge of a verandah with the exotic perfume of night scented jasmine wafting around us. Suzie snuggled up to Juan while I talked to a vulnerable looking girl with torn-open eyes. We had the most bizarre conversation, until she offered me LSD on a tiny piece of blotting paper and I realised she was on acid. She called me Ultra Violet because of my matching eyes and dress. I refused the trip, and went off to explore the party and look for Johann. There were groups of exotic-looking hippies all around, many with distant eyes. Some of the girls were wearing impossibly short skirts and lots of black eye make up. Others were wearing long Indian dresses like mine and looked tanned, fresh and natural. The men mostly wore Indian gear. Some in lungis, long pieces of cloth worn like a skirt, others in loose cotton trousers and thin shirts. A few wore old cut off jeans and T-shirts.

I was drawn to a group dancing to the Rolling Stones' 'I Can't Get No Satisfaction' in the lamp-lit garden. One or two people I'd met on the beach or at the Blue Bar waved and greeted me. I started moving, letting the sounds take me and enjoying the sea taste of the night. Then I saw Johann walking out of the shadows with his familiar loose limbed walk, and by his side a beautiful girl, a tall willowy blonde I'd never seen before. Perhaps she's just a friend, I reasoned. Suddenly deflated, I left the dance patio to find somewhere to sit. I found a crooked pine tree overlooking the dancers and took out a cigarette

'You don't look too happy.' It was Jacquie. 'You must have just heard the news.' She sounded sad.

'No, what?'

'About Graham. We heard the other day that he's been busted.'

'Busted? I thought he traded in ceramics and rugs.'

'And dope,' Volker added miserably. 'Some friends of ours have just returned from Marrakesh with the news. He's in prison waiting for the trial, but at least he has a good lawyer. I'm going to visit him in a few days. Combine it with selling some leather stuff.' Volker was rolling a joint, sticking the skins together carefully with his square artisan's hands. He passed it to me and I inhaled gratefully.

'I'm glad you're going, I don't think I could get it together now,' I said feeling a pang of guilt at not even missing Graham any more. Looking up I saw Johann and the blond strolling towards us hand in hand. He gave me his sunny smile as he introduced her.

'Maya this is my friend Cathy, and you know the others. Maya's just arrived from the States.'

Maya smiled widely, saying 'Hi.' She looked like a model, perfectly proportioned and silky, making me feel like an unkempt gypsy. My smile felt like a grimace.

'It's a beautiful place isn't it?' She had a surprisingly harsh American drawl. I looked away swallowing.

'We've just told Cathy the news,' Jacquie put her arm around my back.

'Yes it's a bad scene isn't it? You got quite close to him when you first arrived,' Johann replied, trying to look me in the eye. 'Anyhow, we're on our way to get some food'. He took Maya's hand. 'See you later'. They disappeared into the moving mass of dancers. Soon after midnight I walked home with Jacquie and Volker. It was early hours for the party but they needed to get home for Sky, and seeing I was upset they invited me to their place for the night.

I spent most of the night sitting on the patio watching the moon. Seeing Johann with someone else had shocked me. It felt like a mistake, and my heart ached. I left at dawn, scribbling a note of thanks, and walked along the beach homewards. Paddling that fine line of froth which marks the passage of water to shore I did something I hadn't done since I was a child. I prayed. I prayed fiercely, trying to invoke the Divine in deep bursts of breath and movement. I found myself chanting out loud with my arms stretched towards the sea and sky.

'Dear God, Divine Infinite Spirit, if I am meant to be with Johann please bring him to me. Please bring him to me.'

Two days later the word reached our camp that some 'super freaks' had just flown in from California with some mescaline. Suzie had gone to stay with

Juan in Ibiza, so I went with a few other friends to meet these travellers in a communal house. I got butterflies in my stomach as I saw Johann arrive alone.

'You gotta have some of this,' they said. 'It's deep and gentle, mescalito, like nothing you've experienced before. You can have a contact with nature like you wouldn't dream of. Take it.' A bushy haired young man pushed a little bit of blotting paper into my hands. 'It's a gift.' I looked doubtfully across at Johann.

'Don't worry,' he said quietly. 'We'll take it together—It's not like LSD—much more gentle—there's nothing to fear.'

We started the trip walking amongst the trees in the small pine wood bordering the beach with the strong scent of pine resin mixed with an undertone of sand. The trees seemed like a group of gnarled old men. Some were kind and wise. Others, in our heightening state of consciousness, appeared frightening and twisted like grotesque trolls. As we walked towards the sea on the strange white lunar rocks Johann took my hand and my stomach contracted.

'What happened to Maya?' I couldn't relax until I knew.

'She left for Ibiza the day after the party. She was meeting her boyfriend there.'

'You looked like you'd really fallen for her at the party. I thought you two had got it together.'

'And she was just playing,' he sighed, 'Making me into a fool.' In his emotion his syntax went German. The colours of the landscape had begun intensifying, details sharpening like binoculars focusing. I felt a new space in my chest as I squeezed his hand.

'Look at that water.' I pointed to the shimmering sea. 'Those silver patterns dancing on the waves are amazing.'

'It's all becoming alive.' He smiled and fondled my hand gently. 'I'll forget her now. It was just a beautiful dream but this is real. Let's walk on those rocks.' He gestured towards an outcrop near the sea. We picked our way barefoot across rock worn down into sculpted shapes by centuries of moving water. We found a smooth flat surface of sand where we built piles of flat stones, each one smaller than the one below it, like little Tibetan chortens.

As we sat kneeling and building we looked at one another and smiled as if we were sharing some deep universal secret. The sea became an iridescent blue breathing creature patterned with silvery lights. The sun on my back was an embrace of warmth as it penetrated deep into my bones. We were playing the timeless game of choosing stones of the right size and shape, carefully balancing them one above the other until we had little stone towers perfectly balanced in patterns of white and grey.

Later we lay holding hands on the sand, gazing at the sky and listening to the sea, breathing with her, absorbed in a sense of eternity. The sea seemed to be breathing us, as if we were part of one vast vivid energy of life, connected to everything. I looked towards Johann and he looked at me. The same energy seemed to be happening between us. He and I were intricately connected in this divine web of love. Our separateness was an illusion. He gently pulled me towards him and we lay face to face, looking into each others eyes. I watched his face change from puzzlement to recognition. 'It's you isn't it?' he said stroking my cheek. 'You've got the most amazing eyes. I feel as if I know you.'

'Yes, it's me, and I felt I knew you from the first moment I saw you, even before we spoke.'

'And I thought it was her!' He burst out laughing as if it was a ridiculous joke.

'And I thought I had lost you.' We lay opposite each other, locked in each others eyes in a wordless place.

Evening came and the reflection of the sun made a shimmering golden pathway to the horizon. 'I feel as if I could walk on water, along that pathway,' I murmured, pointing towards the setting sun. He took my hand and silently kissed my palm. As we walked through the thick warm dusk, back to his white *casita,* the silent pines felt like friends, communicating their own life energy through their scent and delicate green needles. His little house was spartan and orderly, except for the living room table which was covered with books and astrological ephemeris and charts. 'So you're an astrologer?' I was coming back to earth, and leafing through one of his books.

'I'm studying,' he replied, getting a basket of vegetables out from under a the small curtained sink. 'It is my main hobby since I came here. And what sign of the zodiac are you?'

'I'm a Cancer, crab, so I love water, and the moon really affects me. And you?'

'I'm Leo, the lion, but my moon is in Cancer, so I have that watery aspect as well as Fire. That's good, we have a good moon and sun connection.

'You can chop these while I get in some wood if you like,' he said, gently handing me a board and a knife. I chopped slowly, becoming completely absorbed in the patterns and colours of onions, peppers, tomatoes and aubergines. He came in with a pile of driftwood and pine cones for kindling. Soon the room was dancing with the flickering patterns and shadows, aromatic with burning pine. 'Do you want to sit by the fire while I cook these?' His movements were smooth and efficient as he tossed vegetables into a wok and put on some brown rice. We sat by the fire eating in silence and the simple food tasted like a feast.

'I'll get my guitar,' Johann took the plates to the sink and ducked through a low arch into the dark bedroom. We sat opposite each other on a coloured woven rug in front of the fire singing Donovan, 'Sunshine fell softly on my window today.'

As we sang our energy touched and rose in the gold and shadowy play of the flames. The mescaline was wearing off but colours were still deep and vibrant. Words seemed like pebbles, a small currency that we exchanged when we weren't immersed in our vast ocean of togetherness.

Johann put down his guitar and sat next to me, stroking my hair as we gazed into the fire. When we looked into each other's eyes again I saw myriad different ages in his face: a baby, an adolescent, a middle aged man, then old and skeletal. I saw him in an Indian life, dressed like a prince, as a woman, and as a Tyrolean peasant. But all through these faces there was a thread, the knowledge that I'd always known him and loved him. Then he tenderly cupped my face in his hand and we were kissing. This was more than a sexual encounter. It was tantric. The meeting of the divine male and female energy, in spirit as well as body. That night I had a glimpse of paradise.

When we woke the next morning he said he had to go away to work for a day. That was OK, I needed to be alone to absorb everything that had happened and I went back to the *casita* I was now renting. But when he didn't appear at nightfall I was thrown from heaven into hell. How could I have believed that he would stay when everyone else had always gone? That night I had my nightmares again and in the morning remembered the shadows.

I'm standing at the top of the dark brown stairs screaming for my father. I'm only three and I know something momentous is happening. 'Haro!' I scream as he slowly walks down those stairs, looking back at me with broken, beseeching eyes.

My mother picks me up. 'It's all right darling,' she keeps repeating, stroking my dark curls. She is weeping. Robbie is clinging to her skirt. My father is leaving.

'Where is my daddy?' I ask every night after that, and 'Why has that man come?' My stepfather has moved in almost immediately.

'Harold will visit in a few days,' my mother reassures me. 'He's just gone away for a little while. And that man is Terence,' she smiles towards the stranger, 'Your new father'

I know it's all a terrible mistake.

Me as a baby   Bathing in the garden at the age of two

Johann returned the following evening. He had arranged to work for a day and thought he'd see me that night, but there had been a lot more to do than he thought so he'd had to stay. He had no means of contacting me. When we made love I felt whole again.

A few days later we went to Ibiza market. It was a short crossing on the ferry. The town of Ibiza was a fishing port with a medieval fortress

Holidays in Cornwall with Harold

high on a hill and narrow winding streets below. Old ladies in long back dresses sat outside their simple houses making lace while children ran around playing and asking foreigners for pesetas. A group of artists and hippies had come to the island, bought up dilapidated old farmhouses and managed to make a living by arts and crafts, which they brought to the market. Others made money in northern Europe and then lived cheaply on the island, renting a place for summer or winter seasons. The market stalls were vibrant with colour. As well as baskets of gleaming fish there were piles of oriental spices, red and green peppers, grapes and fresh green autumn figs. The craft stalls were selling baskets, slippers, sandals, nick-knacks and hand made jewellery. Jacquie and Volker were there touting their decorated leather belts and moccasins. Suzie and Juan were wandering around hand in hand. Suzie told me excitedly that she and Juan were in love and she had decided to stay with him in Ibiza for winter. I was pleased for her, though sad to lose her, but I was soon holding Johann's hand again and we were lost in the hubbub. It was obviously Formentera's day out.

In the heat of the day Johann and I sat in a café overlooking the brilliant turquoise sea and the higgledy piggledy town of white one-storied houses. Johann turned and looked seriously into my eyes. 'I've got to go back to Frankfurt next week. I've fixed up a job at Frankfurt airport to save up money to go to India. I'm going to travel there overland with my friend Klaus.' I looked away, at the sun shimmering on the sea, trying to swallow the impulse to cry. The sea was constant but everything else changed all the time. He pressed my hand to get my attention back. 'Would you like to come?'

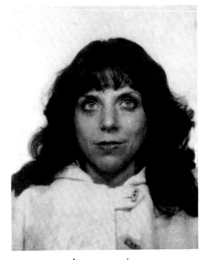

At sixteen   At twenty-nine

'Yes I'd love to!' I replied laughing as goose bumps appeared all over my arms.

It seemed ordained, as if the script were already written. When Johann left for Germany a few days later the first autumn storms broke and I felt bereft. A cool north wind whistled in the pines and a first few purple olives blew off the sparse trees. He left me a note on the bare scrubbed table in my tiny *casita*.

'I love you. You are beautiful.'

Arriving back in London was like going from colour to monochrome. I needed to save money so I went back home. I wasn't sure if my mother really liked having me there. With her strong Swedish reserve she never was able to talk about feelings. She hadn't been the sort of mother you could go to with your problems or for a hug, and she certainly never would approach me. Traumas were suffered in silence in that house. Even when I finally left home it wasn't discussed.

I realize now how hard it was for her to be a mother. She'd had her first child at the age of twenty-two, a very young woman. She'd moved to a England with Robbie, then a two-year-old, and me a baby of a few months.

While I was in the womb Harold started having an affair. I was born with the burn of infidelity in my cells. It was hardly surprising that my mother needed to escape her pain by falling passionately in love with Terence, a dashing stranger she met in London. Through him she had the courage to leave Harold and in her insecurity she focused most of her attention on her new husband and then on their son Sven, who was born a couple of years later. Robbie got his share of her attention because he was highly strung and 'difficult'. But I was cast in the role of the good girl, sandwiched between her two love children, and was left out in the cold. I was the one who could be relied upon not to make a fuss and to 'understand' the needs of the others. It took something totally out of the ordinary to make her take an interest in me.

It's 1964, I'm eighteen and in an attic room in Clapham with Mike. Although I'm still living at home I visit him every night. It's winter damp and we're making love. I know we must stop. I'll get pregnant. I've forgotten my cap. But part of me knows that I'm desperate to get pregnant while another part of me knows that if I do I can't possibly have his child. He's aggressive and verbally abusive to me. I'm only eighteen. If I get pregnant I'll have to abort the baby, and it will be like killing myself. But the other part of me goes on making love. I can't be bothered to take care of myself. I want to kill myself. I'm crying out for love but no-one seems to hear. My mother's not interested, my father's not there, my stepfather's an impostor and my brothers are lost in their own worlds. Mike says he loves me but just wants sex and then puts me down all the time. Perhaps if I do something dramatic they'll love me, notice I exist.

Six weeks later I know I'm pregnant. One evening my mother asks me why I'm behaving secretively and look so pale. For once she actually notices that I exist. 'Are you pregnant?' she asks.

'Of course I'm pregnant and what do you care!' I scream, storming out of the room.

Later she comes to my bedroom. She looks nervous and tense, frightened of me. All I want is for her to hold me and reassure me and tell me that she'll help me be a mother. But instead she asks, 'Now Cathy what are you going to do about this? Do you love Mike? Do you really want his baby? I thought you wanted to try to get into drama school or earn some money, when you've finished your secretarial course. Go travelling?'

'I hate Mike and I don't know what the fuck I want to do,' I yell, trying not to cry.

'Well think about it. The decision is yours of course but we don't want to waste any time if you're going to have an abortion.' She leaves the room nervously with that word hanging between us like an axe.

Two weeks later we're heading for the psychiatrist. I need him to prove I'm not mentally fit to have a baby. It's the first time my mum and I have been out together for months, I think bitterly. Soon I'm sitting stoically in the psychiatrist's office, trying not to weep as he signs the papers. I can see my mother's relieved, but I feel like I'm going to die.

My mouth is dry. It's the day of the abortion. I'm feeling sick with fear. Perhaps I've made the wrong decision and this is all a big mistake. If only I'd been able to talk to someone. If only Mike was different and loved me instead of being angry—then I could have had his baby. But we're already at the clinic door. My mother comes in and then says goodbye.

'Miss Lowenstein, please follow me to the changing room. Take everything off and put on the white gown with the tags at the back.' The nurse is curt and crisp. I feel she disapproves of me. But why the hell is she working here then? There's still time . . . I want to run out and follow my mother, crying like a child . . . Help me . . . Look after this baby and me . . . We could live together and be happy like a proper family . . . 'Now follow me through to the next cubicle where we'll give you a pre-med injection. It'll make you relax and feel drowsy.' I'll run out now, screaming down the street in my gown . . . Tell them it was all a mistake . . . I made the wrong decision . . . I want to go home . . . But no, it's right . . . I must do it . . . I can't live with Mike and I can't manage on my own . . . If only . . . And it's too late . . . The nurse is finding a vein and I'm shaking. I'm floating. It's all OK now. I'm above my body and I don't have to worry. It's better than dope. Maybe I'll die anyway but now I'll fly . . .'

I wake up in a sickly yellow haze. My womb is screaming, my is mouth parched and there are pads between my legs. I feel emptier than I've felt all my life. I feel like I've entered a barren desert. All I want to do is sleep and sleep *and never wake up to this pain again. But they're bringing me tea and biscuits. A bright nurse takes my pulse and asks me how I'm feeling. I feel as if a shadow has entered my heart. 'OK,' I mumble.*

A week later, I'm crossing the road with Mike. I'm weeping and it's freezing cold. He's been shouting at me for destroying his baby. We're on the way to a Soho pub to meet friends. I step out into the busy road and keep walking into the traffic. A car screeches to a halt.

'Do you wanna kill yourself? Idiot!'

Yes, at this moment that's exactly what I want to do. But I only have the courage for a half-hearted attempt.

Back in London, living at home and working in a boutique would have been unbearably boring if I hadn't been dreaming and planning my journey to India. Sometimes, when I hadn't heard from Johann for a while, I'd lose my nerve and wonder if the whole thing was just a fantasy. It all seemed unreal and improbable, a holiday romance coloured by mescaline. After all, I hardly knew him, and if he'd switched from being infatuated with Maya to being in love with me so quickly, perhaps he could switch again and call everything off. And yet our time together was the deepest experience of my life.

Meanwhile he and Klaus bought a Volkswagen van and kitted it out for our journey.

A fine April drizzle made everything look drab as my mother took me to Liverpool Street station. I couldn't wait to be out of there. She looked drawn and pale, trying not to appear anxious, and my stomach was churning uncontrollably.

'I may not be long,' I said trying to be reassuring. 'If we don't get along I won't even travel with them. I'll probably be back in a couple of weeks.' She looked unconvinced. We hugged briefly and I carried my rucksack onto the train. She looked small and forlorn against the grey platform as the train pulled out. A knot of nervous excitement exploded in my belly and carried me to meet Johann in Germany.

Overland to India, 1969

Mother India

Oh Mother India
I have danced my life
In the shadow
Of your divine dance
Your spirit my guide
Your devastation
My teacher
In my cells
I carry your dreams,
Your chaos and healing
I was one of the seekers
Who lost and found

Her Self in you
Still
With Shiva's scars
In my body
I wonder at your power –
Your poverty and colour
Clothed in veils of
Squalor and desperation
Beauty and splendour
You hum
With a heart
Of Spirit

'At last I feel we're really in the East,' I said excitedly as we wandered hand in hand around the bazaar of Istanbul, with its hot, perfumed air, hubbub of pulsing crowds and vivid colour. Young boys pulled at my skirt, trying to sell me sweetmeats. Dark skinned men appeared from the shadows trying to entice us with exotic rugs, and people huddled around braziers roasting maize and fish caught in the Bosporus earlier that day. There were cluttered cafés where bearded men sat smoking black tobacco in hookahs and playing backgammon while drinking cups of sweet black coffee.

'And it all just gets better,' Johann replied, looking quite at home amongst the noise and crowds.

'Look at those fabrics.' We were passing a stall draped with luscious silks and immediately a couple of swarthy moustachioed brothers were beckoning us in with offers of 'winning bargains'!

'Let's get away from these guys. I'm hungry.' Johann led me through the narrow maze of stalls. We hadn't had breakfast. 'Let's get some goat's cheese and yoghurt. We've still got some bread back at the van.' We stopped beside a slightly rancid smelling stall near the end of the market. 'Don't worry. It's delicious,' and he started bargaining. We sat eating our breakfast with the Blue Mosque shimmering in the distance.

On the outskirts of Istanbul we tried busking outside an affluent hotel with uniformed doormen. 'You can dance while we play guitar.' Johann gave me his cheerful smile. I started moving shyly. 'Don't worry. You look great in that embroidered dress,' he reassured me. A crowd was gathering, watching curiously.

'Come on, Cathy. You're a good dancer. Just relax and pretend they're not there.' Johann smiled encouragingly, and soon we'd earned enough money for our next couple of meals.

Whenever we were near a town in Turkey we heard the call for prayer, five times a day—*Allah Hu Akbar*—God is great—and we would see the men kneeling towards Mecca in prayer. I wondered what this must do to the psyche to be so focused on God. In the end I decided it was a good thing, as long as it was free from fanaticism and if Muslims accepted the unifying spirit behind all religions. Even as a child I had felt drawn to the sacred in whatever form it took. My parents were agnostic, and yet when I was quite young I crept into our nearby synagogue one day, and on another occasion ran to church at Easter.

We drove through the desert, stopping at small villages for food. Wherever we stopped curious crowds gathered to gawk. Gangs of kids watched me as I tried to find somewhere to pee. Voracious men continually tried to sneak up on me to get a quick grope whenever Johann and Klaus were looking the other way. Western women, even accompanied by men, were easy prey, while their own women flitted around in purdah like shadows.

When we drove away from the towns this stress seemed irrelevant against the huge quiet beauty of the desert. It was a vast smooth landscape where sandy earth and sky made us feel insignificant and vulnerable in our small van. Here Johann and Hobbit the dog would run around, laughing and playing together. In the evenings we would stop and spread our sleeping bags on the ground. We cooked on a little calor gas stove in the van or made a fire. We ate outside, watching the sun set in a landscape of strange shifting sands. The men got out their guitars and we all sang into the dusk. Then Klaus disappeared discreetly and we made love under the vast dome of stars, falling asleep in each others arms.

Afghanistan was wild and rugged. In the great stretches of silent desert we saw the occasional goatherd, wandering tall and proud like a moving statue amidst the harsh sand and stone. In Herat we shared a smoke with fellow travellers on their way to India against a backdrop of the all-pervasive mosque and the tall white-turbaned Afghanis. Kabul was alive with colour and trading, a city of donkeys, which brought in the fruit, nuts and vegetables from the surrounding countryside. I remember the huge rock formations which surrounded us as we drove through the Khyber pass into Pakistan.

In Pakistan the heat hit us like an open oven so we decided to drive straight up to Nepal. Kathmandu nestled on the edge of the majestic Himalayas, surrounded by terraces of vivid green rice paddies. In 1969, the year that a man first landed on the moon, the town was a small vibrant hotch-potch of wooden houses and narrow streets, filled with rickshaws, bicycles, beggars, monks and wandering white cows.

It was full of hippies from all over the world, a motley crew with unkempt hair, some of whom had been on the India trail for years. Some were seekers who had spent long stretches in ashrams, or living rough, half naked and half starved with the renunciant *sadhus*. They often wore saffron clothes, had ash smeared foreheads and went barefoot. Others were wide or dull eyed, high on drugs, and others like us were more like flower children, reasonably clean with colourful clothes, beads, head bands and bangles. We would sit in cafés drinking chai, served by young boys in dirty rags who ran in and out of the tables as we sat chatting, smoking dope, and strumming guitars. There we shared our stories with fellow travellers. Some had travelled on the legendary Magic Bus, in groups with guides. Others were loners who had hitched or even motor cycled through the desert.

We were recommended an area a few kilometres outside Kathmandu. There we found a small stone two storey house for rent near the picturesque town of Boudhanath, which has the most famous Tibetan Buddhist temple outside of Tibet. It had a huge white stupa, a monument consisting of a spire on top of a cube, designed to represent the four elements. Amid the warm earthy scent of cow dung you could see Tibetans wandering around turning their prayer wheels, while the cacophonous sound of long Tibetan horns and drums played like the sound track to a strange movie.

As we unpacked the van a crowd gathered. What a change from Germany, I thought, as these small, dark, bright eyed people laughed and offered us cigarettes and vegetables. Here they laughed *with* us—there passers-by had laughed *at* us when they'd seen us packing up our van in our coloured hippy clothes.

The house had the minimum of furniture: mattresses to sleep on, a couple of chairs and a simple wooden table. But for us it was luxury after living in the van for six weeks. We overlooked brown mountain slopes and green terraced hills where women worked the land, cultivating their vegetables and rice, looking graceful with long black plaited braids, vibrant bright blouses and colourful skirts.

A little track wound around the side of the house where both men and women passed by carrying huge bundles of wood in baskets on their backs, with leather supports around their bent heads, wood to cook with and in preparation for the coming winter. They were always smiling, laughing and singing like the exotic birds we saw flitting above the fields. The dark eyed children played like nature spirits around our house and peeped through the windows.

We didn't do much. It was a relief to rest after the long journey. We read, went for walks, explored the beautiful terraced land, visited the local temples and stupas, and of course spent time in the chai shops with other hippies, smoking dope, listening to music and talking. It felt completely right to be setting up a temporary home with Johann. In my heart it was as if this was what we were meant to do, and for me it was like a practice run for things to come, when we would settle in the West and have a family together. Here at last I made time to write home and reassure my mother and Harold that I was OK.

One evening after we had spent the day wandering around the temple, watching *sadhus* and monks meditating and white cows grazing, Johann and I were reading, lying on a mattress covered by sleeping bags. He was propped on one elbow, his face looking serious and refined. As I looked at him I felt that overwhelming sense of having known him through many lifetimes, of having always loved him.

As he looked up I said, 'I love you so much. I've never felt this about anyone before.'

'I love you too,' he replied. 'But maybe it's different. You are only the second woman I've really had a relationship with. I was very shy until now, and I feel I need more experience with women.'

'I'd have a child with you tomorrow if you wanted one,' I murmured half to myself.

'I wish my feelings were as simple as yours and I could just completely commit myself to you,' he replied, looking out of the window. A dull coldness crept into my womb and I looked out of the window too. Outside, wiry farmers walked on the path carrying their great bundles of firewood, looking like pack animals.

After a few weeks of living in the country we were all beginning to get restless. We had heard that Kathmandu would be a good place to sell the van to other travellers and that's what we did. Klaus decided he would like to travel on alone. Johann and I felt we wanted to explore India now it was cooler. We headed south by train with Hobbit on a lead. No one here travelled around with a dog and on the trains fellow passengers laughed and pointed at us as if we were crazy.

After a few days we arrived in Rishikesh, a sacred place of pilgrimage by the Ganges. The streets were teeming with bicycle rickshaws, with wiry sweating rickshaw wallahs carrying tourists and wealthy Indians, dodging holy white cows and loin-clothed, matted-haired holy men. Lining the road by the river was a shocking display of every form of human suffering. Hundreds of beggars with pleading eyes and leprosy'd limbs, people with no arms or legs just using bits of wood on wheels to get around and starving mothers holding elf-like children with fly-diseased eyes and distended bellies. It seemed relentless. All of them had outstretched arms or piebald stumps begging, *'Pais, mem sahib, pais.'* I dropped some coins as we walked silently past but I felt sick at the impossibility of it all.

'It's hopeless isn't it?' I took Johann's hand.

'It's India,' he sighed reflectively. 'As long as they have the caste system of untouchables and believe it's inevitable karma, I think it'll just go on the same.' He steered me away from a boy in rags with an empty coconut shell bowl in hand.

We walked up a track to the ashram of Maharishi Mahesh Yogi. The previous year it had become famous when the Beatles were there learning transcendental meditation. I'd seen pictures of this ashram and the Beatles with their long haired guru in the papers in London. I could hardly believe we were now in that same place. Strolling through the wrought iron gates we entered another world, one of lush tropical gardens and opulence. We were greeted with a *namaste* (the hands in a prayer position) from a friendly looking monk. 'Could we be initiated into meditation?' Johann asked, looking down at the serene saffron-robed man.

'Yes you are welcome. Is it from England you are coming?' he asked, smiling kindly.

'Yes I'm from England,' I replied, returning the smile as Johann didn't say anything.

'Very good place isn't it?' He paused and looked into the distance. 'That is where the Maharishi is now,' he added, nodding his head from side to side. How ironic, I thought. Here we are in India and the guru is in England when we have come all this way!

'Here is a room for you to be sleeping.' He showed us a clean bright room with a couple of metal bedsteads where we could stay for a small charge.

'I will be initiating you in the morning.' He put his hand to the centre of his chest. 'But tonight you will fast and take showers.'

In the morning the monk took us into a cool marble floored room that looked like a temple. At the far end was an altar with pictures of the Maharishi and other saints, vases of flowers and offerings of fruit and rice. There we sat cross legged on the floor while he told us that he would give us each a secret mantra which we were to say over and over again inwardly with the breath for at least half an hour every day. A mantra is a Sanskrit word which contains a mystic sound vibration, the Sanskrit language being one in which the vibrations and the words correspond. So, for example, the word 'truth' in Sanskrit corresponds with the vibration of Truth and thus helps you realize the nature of Truth.

'Through repeating your mantras you will begin to quieten your thoughts and feel your true Self.' The monk looked at us benignly. 'This is the Self which is beyond the mind, always present and peaceful,' he chuckled.

The monk knelt opposite us, touched the crowns of our heads and whispered in our ears individually. He told us our sacred mantras, which we pledged to secrecy and asked us to repeat them silently for fifteen minutes until our minds had calmed. I felt a warm watery energy enveloping me as he initiated me, and as I began to say the mantra I felt a sense of homecoming.

Later we sat cross legged under a bodhi tree the sacred tree of Buddhists, watching the sun set and saying our mantras inwardly. It was my first taste of meditation. After a while, my mind stilled. I felt close to the pulse of the universe, and close to Johann sitting beside me as an inevitable part of that pulse. It was like our mescaline trip, and probably that was why we slipped into it so easily, only this was gentler. We held hands enveloped in a deep calm as we watched the darkening sky and heard birds settling for the night. The scent of frangipani perfumed the air and the sound of tabla and singing drifted from a nearby shrine. Flies buzzed and settled on my bare legs but I felt no need to dust them away. They too were a part of the tapestry of nature. We spent that night sleeping in our separate narrow beds in the quiet ashram and I woke up feeling a sense of peace that I hadn't been aware of before, amidst the noisy thrum of my emotions and the distractions of travelling.

This peace was the heart of India, the spiritual essence and life blood running through that vast continent, amidst the anarchic chaos and craziness, the devastating poverty and suffering. This was what us young Western hippies had really travelled here for even if we didn't consciously know it. This peace, from whatever source, is what we all need in our lives.

The following day we strolled down the hill and walked through the colony of leprous beggars. I emptied my purse but this time I felt a spaciousness in my heart.

From Rishikesh we took a train south to Agra to visit the Taj Mahal, that exquisite marble wonder of the world, which glows in the moonlight like something out of a fairy tale. Then we braved a chaotic station which teemed with sweaty crowds so we could get a sleeper farther south. We travelled third class in packed hot trains where wooden luggage racks served as bunks and toilets were a hole with two footholds on either side with a startling view of the tracks running beneath us.

As we travelled farther south towards the famous tantric temples of Mahabhatapurum the countryside became lush with vivid green pastures where buffalo grazed. In the early mornings we saw a parade of bare bums crouched down amidst the fields. We watched statuesque women in bright saris carrying water on their heads in copper pots, and gangs of thin worn women breaking stones to create roads, toiling in the wide forbidding sun. Sometimes we had to sleep amidst the crowds on station platforms, as the trains had their own itinerary, sometimes arriving a day late. Families set up camp and cooked on the platforms, while we bought chai in cheap earthenware beakers which were to be thrown away and ate sugary sweetmeats from emaciated vendors. The only possessions we had were small overnight rucksacks with a change of clothes, a toothbrush and shawls for sleeping.

After long journeys, even sewage smelling hostels were a relief. We would wander out at night to find a cheap restaurant, where strings of fairy lights lit up a few outside tables and we ate chapatis, rice and dahl and drank the liquid yogurt called *lassi*. Sometimes we would peep into simple shacks where families sat on the floor eating off huge leaves with candles lighting up their little shrines. Outside ebony children played games with a few coloured stones.

When we reached the south we stayed by the spacious beaches of Puri, crossed over to Ceylon and went snorkelling in the clear seas. We ate mangoes, bananas and coconuts and purified our water, trying unsuccessfully not to get dysentery. I loved the freedom of it. In India you could look like and be whoever you wanted without standing out. Hippies were certainly less bizarre than the sadhus, standing or sitting in yogic postures half-naked and smeared with ash. I felt completely at home among the chaos and colour. Eventually I became brown and very thin with chronic diarrhoea, but this didn't seem to matter because I was having the adventure of my life with the man I loved.

Johann in India

Hobbit, Johann, me camping on the beach in Singapore

Months passed and our money began to run out.

'Lets go to Japan,' Johann suggested enthusiastically as we sat in a chai shop in Calcutta. 'I've heard you can make lots of money there teaching English as a foreign language and girls make a fortune working in nightclubs in Tokyo.' I felt confused. I'd never even thought of going to Japan. But we'd already been away for six months and India was weakening me. I knew I really didn't want to go home. Travelling with Johann had become my life.

'We can fly from here to Bangkok, get a boat to Singapore, then one to Hong Kong and then to Kobe in the south of Japan'. He seemed to have worked it all out.

'What about Hobbit?' I asked nervously, feeling overwhelmed.

'Hobbit can travel with us. I'm sure we can arrange it. He can go in the hold of the plane and then in kennels on the boat.'

Bangkok was a kaleidoscope of old and new. Ancient Buddhist temples glowed golden against the backdrop of a newly westernised city, where GIs on leave from Vietnam wandered hand in hand with young, flower-like prostitutes. From Bangkok, we took trains down the tropical coast of Indonesia to Singapore.

As we neared Singapore we wondered how we would get Hobbit into the country, as we knew they had strict quarantine laws. When we arrived at immigration we let him loose in the hope that he wouldn't be noticed. He sauntered through ahead of us, the immigration officials taking no notice of him, obviously thinking he was a local stray. He played the part wonderfully, wandering around, nonchalantly waiting for us as we walked out of the darkened building. We quickly found a room in an apartment house and lay low for most of the next day, with brief forays into the exotic tropical city. Two days later there was a violent knock on our door. The landlord had told the authorities that there were a couple of hippies staying there with a dog. The 'dog police' took Hobbit away to quarantine there and then, and we were grounded for the next six weeks. It felt as if he'd been taken to prison.

We couldn't afford to rent for six weeks in Singapore, so we bought a small tent and found a place to camp on Changi beach, which was at the secluded end of the island. It was a sweet sandy backwater of coconut and banana trees, where we swam in translucent seas and lived on tropical fruits and local fish which we cooked on our small open fire together with a pot of rice. We lay under the stars together sharing stories from our lives. But Johann wasn't his usual cheerful self as he was missing his beloved Hobbit. Every few days we travelled across the island by bus to visit him in his kennels. He always leaped with excitement when he saw us, wagging and barking with joy, expecting that we'd come to take him home, and it was painful to see his confusion and upset each time we left.

One day we decided to visit the little island which shimmered invitingly a few miles across the sea from our camp. 'We can get a fishing boat there and it only takes about half an hour,' Johann pointed across the water. The next morning we got up early and took the boat across to the island. It was alive with forests of banana palms, guavas and jack fruits, with sand dunes leading down to deserted white beaches. We explored the island for a couple of hours until we found a perfect secluded beach surrounded by a crescent of dunes. Johann produced a little metal box from his pocket. 'This is the perfect place to take a trip,' he said offering me a scrap of blotting paper.

'I'm not sure. I didn't know you had any.' I was surprised and didn't immediately take the blotting paper. 'It's been such a long time'. I hadn't taken LSD since my London days. 'But maybe we'll feel that old Formentera magic again,' I added, laughing to reassure myself. I'd been concerned that our relationship was becoming too humdrum, and we'd had a few misunderstandings. Perhaps this would be the answer.

We sat silently watching the sea. 'OK, I'll take it,' I decided. 'This is an ideal place,' I said, convincing myself as Johann looked at me persuasively. We swallowed the blotting paper and waited, wandering around the beach half naked. We explored the sand with our feet, and calmly gazed at the patterns and textures of shells, sand formations, and miniature pools. We swam and dried off in the sun, lying together, watching the quietly murmuring aquamarine sea. Later I found myself sitting cross legged, meditating on my mantra, my breath synchronising with the gentle waves. I experienced the vastness of the ocean reflecting the vastness in me. All thoughts gone, I was beyond mind, in an ecstatic state of simply Being.

The afternoon passed and shadows were lengthening when we found a sheltered dell at the top of the sand dunes where we could sleep. We shared water and guavas and snuggled down on my sarong in a hollow, watching the sun, a dark rose disc, sinking into the ocean. The whole world seemed to have gone silent, apart from the constant murmuring breath of the water. We lay in each others arms as the tropical dusk began to fall like a comforting blanket. We had no use for words, wrapped in our cocoon of togetherness.

We were naked in the warm balmy air of evening. In this deserted place it felt as if we were the only people on the island. There was not a house or track in sight, so we felt quite safe. In the gathering dusk we started caressing each other and I no longer knew where Johann began or I ended. We were an undulating wave of intense sensations. At last we were back in the magic we'd lost over the last weeks, in a state of complete abandonment.

Suddenly we heard footsteps above us in the growing dark. Two burly Chinese guys were staring down at us with a torch. We quickly disentangled ourselves and sat up feeling guilty, thinking they'd found us making love on their land. But before we knew what was happening I saw a bamboo pole coming down towards Johann's head in slow motion. Then it crashed against his skull and he collapsed onto the sand, bleeding from his head and unconscious. I put out my hand trying to see how badly he'd been hurt when the other guy leaped on me trying to force my legs apart while undoing his trousers. In that searing moment I realised what was happening and started screaming. But there was no-one to hear. Johann was lying unconscious and the other man was watching impassively. I started kicking and screaming but one of them shoved the bamboo pole roughly across my pelvis so I couldn't move. Hot hands wrenched my thighs apart and the man's weight was on me, his face sneering and greedy as he tried to force his penis into my refusing vagina.

I flew out of my body as an eternity seemed to pass. I looked down at the scene below me, playing out in slow motion, me pinioned against the sand, a greasy man kneeling above me with a grotesque red penis thrusting towards my vagina and Johann lying inert beside me. It seemed then that my screams reached through his unconsciousness, as I saw him slowly sitting up. He was dazed, rubbing a great lump on his head, with a smear of blood on his lip. He yelled as he realised what was happening. The sound of his voice brought me closer to my body, and I started struggling again. With a desperate energy he staggered to his feet and grabbed the bamboo pole off the guy who was watching and tried to hit the one who was about to rape me. In a flash they were both running away into the darkness with Johann chasing them with the pole. I heard dull thuds as they fell down the dunes.

Then there was silence, broken only by the sound of the breeze on palm leaves. A minute later Johann reappeared out of the darkness like a ghost and dropped to his knees next to me.

'How could they do that?' he sobbed. 'How could they do it?'

In the distance we heard the gentle breath of the sea. Above us the stars were glowing in the lapis blue night. I wanted to speak but no words came. I was looking down on us as if from a great distance, observing sadly. We held each other crying and shaking. It felt eerily quiet after the storm of violence. Johann had a huge bruise on his forehead and his eyes looked shattered. I looked at my naked body by torchlight, as if it belonged to someone else. It looked so delicate, with bruising and scratches over my pelvic bones. I was trembling. Johann held me, picked up our water bottle and lifted it to my mouth.

'We've got to get off this crazy island,' he said. 'You're in shock. Can you walk? We'd better get home.' He gently helped me to my feet and shook out the sarong.

'What about your head?' I whispered, realizing that he must be in shock too and could be badly hurt.

'I think it's OK.' He rubbed his forehead.

'I must get to the sea and wash. It feels so disgusting.' I was trying not to vomit. We staggered down to the water, where I sat letting the cool liquid wash between my legs. Johann sat beside me stroking my back, and I looked into his face and washed the blood off his forehead with a handful of sea water.

We walked slowly back to the little port, supporting one another, my legs dragging like jelly. The lush trees looked like a sinister stage set as our torch pinpointed the way through the darkness. Finally we caught sight of the lamp-lit jetty where a boat was waiting with a few cheerful Chinese fishermen standing nearby smoking and chatting. It had seemed like the middle of the night but it was much earlier. We stepped shakily into the boat, where a few locals eyed us curiously. Then a swarthy fisherman revved the engine and we sped off into the darkness.

For the next few days I felt strangely detached. Johann and I were tender with each other as if we lived in each others hearts. Only at night I woke screaming with greasy Chinese men pinning me down like a captured butterfly.

Japan, 1969

Maple Leaf

A maple leaf in the temple
The shakuhachi disturbs a pool
You left me with a heart so hollow
Like bamboo

After the wild chaos of India, the mannered order of Japan was a peaceful relief. We arrived to golden displays of autumn maple trees in Kyoto, the ancient capital of Japan. We chose Kyoto because we'd heard about its sacred Shinto shrines and Buddhist temples with raked stone meditation gardens and bonsai trees.

While Johann stayed put looking after Hobbit, I hitch hiked around asking people if they knew anywhere we could rent. I must have looked bizarre, a tall unkempt foreign hippy in Indian clothes hitching on her own in the neat Japanese countryside. I was totally fearless and strangely hitching seemed easier than finding out about local transport! Somehow, despite my complete lack of Japanese and the locals almost non-existent English, I found a room in an apartment house in a small town about twenty miles from Kyoto.

There was one major obstacle which we had overlooked. Dogs weren't allowed in houses in Japan! Even we weren't allowed in the house without changing into the slippers kept by the front door. Floors were covered with a fibrous matting called *tatami*, and this had to be kept clean. The first night Hobbit was tied up whining outside. He was used to being wherever we were. The following night he whimpered for hours, and it was getting cold. 'I can't bear any more of this,' said Johann angrily, bending to feed Hobbit a bowl of rice on the pavement while I stood by watching.

'It seems impossible to keep him here,' I agreed sadly. 'What do you think we should do?'

'I'll phone my parents and see if they will look after him—see if we can fly him back to Germany.' Johann looked up at me, pained and resigned as he petted Hobbit.

A few days later his passport and injections were organized and we left him at the airport, feeling gutted and guilty as Hobbit looked beseechingly at us from his wire kennel. Two days later we went to check that all had gone well and poor little Hobbit was still in his cage whimpering. Johann exploded in anger at the airport staff, towering over them and shouting. We both felt sick with anger and remorse that we hadn't checked sooner. This time we waited half a day to see he was safely on his plane and phoned Johann's parents the following day, to hear he had arrived safely. Later I heard that he lived a happy life in Germany for the rest of his days.

We put cards around in the shops and Johann soon found work teaching English to students in their own homes. I was less successful. I felt uprooted after India and unsure about teaching. The Japanese were so formal, which made me nervous, so I didn't bother trying to get many students, and just had one businessman for English conversation. He brought us presents of big steaks!—the first and last time I have eaten steak in my life, always having been predominantly vegetarian.

The only time I got beyond polite bowing and English conversation classes, was with the women in the communal baths near our house. I went there almost every night, as there was no bathroom in our flats and nothing much else to do in the village. The public bath house had a white tiled hall where we washed, kneeling and soaping ourselves by individual taps. Then we soaked ourselves in a hot swimming pool or sat in the sauna and used the cold plunge pool afterwards. The local women spent time in the bath house, gossiping and holding their babies. I could see that I became a topic of conversation with my long legs, wavy hair and thin body, but I didn't mind as they were always friendly. I was soon able to recognize women from our apartment house and we would speak in sign language. They would smile and pass me their babies to hold.

When Johann and I weren't working we would explore Kyoto, walk around the temples, or spend time in the one coffee bar where western travellers hung out. Johann started to learn Japanese but I knew such a difficult language was beyond me. I had a few lessons in Ikebana, the Zen art of flower arrangement. One day my teacher invited us for a tea ceremony in her home. I remember the precision and awareness with which she performed every action, stirring green leaves into a pot which exuded a pungent, slightly scorched smell, and pouring it into tiny delicate patterned china cups. We had to turn our cup, savouring the aroma before sipping the hot refreshing liquid. By doing every action with total awareness one can enter a different and wider state of consciousness. This is the foundation of such Zen practices as the tea ceremony, Ikebana, and Zen archery.

Over the winter I noticed Johann withdrawing and distancing himself from me, but I tried to ignore it until one dull April day when he had been particularly silent. 'Don't you like it here any more?' I asked him as we lounged on the futon. We had been living there for seven months now and I wasn't enjoying it very much myself, but as long as I was with him I was usually content. But that day we both felt depressed and hadn't even bothered to roll up the futon. There was an unusual uneasiness between us.

'I'm just bored with it all. It's not our scene here, trying to look straight for clients and being cooped up in this little room together the rest of the time. I want to leave Japan, go travelling again, have some adventures, I . . .' He looked hesitant and sheepish.

'It's OK,' I said, putting my arm around him. 'I don't mind travelling again. Where do you want to go?'

'You don't understand.' He wouldn't look me in the eyes. 'I want to go alone. I need to feel how it is to be just myself again. A year is a long time for me. You know I've never lived with anyone before.'

I felt as I'd just been in a bad traffic accident and I was spacing out above my body. 'But I thought you wanted to be with me. I thought you loved me.'

'I do love you, but I need adventures, other women . . .'

'I can't believe you're saying this!' I was falling into a vacuum of shock. 'You mean you want to go away and have affairs?'

'No, I just mean if it happened I want it to be OK. You don't seem to be very interested any more.'

'I just need to be really close when we start, otherwise it can just remind me . . .' I was doing my best not to cry.

'Look, can't you see this as just an experiment? It doesn't have to be the end. Let's see how we are alone for a while, maybe a few months.'

I couldn't imagine being separated from him for a few weeks, knowing he might be with someone else, let alone months. I grabbed my shoulder bag and walked out of the room, trying to hide my tears as I ran downstairs past the staring eyes of the neighbours. I ran to the local station and jumped on a train—I didn't know where I was going. I got out at a familiar stop and found myself walking round the temple unseeingly, trying to avoid the groups of bespectacled tourists with cameras. I found the secluded raked stone meditation garden where we had been before. I sat there gazing at a grey stone Buddha, trying to quieten my mind, but my emotions were screaming.

I'd always felt Johann was my soul mate, the one I would stay with for the rest of my life. I'd been dreaming of living with him in the UK after our travels and having his children. But I'd never actually told him that—I'd always been too insecure. Now he was casually saying he wanted to go and be with other women if he chose!

By evening I was back in our room. Johann was weeping. 'I never wanted to hurt you like this. Maybe we'll be together again afterwards. I just feel so young. I need to explore.' We held each other, shaking and weeping. The pain continued like an open wound.

Two days later we were on the fastest train in the world, on our way to Tokyo. It was like arriving back in the West. High-rise buildings, traffic jams, neon advertisements, and always crowds of hurried, harassed looking people. We found a cheap hostel slightly out of town. It only took Johann a couple of days to get himself ready to travel. On our last night together I stayed awake feeling as if my heart was being clawed out bit by bit, like a dreadful amputation without anaesthetic. But I didn't wake him. There was nothing more to say. We'd talked it through and he knew how I felt, but still he wanted to leave alone. There was nowhere to go apart from the dark kitchen where I spent the night sobbing and praying. I remember hearing a cock crowing at dawn and feeling that life had betrayed me.

On the hippy trail it was well known that western girls could make good money as hostesses in Japanese nightclubs. It was a venue for Japanese businessmen to meet foreign women and practice their English. The evening after Johann left I found work and dressed up for my first night at a club in the centre of town. I wore a mini skirt and, for the first time in my life, a wig, a long straight one, like the hair I'd always wanted. Carefully I put on heavy eye make up and even tried to stick on impossible false eye lashes. I felt as if I was in a movie, totally unreal and blank with shock. When I went to the ladies to check my make up it was a comfort to look like someone different, but also disorientating.

I poured drinks for dark-suited businessmen, lit their cigarettes and talked to them with false gaiety. I've never been able to drink, it's always made me ill, so I stuck to glasses of sweet lichee juice. When I was asked to dance I felt awkward, as I was about six inches taller than my partner and looked down on him. I longed to be dancing with Johann's tall, familiar body. In the early hours of the morning I got the subway back to the hostel where I was staying feeling completely washed out, and fell into turbulent dreams.

One evening, a week later, I felt dizzy and faint and had to run to the toilets. Next day I had a high fever, a sore throat and all my bones were aching with some sort of a flu virus. I couldn't get out of bed and had no-one to help me. The other people I'd seen in the hostel left early for work and came back late at night. I drifted in and out of fevered dreams and nightmares. One moment I was back with Johann against a backdrop of trains and strange exotic places, holding each other and laughing together. The next moment he was ignoring me, walking away without looking back and I was running after him distraught and screaming. But no sound came out of my mouth as he disappeared into a crowded Indian station. I woke up covered in sweat and weeping. If only I had a friend to talk to, if only my parents were closer. For the first time in eighteen months I missed my mother and found myself remembering some of the green sweetness of England.

I'm back in Palm Tree Cottage, an old Tudor cottage in Kent which my mother bought for a thousand pounds in 1956. It's our holiday home with no electricity or bath. We arrive, as usual, late on a Friday night and she shows us how to light Tilly lamps with paraffin and we make a fire. In the morning my brothers and I go to the Gilbert's farm down the road to collect fresh milk and eggs. We greet the cows in a nearby field and say hello to the chickens pecking around the yard. Later we make a camp in the garden.

I love the countryside here, waking with the sound of blackbirds and cuckoos in the morning, pulling on old dungarees and running with my brothers up the steep hill where we search for the secret white topped mushrooms hiding early in the morning light. It's a reprieve from my fearful stepfather, who never wants to come with us, and a relief from the drone of London traffic.

Somehow I got through the fevered days, staggering to the kitchen for hot drinks when I had the strength, and eating the little fruit I had left in my room. I had never felt so alone. Some days later I was able to have a bath and get dressed. Looking in the mirror I saw a stranger, gaunt and thin with dark smudges under huge frightened eyes. I felt starving and knew that I had to go back to work before I lost my job.

Back in the club I made a new friend called Jane, an American traveller from California.

'Why don't you move to the hippy hotel where I'm staying?' she encouraged me when she found out I'd been ill and alone. 'We share food and hang out together when we're not working.'

I moved a few days later when I felt stronger and was suddenly back in the familiar traveller scene. I hadn't realised it existed in Japan. Everyone was smoking dope, playing psychedelic music and drifting around in Indian clothes when they weren't dressed for work. I felt at home with the other girls. We were all saving up to go travelling again and we would get stoned together before we left for the clubs in the evenings.

During the next few weeks I had several offers of money or tickets to America if I'd go to a hotel with one of these men. But I wouldn't sell myself, however desperate I felt. The pain of missing Johann was like a chronic physical illness. I still hadn't heard from him.

One night Jane and I were sitting talking with a dark suited business man, Mr Kashimoto. He kept fiddling with his gold cuff links and wiping his thick tortoiseshell glasses.

'Do you girls want to come work in my bar in south near sea?' He asked. 'I fly you there and back, you stay month with me and family and I pay you good money.' We wondered what the catch was, but he seemed genuine and was very charming. Jane and I discussed the offer later. She was a veteran traveller, a bit older than me, having left the USA after the break up of an unhappy relationship. Now she wanted to get back to see her family. For me the money would be enough to get me back to India.

A week later we were met at a small airport in the south by a tall stocky man with scheming eyes and a Mercedes. He drove us to the Kashimoto's home, a two story traditional wooden house in the suburb of a small town. Mamasan, the wife, wore a long dress and bowed formally as she greeted us. Soon we were settled in a comfortable *tatami* matted room with rolled up futons which we took out at night. We ate with the family, mostly rice, sushi, noodles and vegetables. They had two extremely well behaved girls and the whole household appeared orderly and correct.

On our first day there, they took us to a beauty salon. They didn't want hippy looking hostesses in their bar, so we were treated to hair cuts and make up Japanese style. Then we went shopping and they bought us both mini dresses. Looking at the new Jane and Cathy we couldn't stop laughing, we looked gorgeous and glamorous. Much as we'd tried to look straight before there always seemed to be give-away signs that we were really travelling hippies.

That evening we were shown into a rather tatty bar. It was all Formica and plastic. At that time the Japanese thought this was very impressive compared to their tasteful bamboo furniture and paper screens. We sat there like fish bait, dolled up and nervously drinking our fruit juices. About an hour later a woman with short hair, short skirt and high heels came into the club with two men and started introducing us to them. Suddenly I realised it was Mamasan, in a wig and dressed to kill! She had been out on the streets touting for business. She'd picked up the men and was now asking them and us what we wanted to drink, acting as if she'd never met us before. Once the men were happily chatting to us in their broken English she left and went out to bring in more customers. And so it went on through the evening. It was unnerving to see this schizophrenic change in Mamasan. Jane and I giggled about it, but it was exciting to be working there as part of her conspiracy to make money, and fun to be the foreigners, like celebrities, getting all the attention. Life in the Kashimoto's household became more and more surreal. 'You want go beach?' Mamasan would ask. 'We get car for you.' Whereupon a heavy, shifty looking man would arrive in an expensive Mercedes.

'I back at four,' he would say with a little bow as he left us. We swam and sunbathed and smoked a joint before he picked us up. Back 'home' we showered, changed and made ourselves up. Mamasan served us a meal before we left for the evening and then another shifty looking guy would roll up in Jaguar to take us to the club. There we would pretend we didn't know Mamasan as she appeared in her evening disguise with the men she picked up on the streets. And so it went on. Before long Jane and I noticed that all these strange men had a ring tattooed in blue around their third fingers.

One night after we had been there for about a week I woke up needing to go to the bathroom downstairs. I was hovering on the landing when I saw the sitting room crowded with all these dangerous coarse looking men, obviously having a meeting. I was scared, but when I woke Jane up to tell her about it she just said I'd been smoking too much dope. Two days later I proved her wrong. We'd been working in the club all evening and I had made my début as a singer, strumming the five guitar chords I knew and singing 'House of the Rising Sun', when a handsome older man invited me up to the bar for a drink. He was very drunk and we had the usual disjointed monosyllabic dialogue of those who don't speak each others language.

'What do you do?' I tried to make polite conversation.

'We are Mafia,' he replied. 'Yesterday we kill man.' He banged his glass on the counter emphatically.

'Oh . . . er . . . well . . .' I went hot. 'You have an interesting life. Could you get me another drink?' As soon as he was busy ordering I signed to Jane that I wanted to meet her in the loo. Five minutes later we were standing by the mirrors giggling hysterically.

'We must be some kind of a front. It could be dangerous.' I heard my mother's voice.

'Do you think we should leave? Surely they wouldn't have any reason to harm us, because in a way we're protecting them?' Jane was combing her hair nervously as she spoke.

'And there's the money. I need to have enough to get back to India, and you to the USA.' They had paid us a half when we arrived and were going to pay the rest when we left.

'If they pay it,' Jane said cynically, her words contrasting with her innocent blond face in the mirror. 'They seem pretty crazy, with Mamasan acting this way with those men!'

'Let's talk about it when we get home. I can't think straight here.' I ran a comb through my hair and we left the ladies room. My drunken friend had disappeared. Perhaps his mates realised he was too drunk and talking too much.

'It's worth the risk for the money. It would take ages to save this much anywhere else.' We were back in our room and Jane was putting on her night time T-shirt. 'We can always climb out of the window and jump into the garden to escape.' We both laughed, slightly hysterically.

'OK, let's risk it as long as nothing weird starts happening.' I replied as the giggles faded. I had another reason for wanting to stay a bit longer. Here I had an address where Johann could easily write to me and I was desperate to hear from him.

A week later my wish was granted. The letter I had been waiting for, hoping and praying for, arrived.

I'm missing you. Perhaps it was a mistake. Please come back to India. Why don't we meet up in Delhi when you arrive? Then we'll go up north together, go to the mountains again.

I danced around the room. 'He still loves me! I'm going to meet him in India!' I looked into the mirror and saw my wide blue eyed reflection glowing back at me, and felt beautiful again.

'Take care, Cathy. He sounds a bit too changeable to me,' Jane replied sceptically.

'If you knew how gorgeous he is. Not just physically, but it's something in his spirit.'

'Sounds like a heart breaker to me and you're only just recovering. You were a mess when we met. I don't think you should run back to him just because he wants you.'

'Yes, but it'll be different this time. He's had his freedom and now he wants me back.'

Two weeks later we left the Kashimotos' having come to no harm. They put us on a plane back to Tokyo with a wad of money in our pockets. In the hippy hotel Jane and I parted. The next day a guy called John, who Johann and I had known in Kyoto, appeared in the hotel and invited me out to supper. It was great to talk to him. Of all the people I knew in Japan, only he knew Johann and understood what I'd been through. He told me he had some really good gentle acid which he was going to take a couple of days later in a temple.

'It'll be good for you, give you back your power again,' he said. 'You gave Johann too much of your soul. You lost yourself and he lost his respect for you. I'll help you on this trip. Help you find yourself.' It was true. John read me well. He was a strong spiritual man who I'd always respected but had never been attracted to, so it seemed like a good thing to do before my boat left the following week.

That is how I found myself tripping in an old temple garden with John, and it was the last LSD I was ever to take. I remember the powerful presence of a statue of the Buddha. I felt he was giving me teachings on the nature of impermanence, the essence of Buddhism.

On the trip all my past emotional suffering seemed like a distant nightmare and I found myself laughing a lot with John's piercing eyes keeping watch over me. I also noticed that we were in the midst of swarms of mosquitoes which were biting us, bumps were appearing all over me, but I couldn't feel the bites as my consciousness was higher than the pain and itchiness.

That night, still tripping, we went to a nightclub with a large circular raised area for dancers. I went up there when it was completely empty and started dancing to strange erotic music. Somehow I couldn't help myself from becoming the seductress and soon I had half a dozen men watching my every movement. I had never felt the power of my sexuality before, always having been unsure of myself as a woman. But now I felt the powerful

Dancing in a Tokyo nightclub

elemental energy of womanliness and found myself flying higher and higher on my own erotic energy. This is what it must be like to be a famous singer or film star I thought—all this sexual power.

Then John was up there beside me. 'It's time to go. You'll get into trouble. Those men just want sex with you. Come on.' He led me off the stage like a child who doesn't want to leave the party. But he was right. As we passed a huddle of men they whistled and made lewd signs at me and suddenly I was back in my shy self and wanted to get out of there fast.

Back in the hotel John and I lay together gazing into each others eyes and of course I loved him as one does in that high LSD consciousness where unconditional love is the norm and there is no sense of separation. But when he started caressing me sexually I had to say no. My body still belonged to Johann. There was no escaping that.

A week later John took me to the boat which would take me to Hong Kong. From there I would fly to Calcutta. He stood on the quayside in Osaka holding the end of a coloured streamer while I held the other end. As the boat slowly glided seawards, we waved wildly as if we had been lovers. Soon the streamers broke and I felt the tears of separation. My time in Japan had not been easy, but John had helped me find my power and womanhood again. I sent him a prayer of thanks and farewell before returning to the vibrant chaos of India.

Back to India, 1970

Elemental Woman

I move with the wind with shadows with trees
I dance with the tides and changing seas
My ground is the Earth my guide the Sun
The Moon is my constant companion.
I am Elemental Woman
Mad with wounds of chemical
I hide in caves in stones in streams
My voice is weeping in your dreams
But you will not hear me.
Gaia is my mother, lover, my friend
Her body is mine and mine to defend
Her invisible forms I nurture and tend
But you undo me.
I speak through freak storms,
Through floods, through drought
Disease is my damage coming out
But how much louder must I shout
Before you hear me?

Johann was there to meet me in Calcutta, the city awash with monsoon, sultry and humid. I felt as if I'd come home.

'I've missed you,' he said as we sat drinking chai near the airport. 'But I did need to taste my freedom.' He was looking into the distance, inviting me not to ask any questions. But we were back in the magic. I felt complete again, laughing, loving and feeling his body close to mine. No matter that he had been with other women, he had chosen to be back with me now and I wasn't going to ask for more.

We travelled to Delhi and settled down to a few days of reunion bliss in a hippy hotel whilst waiting for permits to enter the little known kingdoms of Bhutan and Sikkim far away to the north. Delhi was actually two completely different cities. The old one where we were staying was run down and crowded, with beggars and street dwellers sleeping in makeshift shelters on street corners. New Delhi was modern, with affluent looking businesses and colonial residences, where beggars were not welcome. But both were oppressive and crowded and I felt exhausted with the constant sweat trickling down my face.

I was glad when we headed for Darjeeling, a cool hill station in the far north on the edge of the Himalayas. The last part of the journey was on a tiny one track railway, snaking its way precipitously up the mountains. We looked out of the window at the bright green terraces where peasants were tilling the land in the sun and smiled at the young Tibetan woman sitting opposite us with her daughter. They had long braided black hair intertwined with coloured ribbons and beautiful slightly Mongoloid eyes. They both wore pinafore dresses and striped aprons with bright silk blouses underneath.

'Lots of refugees came here when the Chinese invaded Tibet,' Johann reminded me. Then he put his arm round my waist and said, 'Perhaps we could buy you a Tibetan dress?'

We found a tiny one storey house perched high on a hill on the outskirts of the town. We woke up each morning to watch the sun rise over the Himalayas in a pageant of colour. We were so high that in the cool of the morning we looked down on a sea of clouds. As they rose like smoke they changed colour and texture, revealing a breath-taking view of the vast mountains beyond. The mountains were like great white angelic beings and seemed to hold the secret power of all the yogis who were drawn there to attain enlightenment. It was early December and the days were short, but translucently clear with diamond blue skies.

On our first day we walked down steep winding roads and tracks to the weekly market. After buying provisions we sat on the edge of the square with some other travellers and some Tibetans who had roadside stalls selling everything from chai to the most beautiful turquoise, coral and silver jewellery. Some of them were brewing the traditional salted butter tea over a fire. I could hardly drink it but Johann didn't mind the taste, or the joints, which he accepted eagerly. Now I was away from Japan and back in India with the man I loved, I no longer felt drawn to the stuff.

We spent hours watching kites flying against the backdrop of the Himalayas. It was the local sport, and what a transcendent one, playing with wind and sky! Each morning we walked down into the village, breathing the clear mountain air and greeting the ever good humoured Tibetans. One day we took a trip to the point where you could see the sun rise over Mount Everest. We went in a tourist bus, and after a short walk in the cold dawn we stood silent with awe and watched the first rays of sun hit those distant blue peaks, transforming them through violet to pale magenta, dusky crimson, and then to pink and a deep rich gold.

After a couple of weeks of being tourists in Darjeeling I felt the need for something more. Something inner was calling me. Many Tibetan monks had fled here for safety when their monasteries were ransacked by the Chinese. They had opened a monastery perched on the edge of these mountains, as if they were in Tibet. One day when we were walking near the monastery we met a maroon robed monk with a beatific smile. We greeted him and were soon chatting together.

'Why do you travel in India?' he asked, genuinely curious. 'Are you seeking something spiritual?' We replied that we were interested in Eastern spirituality. 'You can visit the monastery where I live, and come to meditate with us if you wish,' he said, his eyes twinkling gently. 'We have a few Westerners who study with us.'

'I would like to come and meditate,' I replied shyly, as Johann smiled good naturedly beside me. 'But I don't know how long we will be staying.'

'You may come any evening at seven if you wish.' He smiled as if he was playing a game, but there was only goodwill and compassion emanating from him. His face was brighter than any I had ever seen before.

'I will try to come one evening,' I answered glancing at Johann to see if he was interested.

'Yes, that's good.' He gave me a deep glance of acknowledgement and recognition.

Two days later I was watching kites flying above our house at sunset—men and children dancing around in the distance. Some of them were on the roofs of their houses, holding dragon kites and coloured paper birds. How much better than football, I was thinking, when Johann came to join me.

'I'd like to visit those guys we met at the market,' he said. 'They invited us for a smoke any time.' He put his arm around me. 'You wanna come?'

'I'd been thinking it would be nice to go and meditate at the monastery . . .' I turned away disappointed. 'It's always the same old scene—smoking.'

'Well, I'm not in the mood for meditating. It's not really my scene. But why don't you go anyway? I'll meet you at the chai stall afterwards.'

'OK,' I sighed.

As I approached the ornate building in the dusk I could just catch the shape of the carved wooden roof against the darkening sky. Inside, a friendly monk pointed to a rack where I could put my sandals and silently led me to a meditation room, almost as if I was expected.

The room was large, and glowing with candles and incense. On a small dais sat a serene bronze statue of Buddha surrounded by golden offering bowls filled with rice and water. The walls were flanked with large vibrantly coloured wall hangings depicting various Buddhist deities, some looking violent and wrathful, others benign and compassionate. The floor was carpeted in maroon rugs and I could see splashes of silky amber cushions in the darkening sanctuary. The monk pointed to a cushion, silently indicating where I should sit. There were about twenty people in the room, sitting cross legged or kneeling on cushions. Most of them were Tibetan monks with shaved heads, wearing dark maroon robes and saffron sleeveless shirts revealing cold bare arms. Amongst them were a handful of Westerners and a few Indians. I noticed there were only three other women there, who all looked like travellers.

I sat down and started meditating to my transcendental meditation mantra from Rishikesh. A few minutes later everyone rose as a little bright eyed lama entered. He bowed and walked towards the platform, where he stood for a moment with his hands in the prayer position, smiling at those beneath him in greeting. The audience responded with the same gesture and I found myself joining in quite naturally with the others. He had an aura of peace and presence which seemed to pervade the whole room.

We all sat down and the monks started chanting. I had been feeling a bit anxious and insecure. It was the first time I'd gone out alone in the mountains at night. But gradually the chanting quietened my mind and I felt myself in touch with this ancient lineage, steeped in discipline and peace. The rhythm was touching a deep part of my psyche. It was like the relief of a chronic pain wearing off, a great weight lifting from me. The chanting seemed to be washing me in waves of reassurance. Then I was thrown into the past.

I'm three and crying at the top of that staircase. I'm falling and screaming. I'm not screaming from the fall but with the pain of knowing that my father is leaving. Then I feel the familiar fear creeping into my cells. The fear of my stepfather.

I started sobbing while the soothing chants continued. I opened my eyes to check that people weren't looking, but everyone had their eyes closed and were completely involved with chanting. As my eyes rested on the serene figure of the lama he opened his eyes for a few seconds and appeared to be looking directly at me, but I couldn't be sure in the flickering light. All I knew was that I felt a wave of healing warmth as tangible as warm water surrounding my chest and heart. I felt a deep sense of relief, as if someone was helping me carry a heavy load I hadn't even known had been such a burden.

Looking back, I see that meditation as a turning point in my life. Up to then I had unconsciously been trying to heal the wounded child within me through the love of a man. Now for the first time I experienced the possibility of healing myself consciously through spiritual practice.

Darjeeling

Yoga ashram, Pondichery

'And this is for you,' Johann said the following day as he fished a brown paper bag out of his jeans pocket. Inside was a chunky necklace of turquoise interspersed with bright red coral beads, with a strange wide brown and white bead in the middle. 'It's the traditional necklace which is sacred for the Tibetans.'

'I love it.' I reached up to kiss him.

The next days passed companionably with reading and walks to the local chai shops to chat with the Tibetans.

'I'd like to go trekking in the Himalayas, see if I could be able to visit Bhutan or Sikkim.' Johann was beginning to get bored. 'But I know it wouldn't suit you with your health. I wonder what you could do?' Something was wrong with me and it wasn't only the recurring dysentery. I hadn't menstruated for a year, was painfully thin no matter how much I ate and I was increasingly weak. I knew I needed to look after myself.

'Perhaps I could go to that yoga ashram in the south. I could do an intensive training and begin to get my strength back,' I said nervously, knowing that it would mean us separating again for a while.

'It's difficult being together when we want such different things,' Johann said unhappily.

'I know,' I said. 'It feels so confusing. Perhaps I should go and see the lama again. Maybe he could help.' I was remembering that powerful healing energy which had lifted such a weight off me. 'Maybe things will become clearer.'

The following day we walked together down the narrow cobbled streets to the edge of town. Smoke was rising from the chimneys even though it was only early afternoon. A monk greeted us and told us there was no meditation group at the moment.

'Could I have an audience with the lama?' I asked hesitantly. The monk smiled and left us in a cold room with walls covered with colourful hangings and bookcases crammed with Buddhist texts. The monk returned and indicated that we should follow him. We were ushered along a narrow dark passageway and through a door into a room hardly bigger than a storage cupboard where the lama sat cross legged on a wooden bed, covered with woven rugs and silk cushions. He had a smooth round face with soft hooded eyes and around his wrist were the strings of beads he used for counting mantras. There was an altar in the corner of the room, with an oil lamp burning by a small bronze figure of Buddha, with a bowl of flowers at its feet. The room was heavy with resinous incense. Although it was a completely unfamiliar world, I felt the same deep sense of homecoming I had felt when visiting the Maharishi's ashram. The lama indicated for us to sit opposite him on two wooden chairs. He closed his eyes and started chanting while we sat silently, absorbing the atmosphere and listening to him.

'Where are you from?' he asked after he had finished his chants with a long 'Om Mane Padme Hum' and had quietly opened his eyes.

'We are travelling,' Johann answered. Cathy is from England and I am German.'

'Where do you go next?' he looked enquiringly at us. 'Do you like to stay here and study with us?'

'I don't know where I'm going,' I said, feeling a knot of tight confusion in my throat as I spoke. 'Johann wants to go trekking but I am weak with dysentery and I don't really know what to do. We won't stay here long. Not long enough to study with you, but I thought you might be able to help me.'

He looked directly into my eyes and as he did so he seemed to be transformed from a little old man into an extremely powerful sage who could see right into me. Then he closed his eyes as if looking inward to find the most appropriate response.

'In this lifetime you have chosen many lessons, much karma,' he said gently, again looking as if he could see right through my body into my soul. 'For you it is most important to care for physical body, preparing yourself for higher practices.'

This was a clear answer to the question I was going to ask: whether I should go to the yoga ashram or stay with Johann.

'Your nervous system is too sensitive. You must be careful with emotions as they can harm your body too much and let in disease. Care of body will help balance. Most important.' He looked at me significantly. 'Most important,' he repeated and looked at me with a smile of great warmth and compassion.

There was so much more I wanted to ask him but he had shut his eyes as if the subject was closed. I knew this meant the interview was over and felt both elated and sad as he had seemed to know me more deeply than I did myself. I knew there was so much I could learn from him, but unless I stayed in that monastery I wouldn't share his wisdom, and I knew the time wasn't right for that. Johann didn't want an interview, so we slipped away quietly.

'I've read about meetings like that in Paul Brunton's books about the Himalayas,' Johann said as we walked slowly back up the hill. 'These wise people always seem to give hints, as if they know your whole life but are only allowed to tell you crumbs of information to keep you going.'

'I suppose it's about free will,' I said, looking around at the distant mountains. They were giving out an aura of mystery in the growing dusk as the last hints of rose and purple clung to their peaks. 'We're only supposed to know so much or we wouldn't have the free will to chose our own destiny.'

'But do we chose our destiny?' Johann said thoughtfully.' In those books the wise ones already seemed to know what the questioner would do long before they came into a situation where they apparently made a choice.'

'I just don't know. It's so mysterious.' We walked hand in hand up the steep path which led to our little home. The sky was like a dark shell above us, and I wondered how many wise yogis were sitting in caves or other hidden dwellings in those magnificent mountains, watching the same darkening sky from a completely different level of consciousness. The question hung in my mind like a secret night bird as we walked home in companionable silence.

But our companionable mood didn't last more than a few days and through the next weeks our differences seemed to widen all the time.

'Why do you have to smoke so much dope?' I asked him. 'Why don't you meditate with me sometimes instead?'

'What does it matter anyway?' Johann looked bewildered. 'I don't know why you've got a problem with dope, it grows here, it's harmless and cheap and anyway I really enjoy it. You reach the same place anyway—only it's quicker.'

'I just feel closer to you when you're not stoned. You seem a lot more sensitive.'

'I'm insensitive, just because I smoke? Do you think the thousands of sadhus here are insensitive too?' He shut his book, turned away and started rolling a joint, as if to make his point. I walked into the simple kitchen to put on the kettle.

'Let's not argue.' I was angry at myself for feeling irritable with him.

'I'm beginning to feel like moving on anyway,' he said. 'And you know you want to go to the yoga ashram.'

'And you don't want to come?' I was on emotional quicksands again.

'I've been thinking about Goa. Trekking seems like hard work since the weather's not so good. There's a great scene there, but you'd hate it. Too much dope and living on the beach again.'

'I wouldn't like the dope but I'd love the beach. I'd come with you if I didn't need to go to the yoga ashram for my health.'

'So why don't we go our own separate ways for a while and see what happens?' He didn't seem to realize how much his words hurt me.

It was like an action replay. I felt like he'd stabbed me in the heart but this time I wasn't going to plead or weep. I was trying to trust that whatever happened in life was meant to be.

'Let's just keep in touch by post and see what happens,' he said, avoiding my eyes.

Two days later he was gone and I was sitting alone and in shock watching the sun set over the mountains. My idea of love was obviously completely different from his. For me he was my soul mate, the man I would be with for life, and our differences were just tests we had to work through. But who was I for him?

Heartbreak and Yoga, 1970–1971

I Am Hollowed

I am hollowed
An empty shell
When you say
You don't love me any more
My heart feels torn out
Tangled. Broken.
Words unsaid, now spoken
Reveal seas of separateness
Between us
And suddenly we are like
Distorted watery reflections
Of what we have been.

Never did I want
To touch these
Shores of grief again
Nor lose the threads
Of togetherness—
Yet out of this
Alchemical pain
Like blue in the centre
Of a flame
Comes peace
Which gives it all meaning

I spent the morning walking around the hills in a daze. Then I went to the Tourist Office and bought a plane ticket to Pondicherry in the far south. I'd heard about an inexpensive yoga ashram there which took foreigners for training. I would leave in a week. I was told I'd have to change planes in Calcutta. I needed to stay the night there and get the connecting plane in the morning. As I packed up what had been our little home for six weeks, I felt as if I was packing up my dreams. Then it was time to leave.

I thought Johann would still be in Calcutta. He'd said he would stay there a few days before heading south to Goa. Surely there'd be no harm in trying to find him. I could stay with him for a night and we could try to make at least some plans about the future. I was already aching with missing him.

I arrived in Calcutta airport at night and got a rickshaw to the area where we'd stayed before. The streets were steaming and chaotic and I felt the weariness of the wasted rickshaw wallah who was pulling me through this mayhem. He dropped me off somewhere unfamiliar assuring me the hippy hotels were nearby. I knew there were about six of them all on one street, but soon found myself wandering through dark back streets where beggars slept like discarded piles of clothes in the shadows. The smell of sewage, the heat and incense hit me like a sickening memory as I felt increasingly disorientated and lost. Finally I was in the brightly lit bazaar of a street where I imagined the hippies hung out.

I started asking for Johann at each reception desk and by the time I reached the third hotel I was beginning to feel panic rising. I was in a nightmare. Crowds on the streets were leering up at me and beggars hands were grabbing me. Young men were following me asking if *memsahib* was 'looking for hotel' or 'want to be shown good Western restaurant.' It was nearly midnight and I was exhausted. Finally I saw some hippies sitting in the doorway of an old Victorian building and asked if they'd met a guy called Johann. 'Yes, he's cool, they said. Up there in the lounge hanging out with a girl called Miranda.' I ran up the stairs and there they were entwined and asleep together in an armchair. I went up to them and shook Johann awake. He was obviously confused to see me.

'Johann, I've been looking for you. What are you doing?' His pupils were dilated.

'We took some acid.' He looked at me distantly. 'How come you're here anyway?' Miranda was still wound around him looking up at me pityingly, like the cat that's got the cream.

'Please, Johann, let's just go to your room and sort things out. I've only got one night.' He disentangled himself reluctantly and led me to a box-like airless room with no windows and a large double bed.

I sat on the edge of the hard bed. 'What's going on with you and her?'

'Everyone was taking acid yesterday and I took some with the crowd and then she came on to me . . . so . . . you know . . . You shouldn't have come.' He looked guilty. 'You know I don't like hurting you.'

'How could you? We've only just separated. I just thought we'd have a night together and try to sort things out. I'm on my way to the ashram . . . I wish I'd never come . . . I wish I'd never met you . . .'

'Oh, come on Cathy, she's only a girl I was having fun with, nothing's changed with you.'

But I knew that wasn't true. For me everything had changed. I lay awake rigid with grief as he slept serenely beside me. As dawn approached I started puking and having terrible diarrhoea. In the morning I was too ill to move. I didn't care about the yoga ashram or my health or anything any more. I just wanted to die.

'Let's go and forget all our problems.' Johann said as I lay on the bed crying later that morning. 'I'll take you somewhere you can forget all about everything.' He helped me out of bed and led me down the street to a dilapidated house where we found ourselves in a large attic-like room strewn with soft rugs and cushions. It was an opium den! 'Don't worry, it's good stuff, it'll make you feel better—you'll fly again' He looked at me anxiously. There were several older Indians there, gaunt and dreamy looking. I was the only woman. Johann and I were shown to a space where we could lie. We were also shown the sickly hole in the floor that was the toilet.

'If you sick you running there.' The shadowy grey haired attendant nodded his head knowingly from side to side. Then we were handed a huge pipe with a glass globe of water at the bottom. The wraith-like man stuffed the top with something black, lit it and handed it to Johann. He inhaled deeply and the water bubbled as the smoke went through. He rested a moment and inhaled deeply again. He smiled beatifically and handed it to me. Following Johann, I inhaled deeply, took a few breaths and inhaled deeply again. I put the pipe down and felt violently sick. I rushed to the dirty toilet and threw up, then went back to lie next to Johann. He put his hand out.

'Are you OK?' And suddenly I was. All the pain I'd been feeling for the last few days had disappeared and the illness along with it.

I'm lying in a cotton wool cloud of well being, floating on the edges of lush green English meadows.

I'm riding the waves on a vast Indian beach.

I'm sitting surrounded by vivid tropical flowers at the Maharishi's ashram. A beautiful Indian appears and hands me a succulent yellow mango and tells me I must say my mantra. I try to remember my mantra but it just floats away . . . and I float into a dream of colour images and poetry . . .

It was probably a few hours, but felt as if a day had gone past by the time we stumbled out into the heat and hubbub of car horns, rickshaws and crowds. Johann took my hand and guided me back to the hotel where we lay around in the little room for a while and fell asleep in each others arms. When I woke up he was gone. I lay there thinking he'd probably gone for a shower or some food. But he didn't return. I went to find him but just met a group of hippies sitting in the communal lounge. I sat down there trying to not to cry but tears were falling helplessly down my cheeks. I knew he'd gone to see Miranda. Several people who had seen what was happening came over and laid me down gently on a sofa. They surrounded me in a circle, stroking my hands and hair and feet. They looked lovingly into my eyes and a woman held me and rocked me against her soft breasts.

'You mustn't be sad,' she said. 'We're all brothers and sisters here. We all love each other. We all sleep with each other. It doesn't matter. You think there's not enough love to go round, but there's plenty.' They put a George Harrison LP on an old turntable and I heard him singing 'My Sweet Lord'. I couldn't stop the tears. The group were stroking and massaging me, covering me with a soft rug, and I gradually fell asleep on the sofa. In the night I woke with a shock of pain and crept back to our room. Johann was there sleeping soundly and I curled up next to him, spooning myself into his smooth back. He turned over and pulled me closer to him in his sleep. Perhaps everything would be OK after all.

But in the morning he was cool and didn't want to talk about his feelings for Miranda or our future. 'I'm confused.' He looked at me blearily, as if he was a different man from the one I had known in the Himalayas. 'I don't know what I feel or want any more.' He put his arms around me sadly. 'Can't we just separate for now? I'll go to Goa and you to the yoga ashram and we'll see what happens. I need to be alone to sort my head out and you need to get strong again. Let's live in the moment and we will see what happens afterwards.' A couple of days later he was gone.

I was still too weak with dysentery to travel, I felt my already delicate vitality was slipping away like water, as if Johann's betrayal had sucked away all my life blood. Perhaps I should go home, but I felt I had no home. The hope of the swinging sixties had died in me and most of my memories were of being a nanny, living in a tatty London bedsit, and going through difficult relationships. I couldn't go back. What about phoning my parents just for a chat? But going to a post office to make a long distance call only to hear my mother's distress felt insurmountable.

I was wandering alone and aimlessly on the streets near the hostel a couple of days later when a wiry dull-eyed Indian youth sidled up to me. 'You like cocaine?' he whispered.

'OK, yes, I'll try it,' I found myself saying. I would do anything to get out of this emotional pain, and I was beyond trying to meditate. He handed me a tiny plastic package with what looked like salt inside and I handed him a few rupees. 'How do I take it?' I asked opening my hands questioningly.

'You sniff.' He mimed, holding one nostril closed and sniffing in with the other. 'Only take little.' I went back to the empty room and put a little of the white dust in my palm, held one nostril shut and sniffed it in with the other. Suddenly I was flying. The pain had gone. I went out into the lounge and started talking and joking with the group sitting there. I found myself telling amusing traveller's stories about our journey with Hobbit and having to fly him back from Japan. Everyone was rolling around laughing and an attractive artistic-looking guy was making eyes at me.

'You seem like a different person,' said Annie the American who had held me to her breasts a few nights before.

'It's cocaine all around my brain,' I sang and they nodded knowingly.

The next few days I stayed in the hotel. I'd got no urge to go anywhere and didn't seem to need food. I sniffed cocaine whenever the emotional anguish got too strong and I couldn't believe how easy it was to feel OK again. The crowd in the hotel had become my friends and family. We lay around listening to The Grateful Dead, telling our travellers' stories or reading. Every now and then a few of this itinerant family got a meal together in the communal kitchen and we all ate. It seemed quite a few of us were on cocaine or visiting the opium den regularly.

After some days I'd finished my stash of white magic and went out on the street to look for the young guy who sold it to me before. There I saw a blond haired beggar. He was tall and emaciated and all the life seemed to be drained out of his eyes. He was obviously a foreign hippy of some sort, just got lost on drugs on the streets of India, I thought. Maybe he'll die here and nobody will really know or care.

I stopped and walked quietly back to the hotel. I knew I had to head south and study yoga.

I arrived in Pondicherry just before Christmas 1970. I couldn't start a course at the Ashram until the new year, so I hired an airy room and set out to explore the town. It had been a French colony and still had a European feel. The streets were wide, the houses white with ornate painted balconies. It was a mixture of French colonial mansions and wealthy Indian residences, set in pools of colourful tropical gardens. It felt like an opulent island amidst the surrounding poverty where peasants lived in shacks with a few animals.

I hired a bike and discovered a second hand bookshop where I browsed and chatted with the friendly owner. One day a book called *Autobiography of a Yogi* leaped out at me from a shelf. I had to buy it. It was the life story of Yogananda, a great Indian sage who brought yoga to the West. His life was strewn with miracles and meetings with incredible Masters. This was what I was looking for, the magic mystics of India. Everything else was being taken away from me. My love and my health had gone. It was surely not by chance that I was reading that book just before starting my yoga training. It was only years later that I realised that the Yogananda who dropped into my life with that book was my guru.

On Christmas Day I woke feeling alone and ill with diarrhoea. My constant dysentery was bad enough, but worse was the clawing emotional pain of missing Johann and having no friends or support. I washed in the grimy shower and wondered what to do with the day.

Determined to get out of self pity, I put on my best cherry-coloured dress and decided to go for a bicycle ride along the coast. I was riding by the sea when I passed a group of colourful looking foreigners. As I rode past them someone called out, 'Hey, beautiful, Happy Christmas!' I stopped and got off my bike. When I told them I was alone they linked arms with me.

'Come and have lunch with us, we're eating at the beach restaurant down near the ashram. You can't be alone on Christmas Day.' I could have wept with relief.

Over a Christmas dinner, which was an interesting Indian imitation of British food, they told me about the community where they were staying, a few kilometres outside the town. It was called Auroville. There they were building alternative houses and structures and trying out new ways of living ecologically, sharing resources. That afternoon, merry with food and wine, my new friends took me to the Aurobindo Ashram, which had been the precursor to Auroville. It was a white building perched right by the beach.

'Aurobindo was a great Indian saint, and his enlightened partner, known as The Mother founded this Ashram in his memory. It was through her inspiration that Auroville was founded,' an enthusiastic young woman told me as she led our little group into a small courtyard. A tremendously peaceful energy emanated from the saint's tomb which was covered with fresh sweet jasmine flowers. Later my new friends drove me to Auroville, a few miles away. At that time there were just a few structures being built on land which appeared inhospitable, arid and desert like. Now, forty years later, it's a thriving ecological community, dense with trees and productive gardens, and highly respected the world over.

After my introduction to the Aurobindo Ashram, I meditated by the tomb in the shady courtyard every day. It was a short cycle ride from where I was staying and was a great solace in my loneliness. I walked by the sea, trying to come to terms with the possibility that my relationship was truly over. I was glad when the week passed and I was cycling towards the large flat roofed mansion called the Gitananda Yoga Ashram.

The ashram was in the middle of nowhere, a few miles out of town, surrounded by a dry scrubby landscape. There were no lush irrigated flower beds like at the Maharishi's place, but a couple of banyan trees guarded an outside shrine where there was a small statue of Krishna and Radha and a large fierce one of Shiva, dancing and glowering out at the world. I felt a special affinity for and fear of Shiva. He's the god who cuts through ignorance and I felt as if he was managing my life. The shrine was strewn with flowers, and coloured powder dusted the earth with patches of rich red and saffron. Offerings of rice lay scattered around a circular fire pit surrounded by cold grey stones.

Every morning we woke at six and cycled to the nearby beach. The sand was cool and dry as the sun rose in a great golden lobe over the sea. There were about fifteen of us, all foreigners, and we became a family of moving sun worshippers, doing our salutes to the sun on that beach with our teacher, a plump, grey bearded, long haired Swami dressed in loose saffron robes. Then we would cycle back for a fruit and rice breakfast in an echoey refectory.

In the morning we practised Hatha Yoga, the physical postures or *asanas* we are so familiar with in the West. We were also taught breathing practices called *pranayama*, which help to balance the right and left hemispheres of the brain and still the mind. The theory is that the *kundalini*, or vital life energy, is seated at the base of the spinal column; through balancing and energising the body/mind with *asana* and *pranayama*, the energy of the *kundalini* is gently stimulated and begins to rise; and as it does so it awakens higher consciousness and inner peace.

We learned that yoga means unifying the mind, body and spirit and that the postures and breath are like threads which link all three. In the early afternoons we were given discourses from the great Vedanta teachings, the roots of yoga philosophy. We learnt that Hatha is only one branch of yoga and there are others such as Karma Yoga, the way of service, Bhakti, the yoga of devotion, Jnana, the way of knowledge and Raja Yoga, the royal path. But all these yogic paths have one aim, which is to help us go beyond our illusion of separateness and experience the divine timeless presence within, which is normally hidden beyond our outwardly focused attention.

We also did various cleanses, inhaling and drinking quantities of salt water to clear the nasal and digestive tracts. There was much blowing of noses and rushing to the toilet! In the late afternoons we were free to study or have a siesta. I usually slept on the roof wrapped cocoon-like in a shawl, where I felt like a chrysalis, waiting to transform into a butterfly and find my wings. Evenings were taken up with more postures and *pranayama* on the roof, where we watched the sun set in a palette of apricot and russet as the dusk gathered. Then we would go to our rickety beds in the simple bare dormitory.

I grew to love the quiet rhythm of the days. After the postures and meditations my untamed, unhappy mind would feel stilled and I started to glimpse moments of peace and acceptance. I had no idea what had happened to Johann. I got no mail and there was no way of contacting him by phone. It was a relief, as I was learning that the whole purpose of yoga was to become complete within oneself. I now knew that all other happiness is transient, that the only constant is change and that anything of this world can be snatched away in a moment. I tried to detach myself from my dreams of a future with Johann. After all, I was being taught that thoughts have no more substance than clouds passing in the sky and that a human incarnation is the gift in which to realize this. I felt I had no other choice than to take up the spiritual path, it seemed to be my destiny.

I had been at the ashram nearly a month and it was full moon. We prepared the grounds for a special night, decorating the shrine with flowers, putting offerings of rice and milk in front of the statue of Shiva, the fierce god with his double edged sword. A great soft amber moon rose. The air was thick and rich with the perfume of jasmine and sandalwood. On a brazier nearby simmered a big cauldron of chai, mixing its spicy cinnamon scent with those of the flowers and incense. I was sitting on the dry earth in a half circle of yoga students and the flower-like women staff of the ashram. They were dressed in their finest saris and shawls with deep kholed eyes and flowers in their oiled black hair. We all faced the fiery statue of Shiva. We had pledged to spend the night chanting to him.

A beautiful plump woman with a red bindi on her forehead started to play the harmonium and some of the young male Indian staff improvised on drums and percussion instruments. 'Om Namah Shivaya,' praise to the great god Shiva, we chanted as the night unfolded. The harmonium player sang out each line and we followed in call and response. The moon now hung huge and pale in the cooling night.

We had been chanting and meditating for a couple of hours when the singing changed to a continuous chant of *Om*, the single syllable which is said to represent the vibration of the Universe. I opened my eyes and gazed upwards. I felt a sense of Presence and all the sound was sucked out of me.

I am drifting out of the limited boundary of my body. I am no longer a small woman. I am huge. I am Essence. I am flying free into a sea of stardust, soaring out into the galaxy, vast and super conscious.

I am no longer the fragile I, I think myself to be, but part of the great pattern of life. I feel a great sense of peace, joy and love welling up in me, far greater than the brief tastes I have had before. It is spreading through the cells of my body and reminding me that I am truly a cell in the body of the Universe.

I do not know how long I stayed suspended in that timeless blissful place. When at last I returned the chanting continued gently around me. I curled up in my woollen shawl on the warm friendly earth and fell into a dreamless sleep.

As the weeks went by my delicate body became vibrant and supple. At last I felt strong and healthy. The yogic cleanses—drinking salt water and eliminating toxins—had also cleansed my emotional body. Now my trauma seemed distant and unreal. I lived in this rhythm of sunrise and sunset, of postures, pranayama and meditation, of chanting and sleeping.

Then suddenly one day I felt strangely emotional. I wanted to run, and to make passionate love, I wanted to weep and scream. It was pre-menstrual tension and, though surprising, it felt real and sweet after a year of no moon cycles. And then the blood came. I had returned to womanhood.

As if my newly fecund body had called him, Johann appeared at the ashram a few days later, tanned, strong and magnetic. No letter of warning, no time for getting nervous, and I wasn't even angry or resentful about what had happened before. It just seemed totally appropriate that he was here now and we didn't need to talk about the past.

'Would like to come travelling again? 'he asked me gently as we sat in the ashram grounds the following day. 'I've had enough of that wild Goa scene and need some peace.' He looked like the man I had fallen in love with before our separations and I couldn't help my heart beginning to open again.

'I guess we could try,' I replied hesitantly.

'I know you love your yoga but you've been here for a while now, so I just wondered . . .' He looked at me repentantly.

'Of course I want to if you're sure that's what you want,' I replied looking into his eyes and dissolving into the magic again. 'I was wondering what I would do after this, and now I'm a lot stronger I expect it'll be OK.'

He took me in his arms tenderly, as if to pledge a new commitment. I, who had touched something vast and timeless on that full moon night, believed I could keep my own wholeness whatever happened. I had almost completed my yoga training and thought nothing of missing the last two weeks. I was ready for more adventures and naively thought I would never lose myself in love again.

We headed for the Nilgiri Hills, the blue mountains of the south, in Tamil Nadu. Perhaps they were called blue because of the blue mists which hang in the valleys, or perhaps after a precious blue flower which blooms there every twelve years. It was beautiful countryside and we found ourselves in a rich, high altitude, colonial hill station called Ootacamond. It had luxurious deciduous trees surrounded by rolling hills looking like the English downs, where the wealthy retreated out of the summer heat. For me, that March, I thought it was a perfect environment and climate to heal the past and start a new life with Johann.

We rented a serene room with views over the hills, above a courtyard filled with pink camellias. We spent time wandering around the town peacefully hand in hand, amidst the incongruous looking English buildings. We found a library where we borrowed books and spent the evenings reading companionably together, avoiding talking about the past or the future. I was still painfully thin so we often went to a café where I drank fresh local cows milk to fatten me up, little knowing that it would devastate my future.

One night after making love, I felt myself soar out into the universe as if I was dissolving into the Divine Mother. In that moment I was part of all mothers, part of creation. I said nothing to Johann who lay quietly by my side. I kept that feeling inside me like a precious gem close to my heart.

'I'm feeling really light headed and sick,' I told Johann a few weeks later as I struggled up the small hill to the library. 'I feel as if all my energy is being sucked away.'

'And you're just getting thinner and thinner,' Johann put his arm around my ribs, which stuck out alarmingly. 'It must be the dysentery again. You know I really think you should go back to England and get proper treatment. You can't go on like this, having to take antibiotics to get rid of it again.' He looked both impatient and concerned.

'You're right, my dysentery has been really bad these last weeks. I know I should go back. I'll cable my mother to see if she'll send me the money to fly home. What will you do?' I asked nervously.

'I'll travel home overland, I've always wanted to see how I'd do on my own, hitching and taking trains. Then we can meet again in England as soon as I'm back.' He hugged me reassuringly.

We spent our last day together in Delhi, in an air conditioned cinema for the cool, a cheap hotel to make love, and a restaurant to eat. My stomach was churning and my heart felt like a desert as we caught a rickety bus to the airport. I felt a sense of ending and foreboding all through my cells. Leaving him felt like a huge act of will.

'I love you,' he said, tenderly putting a thick garland of marigolds around my neck. 'I'll see you back in Europe in a few weeks.'

'I love you too,' I replied, clinging to him in a last hug. I walked up the steps to the plane feeling as if a limb was being severed with leaving the country and the man I loved after the two most incredible years of my life. In fifteen hours I would be in another world.

Part Two: Avalon

Return to London, March 1971

Waiting in the Wings

You have always been there
Waiting in the wings
Understudy of my life
But I could never give you birth
Living in hope that you would
Come through this broken stage
With a perfect body
To be the star of my life
I was so open to creating your beauty
—Calling repeatedly—
But you always left before time
As if you hadn't learned your lines
Easier to dream
Than have a screaming baby—Some said
—Those years of sleepless nights—
Easier to dream
Than have those terrible teens
Of secret smoke and deodorant—Some said
And it never ends:
The responsibility

They are still borrowing money
At thirty-three!
They add indignantly
But I would rather have had all that
Than compensating for a barren life
With you, my son, always waiting in the wings

I arrived back at Heathrow on a grey March day and my mother was there to meet me. There were no warm hugs or her saying how wonderful it was to see me. Just a nervous peck on the cheek and her confused frightened eyes. The change in me must have been a shock to her. I was skeletally thin, weighing about seven and a half stone to my normal nine. I talked with a strange travellers accent, a conglomeration of all the foreigners' accents rolled into one. My skin was darker than she'd ever seen it before and I was wearing thin threadbare Indian clothes. She told me later that she thought I had become a junkie. In fact I had become a yogini.

I was shocked too. London was so cold, it was like walking into a fridge. It appeared grey, sterile, clean and very empty after the teeming streets of India. It was also a different place from the one it had been for me in the days when I was filled with my flower power dreams and hopes.

It's 1968 and I'm living in Notting Hill Gate, near the Kings Road, epicentre of the swinging sixties. I'm working as a nanny in the weekdays, enchanted by the little girls I care for and take to the park. I'm wearing my long embroidered Israeli dress and silver anklets. It's a Saturday and there's going to be a free concert in Hyde Park. This morning Becky, my flat mate, and I went bargain hunting in Portobello Road market and she bought a Victorian cape. I bought a pair of Venetian glass ear rings with swirls of embedded blue which bring out the blue of my eyes. It's a hot summer afternoon as we head for the park.

Pink Floyd unpack their instruments from a van and walk up to the small stage. Then we're dancing, swaying and spacing out into the cosmos. A man with a silk ruffled shirt and skin tight bell bottoms is dancing close to me. He picks a rose from a nearby flower bed and hands it to me, saying, 'Peace and Love babe.

Peace and love.' We're all stoned and it seems as if this party will last for ever. We will bring peace and love to this planet. The Beatles have sung it. That's what first woke me up, seeing them on our black and white TV screen when I was thirteen singing 'All You Need is Love'.

My mother took me home to a bedsit in the house which she and her new husband, Ivan, had bought since I'd been away. I didn't even know she had remarried. I settled in there, feeling disorientated, friendless and unwelcome. I had no idea what I was going to do next, apart from wait for Johann so that we could find a home and start a life together.

Nothing was said about my health, but I took myself to the hospital for tropical diseases and got some treatment for my dysentery. I slowly improved but was soon overshadowed by other changes in my body. My period was late and I was beginning to feel different. My breasts were tender, and I felt sick in the mornings. 'I must be pregnant,' I told the doctor insistently when a test came out negative. 'I've got all the symptoms and I feel different.'

'Maybe you are just feeling different because you've just returned from India and your body is adapting,' he said patronisingly. 'Come back in another month if your menstruation hasn't resumed and we will do some tests.' I came home confused. I desperately wanted Johann's child, could it be that this was creating my symptoms?

'Phantom pregnancies are quite common you know, and you told me you had a year without menstruation before,' he said when a second test came out negative. I came home feeling stupid and bewildered—he hadn't bothered to examine me. May began and I didn't feel well enough to go out and look for work or a different flat. I had a small income from some money my grandmother had left me and with that and the free bed sit I could manage.

The worst thing was waiting to hear from Johann. I had no way of getting in touch with him and, apart from a brief card I received a couple of weeks after I got back, I had heard nothing. I needed to have him confirm my reality about the pregnancy, to tell him about our baby. What was happening to him? Why couldn't he get in touch? Surely after two months he could have written or found a phone? Every time I heard my mother's phone ring upstairs my heart would jump, and every morning I would go downstairs hoping to see a foreign stamp on a letter.

The letter arrived at last. I ran upstairs, prolonging the pleasure by making myself breakfast before sitting down to open it. The room was full of spring sunshine, I had my window open and I could hear a blackbird singing against the distant roar of London traffic. My heart was beating with excitement as I tore open the blue airmail envelope.

> I am in Greece, living near the beach with a Cretan girl I met here. I'm so sorry to hurt you again but I thought I should tell you, and we can talk about it when I come to England.

I tore the letter up and pummelled my pillows. How he could do this to me again? Outside I could still hear the cheerful birdsong, but it seemed to be coming from another world, another time, a time when I had hope.

I wrote back to an address in Greece, not knowing if the letter would ever reach him.

> I'm sure I'm pregnant, but I'm confused because the tests say negative. What do you think I should do? I want our child but can't bear the pain of you being unfaithful, so please don't come to England unless you can really commit yourself to me. I love you and can't take any more.

By the middle of June I hadn't heard back from him. There were more symptoms of pregnancy and no sign of bleeding. I felt completely claustrophobic cooped up in my tiny bedsit. I had to get out of London. I had heard that there was going to be a festival to celebrate the Summer Solstice near a place in the west country called Glastonbury, an ancient town of spiritual pilgrimage with a sacred hill called the Tor. I borrowed a tent and a sleeping bag, packed them in a rucksack with my best Indian clothes and set off in a coach from Victoria.

This was the second Glastonbury Festival, and it was comparatively small, just about a thousand people, mostly hippies. Arriving in Somerset

Dancing at Glastonbury Festival, 1971

was a relief. The air was soft and the countryside gentle. The hedgerows were creamy and scented with elder blossom. A group of us hippies got off the coach at Glastonbury and I paired up with another young woman to hitch to the festival site about five miles out of town.

I put up my little tent amongst a group of others and went to have a look around. It was 1971, and in those days it only occupied a few fields on Michael Eavis' dairy farm. These days it's the biggest music festival in the world. This festival was in aid of the Campaign for Nuclear Disarmament, CND, and there were groups of young people camped in tents or makeshift structures of plastic and tarpaulins. It was a hot afternoon and both men and women were topless, while others were wearing Indian clothes like me, or were scruffy and unkempt. Nearly all the men had long hair and many had beards. There were Hell's Angels in their leathers who, despite their reputation, were chilled out and peaceful. Some people were even wandering around naked and nobody bothered.

To me it was like being in Formentera again, with lots of guys drumming and people dancing into the night. I immediately felt at home and completely safe with my tribe. In the distance I could see Glastonbury Tor, sticking out of the surrounding Vale of Avalon like a great pointed breast. Even from that distance its mystical energy seemed to pervade the place. By evening there were crowds around the glowing blue pyramid stage and I found myself happy and dancing to the sound of Arthur Brown singing 'Fire, You're Gonna Burn'. It was great to hear live music again, to be dancing under the darkening sky surrounded by the gentle green English countryside at midsummer.

Lots of people around me were on LSD and I could feel the energy changing to a higher frequency, even though I took nothing. Men and women came up to me and we would dance and meet wordlessly in movement, then drift off again into our own worlds. I ate supper in a small café where some musicians were playing Irish jigs. Later I sat around one of the camp fires with a group, chatting and drinking tea. Most of them were smoking dope but smoking held no attraction for me any more.

The following day everyone was talking about an enlightened young Indian guru who was coming to give his blessings to the people at the festival.

He was called Guru Maharaji and although only fourteen years old he was the teacher of an organisation called Divine Light. It was said that if you took an initiation into this path you would be shown how to access the inner light, hear the inner sound of the cosmos, and taste the inner nectar. He mounted the stage quietly with his followers while loud chanting rose from a group of Krishna devotees in the audience. I was interested in all this, but I didn't get much of an impression when the chubby adolescent guru gave a brief introduction to the teachings of Divine Light. Much more impressive was the appearance of two miniature rainbows above the festival grounds while he was speaking. Soon the word was out that these were angels, blessing our festival, and we all went around saying, 'Isn't it great that the angels are with us?'

That evening we celebrated the Summer Solstice, the longest day of the year, with Fairport Convention and Melanie playing into the night and a great group of stoned hippies dancing hedonistically around those Somerset fields until dawn. We all cheered the rising sun as it lit up the distant Tor with silver and finally reached us, where we were dancing or sleeping in huddles of warmth. In a state of near ecstasy, I felt that we really would change the world with our loving vibrations.

The following day I was feeling happy but exhausted. In the afternoon I strolled back down to the pyramid stage where a small band was playing, and started swaying gently to the music. After I had been dancing for a while I suddenly felt something tear and snap inside my belly. Oh God it's the baby! I thought, and immediately went and lay down in my tent. I felt a pulling pain in my pelvis. I was weak and light headed. Everything around me was swirling and I fell asleep, completely drained.

I slept until the following morning, when I woke up to find that I had been bleeding. I knew this could be a miscarriage, but instead of keeping completely still, which would have been wise, I felt I needed to get back to London. I managed to get a lift to Glastonbury with someone who left me by the Abbey and found myself sitting in the famous Abbey ruins disorientated. Many hippies who were returning from the festival were there while they waited for the London coach, and I watched them as if from a great distance as they danced around the grounds, played flutes and sat in groups smoking dope.

I was alone, in pain, and didn't have the energy to talk to anyone. A couple of hours later everyone piled into the coach and I sat there weak and dazed as we slowly made our way towards the city. By the time we arrived I could hardly walk, so I took a taxi and soon I was lying alone in my little bedsit, as if the festival was all part of a sweet dream which had never happened.

Looking back it seems amazing that I didn't tell my mother, who lived upstairs, but then it made sense not to disturb her new marriage when I knew she didn't want to be bothered with my problems. Instead I staggered to the doctor and told him I was having a miscarriage. He looked at me sceptically and said, 'Your pregnancy tests were negative, so you can't be having a miscarriage. These are obviously severe period pains as your menstruation is months late.'

He was the same one who never believed I was pregnant, and I saw he regarded me as some drug crazed hippy who didn't know what she was talking about. I went back to the bedsit half believing him. For two days I lay curled up in that darkened room in pain, dizzy with weakness, only crawling to the bathroom with the bleeding. On the third day I managed to crawl up the stairs to my mother's flat. She looked at me in horror.

'What on earth has happened to you?' she asked shakily. 'You look like a ghost.' I burst into tears and told her what had been happening.'Why didn't you tell me before?' she kept asking.

'I thought you wouldn't believe me,' I sobbed. 'And I didn't quite believe it myself because the doctor didn't believe me. And I didn't want to worry you in case it wasn't true.'

'Oh, Cathy, that's terrible,' she replied pale with upset. 'Of course you should have told me. Are you in pain?' she asked fearfully. 'I'd better call an ambulance.'

Within minutes I hear its siren, and I'm being carried on a stretcher out of the house. Then I'm lying on the crisp white sheets of a hospital bed, a nurse holding my pulse while a male doctor examines me.

'We'll try to save the baby,' he says. 'You're about four and half months pregnant. So we're going to put you on a drip, give you some pain killers and keep you very still.'

But the contractions and bleeding get worse and the pain is so bad I'm given morphine. I feel as if I'm flying around above my body. My mother sits beside the bed looking worried. The doctor visits and I hear him muttering something about the probability of needing a D and C, that operation they give to clear the womb after a late miscarriage. In the afternoon the doctor visits again and examines me. Another night passes in fevered painful dreams and in the morning a great lump of flesh and blood come out. I know that an essential part of me has died. There will always be someone missing.

I'd received no reply to my letter to Johann in Greece. So I wrote to him in Germany telling him about the miscarriage and asking if he was going to come to England. I asked him if he could commit himself to our relationship. His reply is etched like a burn in my mind.

> I have only just got back to Frankfurt. I didn't get your letter in Greece, so I didn't know you were pregnant. I'm so sad you miscarried our baby. I hope you are feeling better now. I was about to contact you to say I would visit soon. It all ended with the Greek girl and I would love to see you again. But I can't give you that commitment which you need so I better not come.

I paced my small bedsit like a caged animal. I lay on my bed and wept, but I didn't go upstairs to tell my mother. She didn't need a heartbroken friendless daughter. I re-lived all the beauty I'd shared with Johann and it seemed inconceivable that he could throw it all away in not wanting to commit to me. Now London was a world of sorrow. All I'd been doing there was waiting for Johann. I needed to get out of the city.

I arrived at Nanteos mansion in the height of summer and immediately felt at home in a simple room above the stable block, overlooking rolling Welsh hills towards the sea. There was a small community of young people living there at that time, and we meditated and ate together. During my meditations and walking around the gardens I would be besieged by memories from my travels in India, grief about the miscarriage and missing Johann. But I spent my time learning how to garden and enjoying the flirtatious attention of one of the long term residents, a guy who looked as if he had just stepped out of *Lady Chatterley's Lover*.

But sex was not on my mind. I needed to recover. By autumn I was feeling stronger both physically and mentally and I decided to go and visit some friends who I had met a few times in Formentera. Crispin and Jenny now had a baby, Matthew, and lived in a small stone cottage in the elemental countryside in nearby Radnorshire. They welcomed me warmly into their home and we shared all the adventures we had been through since our golden Formentera days. Another bond between us was Divine Light Meditation. I hadn't found the Transcendental Meditation I'd been initiated into in India worked too well for me since all my traumas. But after seeing the young Guru Maharaji at Glastonbury Festival I'd been initiated into his Divine Light Meditation, which Crispin and Jenny also practised

We led a simple life, as none of us went out to work. Crispin and Jenny were signing on and I still had a small income from the money I'd inherited from my grandmother. We baked bread, grew some vegetables in the garden and looked after the baby. The weekly shopping trip took us a whole day as none of us could drive and there were no buses where we lived, so we had to hitch to the nearest town ten miles away. But in those days it didn't matter. We had our whole lives ahead of us. We knew that the most important thing was to see the Divine Light and hear the inner sound, which we practised together every evening once Mathew was asleep.

At the beginning of these meditations my mind would be filled with thoughts and memories, noisy and turbulent. They call it the monkey mind in India. But as I concentrated on the third eye, the space between my eyebrows, I would gradually see a deep indigo colour, the centre of which became a ball of white light. The more I concentrated on that light, the greater it grew, until it would take over and fill me with a sense of peace and bliss. This would only last a couple of minutes and then I would be back in my disturbed thoughts again. But when I felt it, it was the most important thing in the world.

The sweet domestic life we led was a relief after all I had been through. The burnished colours of autumn were especially beautiful that year, and I was beginning to feel at home in the Welsh countryside, with it's rushing streams and wild hills. I decided I would like to live there and started looking around for somewhere cheap to buy with my inheritance. I could have bought a house right then but I thought I had all the time in the world to look and find the right one.

Just before Christmas we travelled up to London to see Guru Maharaji. The hall was packed and the energy high. It was a peak experience and we went back to our little cottage light and radiant, believing we could totally change our reality, and thus the world, with meditation.

When we got home it was a fiercely windy November night and I couldn't sleep because of a sudden deep and throbbing pain in my ear. For some reason I was staying in my friends' caravan that night. I kept thinking of Johann and wondering where he was now. It was past midnight and the darkness seemed to be closing in on me. I lit a candle but it seemed to make no difference. I started shivering uncontrollably in bed. Suddenly a black cat leaped onto the covers and curled itself around my neck until I felt as if it was strangling me. I froze in fear. Surely this can't be Crispin and Jenny's cat, hiding in the caravan. It looked and felt completely different. I tried to push it away, but it seemed determined to stay, like a dead weight around my neck. I sat up and tore it away. I felt as if I was suffocating, as if I was struggling with some huge dark powerful entity. Icy fingers were around my neck. I realised it wasn't the cat I was trying desperately to tear away from me. It was the spirit of death.

The following morning I was extremely ill. My whole world was lurching and spinning about in a terrifying vertigo and I had become deaf in my right ear. The pain and tinnitus were like a nest of wasps buzzing and stinging inside my ear. I felt that a diabolical force of evil had entered me in that caravan and was pursuing me.

'I'm losing my balance,' I said to Crispin and Jenny, shakily holding onto the edge of the kitchen cabinet. 'My ear feels like a hornets' nest. I must get back to London.' I knew I had to get to a hospital quickly and the only one I could think of was University College in London, where my mother was a mature student.

'We'll get someone to take you to the station,' said Jenny nervously.

Three hours later I got off the train in my wellingtons, and wove my way through the Paddington crowds to get a taxi. I was staggering with the pain and felt like a disoriented refugee, wearing a tatty old mack and with only my sequinned Indian shoulder bag for luggage. The taxi driver looked suspicious when I hailed him but there was no way I could use the Underground with the world drunkenly lurching around.

'We'll take you in immediately,' said the doctor at Outpatients after a cursory glance. 'This could be really dangerous.' Soon I was up on the Ear Nose and Throat ward being given an anonymous white nightdress and towelling gown. I was put on an antibiotic drip and felt I was living an underwater existence with strange visual effects and distorted sounds. I phoned my mum who was studying in another part of the hospital. When she arrived I felt guilty for being in trouble again.

'The antibiotics aren't having any effect,' said the consultant a few days later. 'We'll have to do an investigatory operation.' Then he blandly told me that I might be forever deaf in my right ear. I was frightened and had no one I could share my fears with. Harold and Robbie must have visited me but I have no memory of them. My mother visited every day but we could never talk. She masked her concern behind a façade of cheeriness. I was surprised and touched when, years later, she told me she'd felt as though she'd had the flu for the whole year I was seriously ill.

After six weeks in the hospital, with the doctors and nurses treating me as something of a curiosity, the consultant came round to give me the news. 'You have a rare form of bovine TB which you can catch from infected milk.' I remembered all that seemingly innocent milk I had drunk in the Nilgiri Hills, and the love I had shared in that sweet hilltop town.

'Don't worry,' said the doctor reassuringly. 'We'll put you on the TB drugs and you'll soon stabilize.' The TB was in my mastoid bone, just behind the ear, rather than my lungs. It was a relief. At least they knew what was wrong with me. This diagnosis also explained why my pregnancy tests had been negative before I had my miscarriage: TB can mask pregnancy test results and induce miscarriages. Best of all, there seemed to be an easy cure. Little did I know!

I was put into solitary confinement in case I was contagious. Then I was given the anti TB drugs, huge wafers which were painful to swallow and had to be taken three times a day. Within a few days my body rebelled against them in a violent allergic reaction. I found myself thrashing around the bed, every part of me in agony. I was being poisoned.

'It's nothing to be frightened of,' the nurse said cheerily as my body moved around the bed like a crazy clockwork toy. 'It happens sometimes. We'll have to de-sensitise you by giving you very small doses and building them up slowly.'

Several weeks later I was moved to an annexe of the hospital and, since they had discovered that I wasn't contagious, I was allowed to go out for a few hours each day. I really appreciated my new freedom, as I wandered around Regents Park enjoying the trees and spring flowers. There I met a young gardener and we had long conversations while he weeded the beds. I had no other friends in London and he was the only person I could talk to. For the first time since Johann and I split up here was someone who cared for me. But there was no chance of a real relationship with me being so ill.

Finally, after being in hospital for nine months I was fully sensitized and on the dose of anti TB drugs I was supposed to take for the next two years. At last the day came when I could leave. The world looked so beautiful as I emerged like a butterfly from its cocoon. Even the London streets seemed exquisite once I knew I didn't have to return to hospital to take my pills, and I spent a couple of days enchanted by my new freedom. I vowed never to take life and beauty for granted again.

However, it was a brief respite. Soon I was reacting to the drugs again, thrashing around in bed in agony, and then back in hospital. No-one knew what to do with me. I couldn't try the second line drugs because they were even more toxic than the ones I was taking.

'I can't take any more medicines,' I told the consultant on his rounds. He looked apprehensively at his notes.

'We didn't tell you before because it wasn't necessary, but you need to know that we couldn't remove all the tubercular bone because it was too near your brain, so if you don't take any medication it could spread . . .'

'And I could die,' I filled in. He just stood silently looking at his feet.

He knew there were no better drugs to offer me. They had done all the desensitization possible and I had still reacted allergically. There was nothing more to say.

'I will heal myself naturally,' I said.

Looking for a Cure, 1972–1974

Meditation

Stillness only stillness returning
With breath of night returning, turning
Inwards with breath
Exploring expanding stillness
Touched by the Word recurring revolving
With planets with plants with devas turning
Stillness to form from Om creating
Bodies of sun in stillness creating
Worlds of stars of planets revealing
Seas of galaxies revolving
Through form through Earth
Through human awakening
Through cell through blood
Through egos burning
Through birth through death
Through breath returning to stillness

Harold paid for me to go to a naturopathic clinic for a fortnight to get me started on a nature cure regime. Naturopathy takes a holistic approach to healing with non-invasive treatment and avoids the use of surgery and drugs. Tyringham clinic was in a nineteenth century country mansion, set in the picturesque gentle hills of Buckinghamshire. There I was surrounded by mostly wealthy middle-aged women (and some film stars like Julie Christie I heard later) who were on extreme diets for cleansing, slimming, arthritis or rheumatism. The first day I arrived I had a consultation with the naturopathic doctor.

'Tell me your story,' the soft eyed woman encouraged me. 'I want to know what makes you tick.'

I burst into tears. 'Sorry,' I sniffed. 'But you're the first doctor who's really seemed interested in me. Not just treated me like a set of symptoms.'

'It's OK to cry.' She handed me a tissue. 'It's part of your healing. In naturopathy we try to see you as a whole person, otherwise we can't decide or understand what's best for you.'

'It's just that I feel so alone. The doctors have given up on me and no one seems to know what I should do.' I couldn't stop the tears. She handed me another tissue gently putting her arm around my shaking shoulders. I told her my story.

'The first priority is to cleanse your liver from the drugs you were allergic to,' she said compassionately. 'Then we will decide on the best cleansing and strengthening regime for you.'

I was shown to a pretty room overlooking manicured grounds with woods in the distance. I was put on a mostly raw food regime with lots of juices and enemas. There were also gentle exercise classes, and mud or Epsom salts baths every day to draw out the toxins. I loved wandering around in my thick white towelling robe, pretending I was wealthy and healthy, just taking a little time out in a health spa. There was a great camaraderie amongst us women, despite our different backgrounds. Bath robes are a great equalizer and I no longer looked like a hippy, except perhaps for my old embroidered slippers. In the afternoons we had reflexology, a form of therapeutic foot massage, or complete body massages, which were the best.

'Hi, my name is Stephen,' said the young white-coated male masseur. I was surprised because I thought all the masseurs would be women. 'If you'd like to take your robe off behind the screen and you can keep you underwear on,' I had nothing on under my robe so I just wrapped myself up in a thick white towel lying on a chair behind the screen and walked back out to the couch.

'Now if you'd like to lie on your front I'll start with your upper back'. He looked at me appreciatively as I tried to manoeuvre the towel so I wouldn't reveal too much. 'Just tell me if my pressure is too hard or soft or if there's anywhere that really hurts,' he said gently as he laid his warm hands on my shoulders.

After my second massage he asked me if I would like to go out for a stroll in the grounds. I was surprised that a therapist would show such a personal interest in a patient. Nevertheless we went for several strolls round the grounds when it was sunny. But my time there was short.

'Do come and visit me any time you want,' he said as I was leaving. 'I've got a spare room and you can always stay as long as you like.' I had told him I had no home apart from my mother's bedsit and was uncertain about the future. I gave him a quick hug as I left and didn't think much about his offer at the time.

I left determined to follow my cleansing diet, exercise program and positive thinking and I did so for a few months that winter in the London bedsit. But I felt lonely and unsupported, hardly seeing my mother although she only lived upstairs. She felt an allegiance to Ivan and he wasn't interested in getting to know her grown-up children. Perhaps my family had no idea how ill I was. Harold had helped me go to the nature cure clinic and maybe he now felt that I was strong enough to get on with my own life. Perhaps I never really told them how much I needed them, or they would have given me more support.

Physically I often felt as if I was walking along the edge of a cliff and that only the greatest vigilance would save me from a fatal fall. Sometimes I would begin to feel quite good. My strength would begin to return and I would start to pick up the threads of my life again. But then the gnawing weakness would come back, as if some malicious creature was sucking away my life blood, and I was often too weak to get out of bed. I felt frighteningly alone and vulnerable. I lived in a haze of debility and pain, waking at night from feverish nightmares with my ear hurting and my tinnitus a high pitched scream in my head. I wondered how long I could survive.

Nowadays there are many books written about the gifts of illness, of how sufferers have had spiritual awakenings through the experience of disease. I didn't experience my illness like that at all. I had already had spiritual awakenings and being sick felt like a curse rather than a blessing. It seemed to take me away from my spirit into the depths of matter rather than the reverse. Yet I was determined. I had touched places of super-consciousness and light and knew that somehow I had to heal myself.

My Yoga training in India had taught me that we are far more than our physical body. I knew that traumatic emotional and mental stress can precipitate disease, and certainly that was part of the dynamic for me. My immune system had no doubt been seriously compromised by my heartbreak and miscarriage, but once an illness has become physical it's hard to reverse the process.

I found out about some spiritual healers through one of my yoga magazines and contacted them. They sounded warm and caring on the phone and invited me to stay with them for a month paying a small rent. I still had my inheritance to live on and this opportunity for healing seemed like a godsend.

This was my first experience of living with spiritualists. Elsie and Bill lived in a small semi-detached bungalow on the outskirts of London. It was cluttered with nick knacks and slightly crude paintings of American Indians and beautiful Madonna-like women, who they said were their spirit guides. They had a little annexe attached to the house which was their healing sanctuary and in that annexe was a tiny spare bedroom for guests. That's where Elsie led me when I arrived, shivering from the February cold.

'You just make yourself at home here, my love, and when you're settled come through and have some tea with us.' I unpacked my few belongings, feeling alienated and wondering if I'd come to the right place.

'You need anything, my love, you just ask,' said Elsie carrying a hot water bottle into my room that night. 'I can see you've been through a terrible time. Right poorly you've been, you poor love.' I was touched. She was treating me more like a daughter than my own mother. I was so unused to kindness and caring.

'This morning you'll have your first healing,' said Elsie the following day, over a traditional breakfast of bacon and eggs. Oh my God I thought, what about my diet? I decided to tell them later. 'We'll start in the Sanctuary at twelve when Bill's back from his post round. Now don't you be nervous.'

I lay on my side in a darkened incense-scented room with Fauré's requiem playing angelically in the background. Elsie cleared my aura with sweeping movements a few inches away from my body, as if combing away invisible cobwebs in the air around me. Bill held my feet with increasingly warm hands while Elsie put her hands on my spine at the level of my heart and I felt a gentle warmth emanating from her hands.

'I can see a dark line right through the centre of your heart,' she said.' It's like . . . broken in two.'

'I do feel like my heart is broken,' I whispered, feeling that searing emotional pain again. 'I've lost the love of my life and his baby . . . I don't even know where he is any more. We've lost contact . . . And I wanted his child so much . . .' All the dark emotions I'd been carefully suppressing were burning down my cheeks.

I'm seven years old and waking up from sleepwalking, trying to find the lights. I'm wearing a sheet around my shoulders like a cloak. As my mother leads me gently back to bed I keep saying, 'I need to turn on the lights. I'm trying to find the light.' My stepfather is a shadowy figure lurking behind a curtain in the sitting room in the semi darkness.

'You're a very spiritual woman,' said Elsie, handing me a tissue. She placed her hands at the top of my head. 'Now visualize a crystal-white waterfall of healing light rushing down all through your limbs, cleansing every cell in your body.' She gently dusted the top of my hair. Soon I felt as if I was actually standing under a waterfall, with drops of radiant light pouring through my body. 'Let go of all your pain dear,' she whispered softly.

That night I slept peacefully for the first time in months.

After a few weeks I was ready to move on and I left the healers with hugs, fond farewells and an invitation to return whenever I wanted. I hadn't known such caring people existed, and although I hadn't been able to keep up my diet, I'd cleared much of my emotional trauma and felt a bit stronger. I was better but certainly not cured. It was time to meditate again and live somewhere where I could eat well. I needed to find a community of like minded people. I also needed more inner strength to cope with my illness which was still often like a dose of debilitating flu.

Although I was practising the Divine Light meditation I was also drawn towards Buddhism and I travelled up to Samye Ling, a Buddhist monastery in Dumfrieshire, in the stark Southern Uplands of Scotland. From the outside it appeared like a traditional grey stone house, except for the coloured Tibetan prayer flags blowing in the wind. Inside, the meditation room reminded me of the meditation hall in Darjeeling where I had met the Tibetan lama. The walls were covered with *tankas*, colourful silk pictures of deities, and there was a shrine of Buddhas at the end of the room. In front of them were a line of offerings, bowls of rice and water.

I found that Buddhist teachings were more practical than those I had come across before, actually showing methods of becoming free from the mind and emotions which make us suffer. The Four Noble Truths of Buddhism say that there is beauty and pleasure in this human life, but every individual will experience suffering in sickness, ageing and death. We will all experience the gamut of emotions such as fear, desire, hurt, confusion and anger, plus being aware of all the suffering in the world. Buddhism says that the cause of suffering is in grasping and clinging, which becomes extended into greed, hatred and delusion. Most of the problems around the world such as poverty, hunger and war are directly or indirectly a result of this. There are enough resources for everyone on this planet, it's just that many of us, out of greed, take more than our fair share.

I shared a dormitory with six other women. None of them knew what I had gone through nor what I was still facing, but it didn't seem to matter much. I was happy to have company and just to be there. Every day I would meditate in the dimly lit meditation room, watching my breath rise and fall in a meditation called mindfulness of breathing. We were told not to identify with our thoughts and just let them pass through us like clouds in the sky. But it wasn't easy. My mind would rush around in circles and grab any convenient thought rather than follow my breath. I was amazed how hard it was to remember the breath, when the other meditations I had practised, like repeating my secret mantra or seeing the divine light, had been relatively easy. It was like trying to fly a kite in a gale, but gradually it became easier.

Then I would practice the Meta meditation, in which we were taught to develop compassion for ourselves and others. First we would have to ignite this feeling of love and kindness towards ourselves, then imagine love and compassion going towards a dear friend. This was not difficult, but the last two stages were harder. We had to visualize the feeling of love going towards someone we were indifferent to, and finally to an enemy or someone we really didn't like.

When I became tired and my concentration went, I practised my Divine Light meditations, which I found less demanding. They took me way out beyond my body into a transcendent realm of light, bliss and inner sound. It is said that we should commit to one path and stick to it, but I felt I needed the combination of the grounding of Buddhism with the bliss of Divine Light.

When I wasn't meditating I practised yoga, remembering that the lama in India had said it was so important for me. I rested and relaxed reading and writing poetry, or took short walks in the surrounding countryside. One of the long-term residents of the centre obviously fancied me and we started having conversations. He told me that I looked as if I had just returned from living in the south of France and was surprised when I replied that I was returning from living in the hell of TB. It was summertime and I was tanned and looking fit! This has been a problem for me through out my years of illness. Because I'm tall and tan easily people think I'm really well even when I'm struggling with severe physical debility.

There were two gifts I received from my stay at the monastery. The first was the awareness that suffering is universal and I was not singled out as I had previously felt myself to be. This realization dawned on me during an interview with the head lama. When I complained of all I had been through he looked deeply into my eyes and asked, 'Would you like someone else to take on your suffering?'

'Of course not,' I replied.

'Well if it wasn't you it would be someone else,' he replied quietly, turning his prayer beads. 'Suffering is universal and you are just taking your share.' This really woke me up to an awareness I hadn't had before. As the Buddha said, suffering is universal, and there were plenty of other people in the world suffering much more than me. It is all comparative. If I compared myself with most of my contemporaries I was really in a bad way, but compared to the starving and desperate I was living a pretty good life. I needed to see my cup as half full rather than half empty. I needed to appreciate the good things in life. It was all about giving up comparisons and practising gratitude.

The second deep experience was of hearing what I can only call celestial music. It started one night in the dormitory. I was always the first to go to bed and would be there alone for a couple of hours before the others came up. As I lay relaxing and preparing to sleep, I began to hear exquisite symphonic music in my head. This continued every night for about a week, becoming increasingly clear, until one day it just stopped again. It was profoundly moving, like Beethoven or Mozart symphonies. I realised that this was what is called the music of the spheres, astral music. It was what the great composers must have been able to tap into, but the difference between me and those geniuses was that they could write down what they heard!

The music felt like a gift from the world of spirit, reminding me of its presence, making itself increasingly real to me. It carried an energy of joy, comfort and healing. It was the same energy I had felt years before from the lama at the Tibetan monastery in India, an energy of warmth and love.

That summer felt like a reprieve but then autumn set in and I began to feel weak and ill again. My bones ached with the cold and damp of the sparsely heated retreat centre and my tinnitus grew louder. Once again my priority became my physical health and I knew I had to leave and find somewhere warmer. I felt the despair of not having a home but I just didn't know where to go. My father had offered me a caravan in his country garden but a caravan wouldn't be healthy in winter. My distant mother's lonely bedsit would feel like a punishment. I'd lost touch with almost all my pre-India friends. I needed to find somewhere quickly but was not strong enough to look for a place to buy with my dwindling inheritance.

'Hi, Stephen,' I was phoning nervously, not knowing if he would remember me. 'This is Cathy—we met at the Naturopathic Clinic . . . '

'Cathy! How are you doing? Good to hear from you.'

'I've been doing really well, staying up in a Buddhist monastery, but I need to leave soon and wondered if I could visit you for a few days and look around for somewhere to rent farther south. It's getting cold up here.' He met me from the station with a big hug and I immediately felt better. At least I had somewhere to stay while I looked for a winter let. Stephen worked away at the clinic during the weeks and returned for the weekends. The first weekend he came back I lit a fire, put on a skirt and made a good spaghetti bolognaise. At the end of the evening we fell into bed together.

'You don't need to look for anywhere else to stay,' he said lovingly, snuggling up to me the following morning. 'You can stay here as long as you like. I've never liked living alone and it's been great coming back this weekend to find you here.' We both needed intimacy and companionship and so we started our weekend relationship.

While he was away during the weeks I became involved with a healing technique called radionics. I had heard about it at a lecture in London and now I discovered there was a local practitioner. Twice a week I went to a strange little man who would wire me up to a machine. 'The little black box' he called it. 'It's as if we are all part of a huge electromagnetic system,' he explained. 'All our organs have a perfect vibratory rate of functioning, like the channels of a radio, which we can receive loud and clear if we tune into their wavelength. Illness results when the organs aren't functioning at their appropriate vibratory rate. So what I do is project the perfect rates for your damaged organs to resonate with. This then reminds them how they should be functioning.'

'So all I need to do is to sit attached to this machine, and my organs will be rebalanced?' I asked incredulously.

'That's right,' he replied. 'It's the new scientific mysticism at work.' It was weird but I was willing to try anything and I'll never know if it made any difference.

That Christmas I travelled to Buckinghamshire and spent a few days with Harold and his family as well as my full brother, Robbie. I hadn't seen any of them for several months and all was friendly and comfortable. But no one seemed really concerned about my health or itinerant life, and I didn't feel like imposing the details of my life on them, so I suppose they had little idea of my physical suffering and my lack of a real home. They had their own concerns which were far different from mine. My stepmother felt uprooted in the countryside, Harold had a difficult relationship with my youngest half brother, and Robbie was building up his career and involved in a challenging relationship. I left the family feeling unheard and unseen, despite the obvious love Harold had for me.

Months passed with Stephen, and I started feeling better with the warmer weather. I was studying radionics with my strange little healer but I became bored with being stuck alone in the house during the week with little money and no transport. I decided to go back to London and continue my studies on a one-weekend-a-month basis.

'We were good for each other weren't we?' said Stephen as I was about to leave.

'Yes, and I really appreciated you and a home for winter.' I gave him a big hug.

'And I appreciated you being here, so we can always be good friends, can't we?'

'Yes,' I said.

He held me for a moment before I stepped onto the coach back to London.

Fairies, Fantasies and Freedom, 1976–1980

Dragonfly

A dragonfly
Landed on my big toe
His rust red
Exactly matching
My nail varnish
He must have thought
He'd found a mate
Sat so perfectly
Still
With my colours
His silver filigreed wings
Shimmered
As I watched
Spellbound
As if blessed
By this unexpected
Ethereal intimacy
Until I felt
Compelled
To twitch my toe!

My mother had sold the house in London and moved to mid Wales with my new stepfather, Ivan. I moved into a legal squat near my childhood home with a group of Buddhists, which at the time seemed the best option for a cheap and congenial home. It was a friendly atmosphere, with like minded folk, and we spent time meditating together at the local Buddhist centre. I stayed there a couple of years, still not strong enough to work, but then came the famously hot summer of 1976 and I wanted to get out of the city. I remembered childhood holidays in the country and never wanting to return to the city.

I'm five years old, at my uncle Frank's house in the country and feeling blissfully happy to be in nature. Robbie and I have been playing in the chicken house and making a den in the garden. Now I am sitting quietly on the grass, contentedly making a daisy chain.

Suddenly, I have a difficult thought. 'Do you think grass can feel?' I ask our young Swedish lodger who is sitting on a rug next to me.

'Oh, I don't think so,' she replies absent-mindedly. But the thought has grasped me like a clam and won't let go.

'If I can feel then grass can feel,' I reason. 'And then I shouldn't walk on it.' I try and try not to walk on any grass for the rest of that holiday, but it's impossible in the country. It seems huge, realizing that everything feels.

I'm eight years old and Robbie and I are on holiday in Cornwall with Harold and his new wife Marjorie-Ann. We walk along the beaches together collecting shells. We play the game of standing still on the fringe of the waves, looking down at the moving water and feeling as if our body is rushing backwards as the waves retreat.

We wade down the muddy estuary to Padstow at low tide. With Harold to guide us we know we'll get there before the water comes in and swallows us up. I know, because two years ago on a nearby beach he dashed in and rescued me from a huge wave which was taking me out to sea.

I pick wild flowers in the hedgerows as we wander through the narrow lanes, thick with the scent of honeysuckle. Back at our seaside cottage I carefully put the flowers between paper in a little wooden flower press. Marjorie-Ann combs my tangled curls and puts a ribbon in my hair and I feel pretty and cared for.

In the morning we get up early and climb the hills, making fresh footprints in the dewy grass, collecting mushrooms for breakfast. When Marjorie-Ann fries them the kitchen is filled with the scent of melted butter.

One hot June day Harold visited me. We met in Hampstead and drank frothy hot chocolate in the sunshine on the crowded pavement outside Coffee Cup, watching the well-dressed passers-by. Harold looked so tanned and handsome as he flirted with the young waitress and I imagined some folk thought I was his young partner, not his daughter. I felt proud and happy to be with my dad, such a gorgeous older man!

'I just can't go on living here in summer,' I complained. 'But I don't know where to go.'

'I know just how you feel,' he said. 'I've always hated being in London in summertime. You need to get away. You could visit us for a few days.'

'I don't know. I feel I need more than a few days and I need my own space. I've been living in other people's places for so long and it just hasn't worked out.' He looked at me thoughtfully.

'Why don't you go and stay in my cottage in Wales? It's empty now and you could stay there until autumn if you want.' The world lit up again.

'That would be great.' I squeezed his arm. 'Thanks.'

It would be like a spiritual retreat, alone in a small cottage in the wilds of north Wales. A week later I packed my rucksack excitedly and hitch hiked to Snowdonia. With the hot dry weather I was strong enough to hitch. It seemed easier than trying to catch coaches or trains and at that time I couldn't drive.

The cottage was grey stone, in the middle of a field at the top of a hill, two miles from a one-shop village called Maerdy. I opened the door to the small sitting room. It had a simple slate tiled floor with a wooden scrubbed table, a book case and a couple of chairs. There was a tiny kitchen where I had to use an old hand pump to get water out of the tap. Two small bedrooms with sloping wooden floors stood at the top of rickety stairs. There was a chemical toilet outside in the former stable. I loved it and immediately went outside to pick some wild flowers to put on the table in a chipped vase.

The only other habitation was a farm about a hundred yards away. The farmer, his wife and their nephew Colin knew my father quite well and I had met them holidaying there when I was younger. They took a curious but caring interest in this single young woman living alone in the middle of nowhere. They offered me lifts to town for shopping and Colin would come round and fix anything that didn't work. He was my age, well built, with dark brown hair and vibrant blue eyes. He soon became the focus of my lonely fantasies and the high point of my days was collecting milk from the farm and seeing our Col. So much for my spiritual retreat, I was already half in love!

The summer continued hot and dry and I spent hours walking those gorse and heather covered hills. I relished having the strength to walk again and enjoy my body. When not walking I wrote poetry and studied various aspects of alternative healing. When I went to the farmhouse to collect milk the images from the TV stayed with me for hours. I didn't have a radio and had become used to silence. I was still living cheaply on my inheritance.

At Harold's cottage in Wales

One person who visited me while I was there was a blond long-haired poet, an ex-boyfriend who wanted to re-ignite the flame. But I didn't want emotional complications to interfere with my sense of peace, it was enough having my heart moved by Colin. With Col I only had short desultory conversations, but he was always silently in the background of my consciousness, walking with his herd of cows, or standing at my door holding my metal can of milk, smiling silently as if he was part of the hills.

It's full moon and I've been alone for most of the summer. It's so hot in mid-afternoon that I'm sheltering in the cool of the house. I hear music. It has an Irish air, with tin whistles, violins and drums. I think a hiker must be passing with a transistor radio so I go outside and look around. No one is there. But I still hear the music faintly, against the distant clatter of Colin cleaning out the cow shed. I go in again and hear the music loud and clear. I go out again and wander around looking for the source of the music, but no-one is there. Only my friendly rowan tree and the momentary bob of a rabbit. I go in again and hear the music more clearly inside than outside. Then a voice in my head says, 'This is fairy music. We are the elementals who live all around you. We are celebrating full moon today.'

I wonder if I'm finally going mad. But as the music continues I feel a sense of peace rather than fear. Gradually the music subsides and I go to have a nap. In that twilight zone between sleep and wakefulness I sense a great gathering of fairies.

'We are having a ball tonight,' they whisper, 'celebrating the harvest moon. You are most welcome to join us.' In my half sleep I apologise and say I won't be going. I am afraid I might disappear into fairyland and never return.

That evening I decided to light a fire. I needed the company and warmth of the flames and although it was the end of a hot summer, the nights could be cool. I collected a small bundle of dry wood from around the cottage and screwed up an old newspaper which had been left by the grate in the sparse sitting room. I needed to think about what had happened: the other-worldly music and the invitation from what seemed to be fairies.

As I watched the flames dancing I remembered what I had read about elemental beings. They are what we call fairies, gnomes, goblins, elves and leprechauns. These are the earthy ones, who have long been known as the little people, living and co-creating with nature, and are a species of beings just as we humans are. Some people disagree with this and say that it is only human beings who have given them physical form, and that in fact they are just a particular vibration of energy. I had read that the main difference between us and them is that they live in a different and more subtle dimension. This is the reason that few humans are able to see or hear them for they live on a finer, lighter frequency (some call it the astral plane) where they can manifest reality through thought. This is why they are able to help in the co-creation of nature. It is said there are different elementals for each of the four elements. There are sylphs of the air, undines of water and the fiery ones known as salamanders, but the ones who were beginning to touch me were the earth elementals, the ones most commonly encountered by humans.

I went to bed that night aware that a great celebration was taking place in and around my cottage, a celebration that I could have taken part in had I had the courage to let my consciousness truly enter beyond the third dimension. Although I wasn't ready to go to a fairy ball I felt a great sense of joy and gratitude at being allowed a glimpse beyond my normal reality.

Over the following two weeks I heard that fairy music whenever I silently tuned into it. It was like finding the right wavelength on a radio. Then it disappeared and I've never heard it since. Whether or not we believe in fairies and other elemental beings, this was a gift from beyond and confirmed my belief that we live in a multi dimensional universe, where human beings are a small part of a much larger story.

Twenty years later, at a storytelling festival in south Wales, I re-met the poet who had visited me that summer. I hadn't seen him since then. 'Come and listen to a story with me,' he said after we had briefly caught up with each other. We went into a big marquee where a story was being told. It was all about the elementals trying to communicate with humans, and how they used their fairy music to reach us! I came out of there laughing with my poet, only to bump into the one other friend who had stayed at the cottage that same summer. Synchronistic events like this always seem to confirm the truth of a greater reality and reassure me that our lives are part of an intricate design which will one day reveal the meaning and purpose of all we go through.

My mother and Ivan visited me for an afternoon in that that simple stone cottage, just as the weather was turning cool and damp and I was beginning to feel weak again. Ivan chopped me a pile of wood, and we walked up to a high point and gazed out at the surrounding hills. I felt a wave of love for this elemental landscape which had given me such a joyful summer. But I knew I had to leave soon as the house was too primitive for the colder weather. I longed to go home with my mother and Ivan, to be part of a family, or to make real my dreams of living in the hills with Colin. But both were fantasies. I had to leave my summer home and I didn't want to go back to the shabby Buddhist squat of the last two years. If I had been well I would have been able to stay in the cottage, but my illness made me move on. I felt like a health refugee, looking for a comfortable home in the world, facing another unknown winter.

In the event, two years passed in a shared flat in London. Although I enjoyed spending time with my flatmates I still yearned for that elusive home of my own. I really wanted to live in the country and had just about enough money left to buy a cheap cottage. I hardly knew where to start, until an acquaintance told me about Stroud in the Cotswold Hills. She was going to move there as it had a good Steiner school for her daughter, and the school was attracting other alternative people to the area. This appealed to me and on the phone I told Harold about Stroud. He offered to drive me there to look at houses and I accepted enthusiastically.

We spent two days going to estate agents and looking at likely cottages. As we looked I became increasingly discouraged and depressed. I felt a certain sense of failure as I contemplated buying a house on my own. I had always imagined myself excitedly looking for a house with a beloved partner or husband, not traipsing around with my dad looking at sad buildings in the rain! The only places I could afford looked run down and desolate. Moreover the ones I liked were outside the town or on the outskirts and I couldn't drive. I was too weak to walk far or stand waiting for buses in winter and I was afraid I would be isolated there. I also knew that once I bought a house I would have no financial buffer. With such poor health I knew I would be able to claim sickness benefit but I would always be struggling to pay the bills. Nor would I have money for the complementary therapies I felt I needed. I realised I wasn't ready to take this step alone.

Looking back, I bitterly regret not buying a house then. Somehow I would have managed, and I would have got on the property ladder before it was too late. The instability of not having a home of my own has been one of the three big issues of my life, along with health and childlessness.

That trip made me determined to learn to drive. I acquired a second hand VW Beetle and an easy going Norwegian boyfriend who let me practice driving around London with him between driving lessons. In August I visited some old friends who had bought a cottage in Wiltshire. I fell in love with the wide rolling chalk hills, the curling narrow lanes and the abundant wild flowers in the hedgerows. I decided I wanted to live there and within a week I found an old school house to rent in a small village. I went back to London, passed my driving test, loaded the car up with my few belongings and drove down to Wiltshire to start again.

Arriving in September I settled in, not knowing quite what to expect from life in the country. One thing I knew was that I had moved into an exquisitely pretty village of grey stone cottages on the edge of downland where I had wide views of a rolling landscape which made my heart sing.

The other thing I knew was that I had to continually fight against my chronic weakness and yet get on with my life. I wanted to be a yoga teacher, so I immediately enrolled into local classes and started a teachers training course. What I really wanted most of all was to meet a man who could be my husband, so we could create a home together and have children.

I met Jeremy in his workshop just up the lane from me. I needed a chair fixed and he was the village carpenter, with dark enigmatic good looks and sad compelling eyes. He lived in a terrace of small stone cottages and had an overgrown front garden and a large well stocked vegetable garden. Inside, his house was cluttered and uncared for and I wanted to tidy it and make it beautiful, just as I had always tried to do with my home as a child.

Before long he was calling on me in the evenings to have a chat. His wife had recently left him, taking with her their three young children, and he was devastated. With my own story I could identify with his pain and loss. We felt like fellow survivors and both of us had the hope that we could heal the other. In the evenings as we sat by the open fire we would feel a powerful spiritual energy rising within us and between us. When I looked into his eyes I felt a surge of love thawing my heart. It was a gentle knowingness, like a melancholy tune for all we had both suffered. I hadn't loved like this since Johann.

Even when we were apart it was as if Jeremy and I were linked beyond this dimension. We seemed to know telepathically what was happening to each other when he was up in his workshop and I was down the road in my little house. The magnetic energy between us was irresistible. Soon our relationship became passionate and we spent a vibrant summer together enjoying each others bodies, going for walks on the hills with his dog, sharing meals and gardening in his vegetable plot.

That winter, as usual, I spent a lot of time in bed with various infections and flus. Despite a good diet, a healthy lifestyle and yoga my immune system was continually low. The worst of it was that the house didn't have central heating and was cold and damp. Jeremy was fighting to be able to see his children and that took up most of his emotional energy. He visited me when he could but we were both too low to help one another or feel the fire of passion again. He got on with his own life while I got on with mine.

By April I was feeling a lot better. I was getting out and making new friends in the area, studying and practising my yoga. We began to be invited out together as a couple and I hoped that we could repair the damage of winter.

'Why don't you want to go to Doug's party?' I asked him one afternoon when I was visiting, dressed up to go to out. He continued to stomp moodily around the house.

'Because that guy is always eyeing you up and putting on the charm. He's only invited me to get to see you again.'

'Oh come on Jeremy don't be stupid, he's like that with all the women. It's just his way. He needs to feel like the beautiful cockerel amongst us hens.'

'Well I don't like it. I'm not in a party mood anyway. I haven't heard from Jo about the kids for weeks.'

'So why don't you tell me you're feeling sad instead of acting moody and jealous all the time? It would make things a lot easier,' I said.

He called his dog, slammed the door and crossed the road to his workshop. This was becoming an all too familiar scenario. His shadow seemed to have flourished with the long damp winter. I went to the party alone, wishing we could recapture our ease and happiness. I began to realize that it had been a complete fantasy that we could live happily together.

By late summer, with our complicated relationship only seeming to cause me pain and heartache, I decided to take up an invitation to go to Spain for a couple of months. I had met Marion the winter before at a yoga class. She lived in Spain and was visiting England for a few weeks while her partner saw his family. She had stayed with me in my cold stone house for a few days and had seen me so weak I could hardly walk.

'You must get to the warmth and sun,' she said. 'You could house sit my friend Timo's house while he's in India. He really likes people to be there when he's away. Ram Dass was there writing a book last year,' she added, as an extra incentive.

Now seemed like the perfect time for a break. I asked Jeremy if he would come with me, thinking that perhaps this could heal our relationship. But he was busy and didn't seem very interested. He said he might come for a fortnight later on.

I gave up the Old Schoolhouse exactly two years after I had moved in. When I returned it would be autumn and I knew I wouldn't be able to spend another winter in such a cold house. I would be without a home again but now wasn't the time to worry about that. So I set off for Spain, the country which has been such a catalyst in my life.

I got off the plane in Alicante and took the bus to Javea, a small town farther down the coast. There was no-one to meet me. All I had was an address with a hand drawn map on a scruffy bit of paper. When I showed it to the first taxi driver he just looked at it, tossed his hands up in the air and said, '*No lo se.*' I don't know it. I was beginning to get anxious when a mate of his turned up. After a brief conflab the second man came over and looked at the map that I was holding out hopefully. Soon we were speeding up the zigzag slopes in the hot pine scented air. It felt great to be in the warmth again. After a few miles he drove more cautiously down some stony tracks, past a couple of white flat roofed houses, and finally deposited me outside what looked like a stone ruin. 'Aqui estamos.' Here we are, he said happily, asking for some thousands of pesetas, which seemed like a huge amount then, but was probably only a pound or two. I opened a wooden gate in the dry stone wall and was met with a shrubby garden surrounding a circular self-built stone house. Marion had said the key would be hidden under a slab of stone beneath the large window. And there it was, a huge key looking as if it would open the way to a magical land.

The house was simply one circular room with a lean-to conservatory added. Water had to be hauled up by a bucket from a well beneath the kitchen area. There was a large bed made of lacquered branches of wood in strange Tolkeinesque shapes and surrounded by more of the same. Here and there were surprisingly beautiful tiles, tiny stained glass windows and niches occupied with statues of Indian deities. I immediately felt at home in this atmosphere.

Marion lived about a mile away with her partner and two young children. On my first morning I walked there over the herb and shrub dotted landscape. I passed the whitewashed *casitas* I remembered so well from Formentera. The black clad widows sitting outside with their needlework looked reassuringly familiar, as if time had stood still. When I saw Marion's old farmhouse with two little blonde children running around and a workshop with bits of craft work going on, I felt a pang of nostalgia. It was like going back to a time when I still had my innocence on Formentera. The family greeted me warmly and soon we were eating their staple of chapatis and dahl followed by grapes, figs and last autumn's almonds. All around the kitchen were bunches of dried sage, oregano and rosemary along with some tiny yellow flowers I didn't recognize.

Marion was the archetypal earth mother and wise woman, with long black hair, and an air of calm in her gentle liquid eyes. As we sat and talked her children came and perched on her comfortably, like birds perching on a

Outside the roundhouse

branch, before they flew off again into their exciting games. She had a special place under a delicate pine tree where she gave healing sessions and where we sat together talking about our lives and loves.

She gave me healing, a healing which felt quite different from the others I'd had. It was as if the energy of the warm dry Spanish earth was supporting me and the elementals of air and fire, so strong in this sparse rocky landscape, were penetrating into my bones and drying out the dampness of dis-ease. Sometimes I would lie in Marion's arms after the healing, something I had never experienced from my mother. I remembered being told that illness in the bones is a manifestation of the deepest place where we feel lack of support.

So the days passed, with regular visits to Marion's for company and healing. In the afternoons we often made trips to the sea where I would play with the children, sunbathe and swim in the warm Mediterranean. I felt that this was the life I was meant to have, being in touch with my spirit at the same time as being part of a family, having fun, and living in the sun. In the evening we would sometimes arrange to meet at an open air discotheque nearby. I would have a siesta, change into a flimsy dress and walk the half mile to the circular open air dance floor. The proprietors were friends of Marion's family, and would let us all in for free. There we danced around happily with the kids on an empty floor before the well dressed customers arrived for the night.

On other evenings there were communal gatherings on a nearby family's land, where we lit fires and played music together. It was like a grown-up version of Formentera, as many couples had children by then, and were no longer travellers. Most of them still made their living selling crafts, but worked harder and partied less. Sometimes I thought of Jeremy and wondered if he would join me there, but I didn't miss him. I was so much happier in the warmth of Spain and out of the aura of his moodiness.

As for my health, although I was well, I often felt spaced out and disembodied, which was worrying. I couldn't understand it as I felt quite happy. I only had the answer to this this many years later, when I learnt about the volatile solvents in varnishes and the nature of my allergies: it was my reaction to the varnished Tolkeinesque wood all around the bed.

One night I woke to the sound of steps pacing around my house. I must be mad I thought, living here alone in the middle of nowhere, with the door unlocked, no-one keeping tabs on me and no phone. Up to this moment I had been fearless and unaware of my vulnerability. I hid under the sheets holding my breath, my heart pounding. If I were injured or killed tonight, no-one would find out for two or three days. I had just seen Marion and wasn't due to see her again until the weekend. After a couple of minutes, which felt like an eternity, I couldn't hear steps any more. I peeped out from the bedclothes and screamed! A torch was shining directly on my face through the curtainless windows. I hid again, stiff with fear, until I heard men's voices laughing, and their footsteps walking away. I lay awake until dawn in shock.

Next day I went to see a young friend and told her the story. 'It's only the Guardia Civil,' she laughed.' They regularly check all the houses to see what's going on.'

'Thank God,' I said laughing with relief.

'But they're not to be trusted,' she added, 'Especially with foreign women.' Hardly a reassuring thought!

One day when I was feeling bored I walked to the local town to do some shopping. I hadn't heard from Jeremy for weeks, and that had been a brief letter saying he had decided not to join me in Spain. As I came out of the little bakery I caught sight of a motorcyclist across the square. He was just parking his bike and as he took his helmet off he looked directly at me with piercing green eyes. He was remarkably handsome. We smiled at each other and he strolled over and greeted me tentatively in English.

'Are you a foreigner here as well?' he asked in that all too familiar German accent.

'Yes I'm living a couple of kilometres away up those hills.' I pointed vaguely behind me.

'I'm thirsty,' he rubbed his mouth. 'I've been riding down the coast from Alicante. It's very hot. Would you like to go for a drink somewhere?'

'Yes, I know a good bar just around the corner from here,' I replied trying to hide my flutteryness.

We sat drinking iced coffee under a shade outside Juan's bar, which overlooked the cobbled square. I felt that familiar flame of attraction and a little voice inside me told me to watch out.

'I'm riding around Spain,' he told me. 'Probably going south next week. I have a month before I must return to Berlin to start my studies again.'

'It'll be even hotter there,' I replied pulling my hair back from my face.

'Yes, but I have heard of beautiful sandy beaches where hardly anyone goes. You can reach them by foot or on a bike but not by car. Foreigners often stay there and you can go naked and camp in the little caves.'

'It sounds great,' I said wistfully, half seeing myself riding pillion towards Almeria.

'Where are you going today?' I asked, remembering Marion telling me about a gathering near hers this afternoon and evening.

'I'm thinking I will stay near here,' he looked at me invitingly.

'I've been asked to a gathering this afternoon near where I live up on the hills, if you'd like to come,' I ventured.

This was another me, riding up the hills with warm pine-scented air kissing my skin, my arms around a beautiful man's slender waist. This was freedom! I was the woman I was meant to be, not the one who lived in a cold damp cottage in a rainy climate which made me ill, involved with a difficult man.

At Jack's we helped prepare food and then heaped wood into a stack beside the fire pit, which we lit when it got dark. It was already late September and could be cool at night. My new friend Josef seemed to fit in naturally. He chatted and laughed easily with the others as we worked, interspersing English and German depending on who he was with. He played with Jack's kids when they threw him a ball and then he would return to me and we would flirt and chat.

We ate and I shared a joint for the first time in ages. We sat around the fire singing and playing drums. Josef sat next to me and stroked my back in the darkness.

'I'm tired. I need to go home,' I said nervously. 'I live very near here.'

'I don't know where I'm going to stay tonight,' he looked at me enquiringly.

'Well, you could stay at mine. There's a couch in the conservatory where you could sleep. It's quite comfortable.' We got on his bike in the darkness and I rested my head against his shoulders.

We lay on a soft rug on the floor of my cosy round house making love by flickering firelight. We were naked and I didn't think I'd ever seen a male body so beautiful nor ever felt my own body so female and sensual. We were strangers but our bodies knew each other and we were moving together to a perfect soundless tune. I was lost in him, flying, dissolving and dancing into fulfilment. I had energy I didn't know I had. I was a wild woman and goddess and he was my warrior, my consort. When it was over we tumbled back to earth. We were wet with sweat, and fell asleep tangled in each others arms.

In the morning I woke up with a stranger. But, as I looked at him sleeping so peacefully beside me, a muscular brown arm and smooth dark torso revealed casually by the thrown down sheet, I thought I was in love. We spent the next few days together riding to beaches on his bike, where we swam picnicked and sunbathed. We dressed up and danced in the disco in the evenings and went home early to make love. He hardly spoke about himself or asked me about my past. It was a relief. I didn't need to tell him about my illness. I could just live in the present where I felt surprisingly well.

After a few days I noticed a change in him. He was getting restless and starting to eye other women in the disco. Just another egocentric guy, I thought to myself cynically. He was too gorgeous for his own good, and certainly for mine. Then one morning he just told me he needed to travel on. I wasn't surprised but still hurt when he made no move to invite me to come with him or to see me again. But I had always known that this was just a passing passion. So I waved goodbye biting my lip as he rode down the dry track leaving a trail of dust.

Three weeks later my period hadn't come. I had often missed periods, so I couldn't be sure of anything. What an idiot I thought, at the same time imagining a beautiful little boy with startlingly green eyes! That first night I had been too intoxicated by dope and sex to take care, and now he was gone and I didn't even know his surname or phone number.

I felt like staying in Spain forever but the owner of the roundhouse was coming back and I'd already booked my ticket to London. From there I had nowhere else to go but Jeremy's home in Wiltshire, and I landed on his doorstep a few days later. He greeted me coolly. He'd said I would always be welcome but I was feeling pretty confused about returning. I told him a few stories about Spain and he about what had been happening in the village. It felt like we were just making conversation and he seemed uneasy about something.

'I've been having a scene with Rachel on the hill,' He finally blurted out. 'I wouldn't have if you'd stayed.' He raised his eyebrows accusingly.

'And I had a passionate affair and don't know if I'm pregnant!' I retaliated.

A few days later I was leafing through my Yoga Today magazine and saw an advert for a yoga centre. I had a flash of intuition that I should phone them about work. I needed a new home urgently and I needed a source of income if I wasn't going to totally fritter away my inheritance on living expenses.

'What sort of work are you looking for?' asked a friendly voice.

'Anything really, but not full time.' I still wasn't strong enough for full time work. 'I've been doing a yoga teachers' training course for two years and that's why I was interested.'

'So you've been practising yoga for some time, I take it?'

'Oh yes, I started in India about ten years ago, but I've been rather ill so it's been a bit intermittent.'

'Well, it just so happens that one of our yoga teachers is leaving tomorrow and we're looking for another one. Would you be interested in teaching?' I was flabbergasted!

'I've never taught before but perhaps I could try,' I said, trying not to sound too nervous.

'Why don't you come over next week and we'll see how you get on with us and we get on with you. We specialize in helping people with multiple sclerosis. Are you free to start next week?' God knows what I will do if I'm pregnant I muttered to myself putting the phone down with a shaking hand. But by the weekend I knew that I wasn't.

Yoga Teaching, 1980–1982

Whirling Dervishes

Your invisible thread touches the divine
Spinning in white like wind like brine
Your skirt like a sail billowing swirling
One hand raised praising
Floating a greeting
Your feet on the earth
Holding securing
The white bird of soul
Smoothly swooping
Dissolving the mind
Reeling releasing
Remembering love
The Presence of Being
Returning the spinning
Silky cocoon of Self
To God

Ickwell Bury Yoga Centre was in a stately brick-built mansion in Bedfordshire. Howard Kent, the boss, welcomed me in a light and airy room overlooking a field of grazing horses. 'I'd like you to assist with two of the classes for our disabled guests each day,' he said. 'It's quite simple. Dawn's been leading the classes for several years and she'll show you the ropes.'

'That sounds fine,' I replied. Yoga had helped me so much with my own physical limitations I felt I would definitely be able to help others to do the same.

'Then I'd like you to try teaching our evening classes. We usually have about fifteen people come in, of mixed ability, so you can make it simple.' I mumbled a yes, but felt terrified. Helping was one thing, but leading a class was something I hadn't bargained for. But I wasn't going to lose this opportunity out of fear.

A few days later my mouth was dry and my pulse was racing as the participants arrived for their evening class. It was a spacious hall with a polished wooden floor and a low dais at the front from which I had to demonstrate the postures. I was feeling physically weak but I had to make this class work. I had rested in the afternoon and prepared meticulously, with all the postures written down in sequence on a piece of paper. I had bought a new pink track suit and put my unruly hair up in a scrunchy. I just kept telling myself I had to act calmly and confidently, pretend that I was experienced and see what happened.

By the end of the class I was surprised to find I felt quite serene, better than I'd felt all week. I'd hardly looked at my notes and the class had seemed to take on its own momentum, flowing from one posture to another, ending with a gentle deep relaxation. As the participants walked out into the night, thanking me for a great group, I realised I had succeeded. It was my first taste of teaching—and my first taste of success.

Howard came in to watch my second evening class, which made me even more nervous. He told me afterwards that I was a natural and that I had the job for as long as I wanted. I was thrilled. Now at last I felt I could depend on myself. I was making my own living, doing what I loved doing and living in beautiful surroundings with like minded people.

I soon became close to the other staff. We would spend evenings together, chatting, playing guitars and singing, all gathered round an open fire as winter approached. I got to know all about multiple sclerosis. It's a horrible nerve disease, much worse than my own. It gradually takes away a person's capacity to use their limbs, and sometimes goes as far as impairing their ability to speak or see clearly. It was reassuring for me to be seen as a fit teacher. I still felt weak and rested every afternoon in the break between classes. But I managed to keep up with the work and to all appearances I looked well. I really appreciated that despite my illness I was slim, supple and attractive. Except for the weakness, which often had me in bed by 8.30, I was normal.

Sadly, many of the guests who came to the yoga centre although young, were partially or severely disabled. They were in wheelchairs or using zimmer frames to walk. One day soon after I arrived I saw what I thought was a daughter arriving with a bald and immobile old mother in a wheelchair. I asked Dawn who they were. She said, 'Oh no, that's not the mother in the wheelchair, it's the daughter and she's only in her late twenties.' I was stunned. She looked about eighty! Her body had seized up to the point where she could hardly move. She looked as if she was turning to stone.

But we had a lot of laughs and good times with the guests. Barry was in his mid thirties like me, and had obviously been remarkably handsome before his accident. He'd been a sailor and had been hit badly on the head by a swinging boom in severe weather. Soon after he'd found himself lacking his normal co-ordination. His feet had become heavy and his fingers numb. He was diagnosed as having MS and a few years later here he was, completely unable to move or feed himself, with his speech slurred like a drunk. Yet he was happy.

'Come an feed me Cathy,' he would laugh invitingly as if he was asking me for a date. 'Give us a hug.' He did this with all the staff, young and old, and we couldn't help but love him. He had no control of his limbs and would bounce around in his wheelchair like demented clockwork toy. Yet he was always good natured and easy going, seeming to regard his misfortune as some ridiculous joke which he was sharing with us. One day I asked him how he could be so positive. 'I just don't think about it,' he replied in his slow drawl. 'If I thought about it and compared myself with how I use to be I'd be miserable. But this is how it is, so I've just accepted it.'

I felt I had so much to learn from him. If he could be happy with such severe limitations, how could I complain about my weakness and lack of energy? And yet there it was. I still found it hard to wake up in the morning feeling debilitated, and it was often simply a trick of mind over matter that got me through the day.

Obviously people such as Barry could only do a specialised form of yoga. Firstly we would teach them how to breath deeply. Then we would get everyone lying in the thickly carpeted lounge doing simple movements like arm and leg lifts to the limit of their ability, always using the breath. If there was no movement left in a limb we would ask them to visualize the limb moving and often help them move it. After an hour of breathing, visualizing or moving, we would take them into a deep relaxation as they lay on the floor. I was usually an assistant to Dawn, the main teacher. Often it was just a reassuring touch which made the difference or a comforting hand when frustration became too strong and someone burst into tears. We usually only had a handful of guests doing yoga in that sunny room, with a cosy log fire burning in winter.

The joy for me was not just in doing a job that I both loved and was good at, it was also helping me with my own health challenges. Before each evening class I was often so tired that I didn't know how I was going to teach. But by the end of the class I would feel re-energized, calm and centred. I had also long since given up even the occasional puff of marijuana. I knew I was teaching exactly what I needed to learn myself. I have a restless flighty mind and deep strong emotions which can toss me around like the wind. Through yoga teaching I was learning to tame my mind and stabilize my emotions, as well as strengthen my body, just as the Tibetan monk had recommended all those years ago. I was learning what a joy it is to serve those less fortunate than myself. With warmth, stability and a sense of purpose, I managed to get through that winter with only brief episodes of illness and continued to hold down the job.

'Hey, the Uncwell's arrived!' Julie, our buxom cook, called out. It was Harold, who had been named the Ickwell Uncle, shortened to Uncwell. He had taken to visiting quite often, and I was so happy that at last I was becoming increasingly close to him. We had never spent much time together since I left home. Everyone looked forward to his visits, especially Julie, who loved his baking. He would go straight to the big old fashioned kitchen where she gave him a big hug. Loud music would be playing on the tape deck as he started making bread. By lunch time, when I had finished work, he would be there helping to serve up the food with the smell of fresh bread baking in the Aga.

While I had my afternoon nap Harold would spend time with anyone who needed him. He chatted with the guests, listened to their stories, made them cups of tea or helped them up to their rooms. I started seeing him in a different light. He was not only my father but a well loved compassionate and entertaining visitor for whom I was developing a great respect.

The first time he appeared in one of my evening classes I was nervous. There he was, a tall rangy and still attractive seventy-year-old, wearing a second-hand green surgeon's outfit amidst the smooth middle-aged leotarded women. I tried not to get the giggles. Fifteen women looking at me expectantly!

'This is my father, Harold,' I introduced him. 'He's visiting for a couple of days and is going to join our class.' The women turned round and smiled at him appreciatively. Then the class continued. As they left several women said how lovely it was to have such an enthusiastic and open older man in the class.

While I was at Ickwell Bury I was also studying acupuncture part time. I needed a profession which would enable me to live independently. Although I really enjoyed my life in the yoga centre I still longed to have a home of my own. So one weekend a month I went to Leamington Spa to study traditional acupuncture. I started the training with no idea what it would entail or how hard it would be. I had decided on acupuncture because a good friend of mine had recommended it. I impulsively enrolled on a three year course without really considering whether it was the most suitable therapy for a person of my temperament.

It soon turned out that all my spare time was consumed in studies and essays. As summer approached I would take my books out into the garden and work there. Beyond the vegetable garden was a secret walled rose garden. There I would sit, surrounded by the colour and perfume of roses, feeling as if the plants were healing me. For the first time in my life I was really using my left brain, the part which has to do with intellect and logical thinking. The course itself was an intricate mix of left and right brain concepts and the way I studied, immersed in books while surrounded by beautiful plant life, reflected this.

Leading the dance at Ickwell Bury

That year we had two weeks off work for summer holidays and I needed a break from my teaching and my studies. Julie and I decided to go to a Sufi camp at Chamonix, in the south of France. The Sufis are a mystical branch of Islam who believe in the unity of all religions. They practice devotionally through a form of prayer called *zikr* and also praise God in song and dance. I had spent a weekend at a Sufi centre in England during my search for a cure and appreciated the feeling of openness and love which pervaded the place. Now we were on a train to the French Alps, with our tents and sleeping bags.

Soon I was flying high again surrounded by snow capped mountains. Every morning we did yoga in a huge dome overlooking the white rugged Alps, then we would all descend on the communal food tent to share breakfast. Afterwards everyone did their own dishes in outdoor sinks and then it would be time for various study or singing groups.

Sufi camp in the French Alps

Our teacher, Pir Vilayat Khan, radiated joy and compassion as he told us Sufi stories. In the afternoons there was choir. We were learning the Alleluia chorus, to perform at a local church at the end of the retreat. We stood in a huge circle learning our different parts, while Pir, our small bearded teacher, stood in the middle waving his hands gracefully in the blue air, conducting us.

In the evenings we practised *zikr* sitting in a circle chanting '*La illa ha il Allah hu*'—('There is no God but that which is God'). With the chant we did

On holiday in Crete

a circular head movement, which energetically pierces the heart open and brings the energy upwards towards the Divine. While doing this practice it's impossible to think, and soon you become immersed in a sense joy and wonder. During *zikr* I felt that same sense of homecoming which I had felt in the Hindu and Buddhist practices in India, that sense of wholeness where I became part of the intangible thread of all life.

We also learned Sufi dances, accompanied by haunting live music. We would sway in circles holding hands and meeting eyes, honouring the Divine in each of us. With each deep eye contact my heart opened more and more. I felt as if I was falling in love with men and women alike. In fact I was opening to the love which is here all the time. This love which is the fabric of the universe but which we, in our limited selves, find so hard to feel because we are shrouded by the illusion of our ego.

Falling romantically in love gives us a taste of this divine state, which is why it's so seductive and is the theme of stories world wide. Sufis believe that we are all ultimately seeking union with the Divine and that thinking fulfilment can come from an external source, either materially or emotionally, is an illusion. In this retreat the Sufi practices helped me surrender a little more of my ego to a greater power.

All too soon the holiday retreat was over and Julie and I were on our way back to England. We hardly needed to speak to each other as we were in such a meditative state. But we looked forward to returning to the yoga centre and sharing some of the gifts from the mountains with those less fortunate.

'A nice guy arrived today,' Julie said as we sat by her open fire on a cold night in January. 'He's tall and blond and only got a slight limp, so he can't be too ill.' Oh here we go again, I thought, someone to distract me from my spiritual path!

Fritz was a vet who had a practice in Devon and was still working. He had a natural aptitude for yoga, good concentration and a sense of humour. We found ourselves getting close, chatting in the dining room over meals and taking cups of tea together in the snug sitting room. 'Where do you live?' he asked after the first few days.

'Oh the staff have rooms in the old annexe,' I said pointing through the cobbled courtyard to what once had been the servants quarters. 'I have an upstairs room and we can use a kitchen downstairs if we want. We often sit round Julie's fire chatting in the evenings when I'm not teaching. She plays guitar too.'

'I wondered where you disappeared to,' he smiled sincerely. 'I'd love to come and join you there sometime. It gets a bit wearing mixing with the others constantly.' The next evening I invited him to the annexe.

'You're so beautiful, it seems strange finding you living alone here,' he commented casually. He looked around my room, which was decorated with my normal eclectic mix of Indian bedspreads, richly coloured second hand rugs, esoteric pictures and vases of wild flowers and roses from the garden.

'Will you visit me in Devon when I leave?' he asked as we lay curled snugly in my bed, covered with blankets and a golden eiderdown a few days later. My resolve to only go for divine love rather than romance had only lasted a few months—I wasn't cut out to be a celibate yogi!

'Of course,' I replied happily. 'I'd love to visit your place and see your practise.'

'I'm due for a real holiday in a couple of months. I'm going to Crete. Would you like to come? I'll treat you.'

'That would be amazing.' I stroked his hair. It had been so long since I had been treated to anything by a partner, and it was bitterly cold and wintry outside.

So in April I had another holiday, staying in a hotel on the beach by the clear Aegean sea. We savoured every moment of that sensual sun filled break. But when we returned to England it was hard to find the time and energy to meet up. Distance came between us and although we both cared for each other we agreed to separate. Learning to love with detachment seemed to be my constant life's lesson.

I continued living and working at the yoga centre but by my second autumn, I knew I didn't have enough energy for both my job and the studying I had to do for my exams the following spring. So I left the centre to live in a rented flat near Cambridge. I taught some yoga evening classes to earn money, studied hard and passed my exams.

I left Ickwell Bury feeling fulfilled. I had managed to work at a job I loved for two years and had been of service to people less fortunate than myself. My health was improving and I was nearly qualified to be an acupuncturist. The future was looking bright.

Broken Dreams, 1983

Childlessness

In the heart of me is hollow pain
The cold stone of infertility
I look on always from the outside
Exiled from my tribe

Excluded from the web of life
Some say 'You're lucky—free'
Free as the sky without the sun
I'd like to scream
Free as a bird without wings
I weep inside

And it's hard to stay alive
Bleeding each month
When no continuity of blood
Binds me to this life

Only the thin thread
Of spirit supporting me
Like an umbilical cord
Nourishing my heart
With the call of humanity

I was walking down a leafy street in Cambridge singing to myself and suddenly there he was, lying like a fallen god under a car. 'Hi there,' he said as I passed. I looked down into his laughing blue eyes and smooth muscular oil-stained arms and felt that fierce chemical attraction.

'Hi,' I replied. 'What are you doing under there?'

'Oh, just checking a loose exhaust.' Luckily my car needed some attention and I asked him if he could check it out. 'Sure, I'll come round later. Where do you live?'

He came round that evening.

'Do you want a drink of something?' I asked when I saw he'd finished the car and was making small talk, procrastinating. We sat drinking tea in the garden.

'I'm not really a car mechanic,' he said, waving towards my beaten up old Ford. 'I can turn my hand to almost anything but building's the easiest way I earn my living. What about you?'

'I've just qualified to be an acupuncturist. My results came through last week.' I smiled happily feeling again the flood of relief after so much studying.

'So you're going to start sticking pins into people are you?' He smiled mischievously and we both laughed.

'Would you like to come out for a drink tomorrow night?' he asked nervously as he turned to go. I was already hooked.

The sun dusted golden lights onto Pete's hair and skin as we sat in a pub garden by the river, watching ducks drifting on the water. He was so handsome, but unselfconscious and strangely familiar. He told me he'd made a makeshift home on a piece of land his parents owned a few miles outside Cambridge. He'd put two caravans together in an L shape, and joined them with a conservatory in which he kept odds and ends and grew some plants. 'And I love my bees,' he said enthusiastically, 'second to my daughter of course.' My heart plummeted. Maybe he was married. Perhaps he noticed the change in me, he got up quickly and turning towards the back entrance of the pub, offered me another drink. 'I've got a six-year-old—Ishta,' he said returning with beer and fruit juice. 'She's gorgeous, stays with me most weekends.'

'So you're separated?' I was flying again, watching the river, hoping to appear nonchalant.

'Yes, we separated a few months back. It just got impossible. After Ishta was born Rita, my ex, changed—got completely unreasonable.'

'Maybe it was post natal depression?'

'Maybe that started it, but it went on for years. We're much better living apart. Have you got kids?'

'No, but I'd love a family.'

'I love children too,' he said sadly, 'and not seeing Ishta every day is really hard. But I'm getting used to it.'

Soon I was spending every weekend in his funky home, much preferring to be with him in the country than in my shared town house. We gardened together, went for cycle rides and walks with Ishta and Boy, his mongrel dog. We cooked meals with vegetables from his land, and made love in his caravan bedroom where I felt like his eastern consort. We were in love.

When the three of us went on a seaside holiday in Cornwall we made a huge spiral race track with sticks in the sand where we played and

Pete with a pumpkin

laughed for hours. Then Ishta had to be buried up to her neck before leaping out of her sandy tomb and running with Pete to dance in the frothy white fringes of the sea. We seemed like a natural family and far from assuaging my urge to have a child it only made it keener. I was yearning for my own. A couple of months later I thought I was pregnant. Life was turning out perfectly at last.

I woke up on a strange high bed with crisp white sheets. I had been in a light and beautiful place outside my body but now I was coming back in. The anaesthetic was wearing off and there was a thick pad between my legs, a dragging fish hook in my pelvis, and I was feeling very sick. My mother was sitting by my bed with her hand on the counterpane. This must be serious. The Sister came and took my pulse and wrote on the chart at the bottom of my bed. 'The consultant will come and talk to you tomorrow,' she said addressing both me and my mother.

'I'm sorry you had to come all this way,' I said. I was in hospital in Cambridge and she lived in mid Wales.

'I was worried when I heard you had suddenly been taken ill. I thought you were doing so well.'

'I thought I was too. But then I had all these pelvic pains and thought I was pregnant. When I came here to check they just whipped me in, thinking it was an ectopic. I guess the doctor will tell me what they found.' My mother stayed a couple of hours and then she had to get her train. I fell into a lonely sleep wishing that Pete was here. When I woke he was, but he was no longer the golden sun god I had met three months before. He had lost his glow, and his face looked taut.

'What happened?' he asked putting a basket of fruit on my bedside locker. 'Are you still pregnant?'

'I don't think so. The nurse keeps saying I need to wait for the consultant's rounds and now it won't be till tomorrow. But I suppose I can't be, as they said they did a D and C, that operation they do to clear the womb.' He looked out of the window sadly and then came and took my hand and held me. I could see he didn't know what to say. We sat embracing silently for a while, until a chirpy nurse came round to give me an injection. She started pulling the curtains around me and said he needed to go.

When the nurse came round with the night time trolley I took the sleeping pill she offered me. I fell asleep to the hollow sound of nurses' shoes squeaking on the polished floors and the intermittent groans and echoes of hospital nights. It all seemed so familiar. Here I am again. And there I was believing I had finally escaped to start my new life. I felt so alone. I realised I hardly knew Pete and there I'd been gaily thinking of starting a family with him.

'Let's get you up,' said the nurse briskly. 'I'll walk you to the showers and then it will be the doctor's rounds.' I hobbled weakly on her arm. I felt like I'd been smashed in my guts, my body curved over my tender pelvis. After my shower a jolly West Indian woman came round with breakfast. Later a group of white coated men stood around my bed. The nurse drew the curtain discreetly around us.

'I'm afraid we discovered rather a mess when we opened you up, Miss

146

Lowenstein,' the consultant said, looking slightly to the side of me, while his students looked earnestly at their notes. 'We didn't find an ectopic pregnancy as we thought, but a lot of very bad scarring. We've removed what scarring we could, but your left ovary is adhesed to your bowel and we thought it better not to operate on that, as it doesn't look like it's doing you any harm. I see that you have a history of tuberculosis and I'm afraid to say this does look like tubercular scarring, although in my experience I've never seen tuberculosis in the pelvis. We'll send you down for more tests later and I'll come and talk to you again soon. Do you have any questions for now?'

'So you mean I was never pregnant?'

'That's right.' He looked vaguely apologetic. 'I'm afraid to say your pains and lack of menstruation are all part of your illness.'

'But if I do have TB I know I'm allergic to the drugs. I tried before . . .'

'Let's not run before we can walk.' He scratched his chin and looked vaguely out of the window. 'And it looks as if the infection is still active. I'm afraid to say it doesn't look like you'll be having children, Catherine. With this much scar tissue in your tubes and around your womb I'm afraid it doesn't look like a possibility.' I almost looked round the ward to see if this person called Catherine was sitting somewhere else. But no, he was obviously talking to me. I went cold and numb. I don't remember him leaving.

In the evening Pete came and I told him. My words sounded hollow, as if I was telling a tragic story about someone else. We had been living a golden summer dream and had woken to find ourselves in a nightmare.

It's dark and I'm in bed at Pete's place. I'm being poisoned and this time I will surely die. Every cell of my body is screaming. I'm screaming for help in my nightmares. I'm screaming for every wise being and healing angel to help me. I'm screaming but no sound is coming out. Help me, please help! I can hear Pete hammering away in the distance. He's in another world. The world of light and life. I'm lost in darkness. A sinister voice echoes through time. 'You won't be having children, Catherine.' I scream for it to go away. Every cell in my body is weeping. I claw the air and scream for help from all the spiritual teachers I've ever had. Help me, please help. But no one can hear. The light has gone out. There is no one. There is no where. Only timeless despair.

'I agree you can't take these drugs any more,' said the local GP looking down at me sympathetically in Pete's caravan the following morning. My tangled sheets smelled stale and scorched from the night. Pete hovered behind him. 'You seem to be getting the same allergic reaction as before.'

'I think I'll go back to my nature cure,' I whispered from a distant shore. 'I don't seem to have much choice.'

'I think you're right, Cathy. We will, of course, keep monitoring you at the hospital and sending you for tests to see that nothing is spreading, but for now it seems impossible for you to continue with this medication.'

I decided to go for Gerson Therapy, an extreme cleansing therapy which had a reputation of curing cancer and other life threatening diseases. Pete was very supportive, shopping for quantities of organic vegetables and fruits which he put through the juicer and served me in tall glasses several times a day. Then I would lie upside down in the tiny bathroom with a bag of warm coffee propped against the sink and a nozzle in my bum. Coffee enemas would de-tox the liver. Later I went to a top homoeopath in London, who prescribed shots of homoeopathic medicine in the thigh every night, and I faced the trauma of learning how to inject myself. I couldn't ask Pete to do it. Our relationship already had too much of that taut energy of struggle, and he had taken me into his home to care for me when I'd come out of hospital. We were like strangers in this fierce drama, both going through it together but unable to really meet or speak about what was happening.

Despite all, I think some of those wise beings must have heard my call for help. I was given the phone number of probably the only person in the country who had dealt with pelvic TB. Not only was she a qualified doctor but also an acupuncturist. Moreover she practised only a few miles away in Cambridge! Dr Wu was a Vietnamese refugee who had worked with women who had pelvic TB in Vietnam during the war. Apparently it was quite common there and drugs had not been available. She had successfully used a mix of acupuncture and herbs, which is what she did with me now. She saw me twice a week for the next year, hardly charging me anything, as I was now living on sickness benefit. She was a true Buddhist and when I was low she would say, 'You are just a small part of humanity's suffering, try not to take it too personally. It will pass.' Every few months I would return to the hospital for check-ups and be shuttled from the TB clinic to the gynaecological clinic, neither of them knowing quite what to do with me, but both agreeing that I was doing well on my regime of complementary therapy.

By the following spring I was feeling much stronger and was offered a council flat in Cambridge. I was still on sickness benefit, having spent all the money I had inherited on survival and complementary medicine. This was the money that could have bought me my own home and changed the rest of my life. Sometimes I would weep with grief after visiting friends' homes, knowing that I had lost my chance of being able to buy a home of my own.

I had stopped my extreme juice therapy and it seemed a good idea to move into my own space after my difficult months with Pete. We ended up having a weekend relationship, with either him visiting me in town or me spending time with him in the country. We didn't talk about things and slowly we saw less of each other. I think we both hoped that with more time apart we'd recapture our initial magic. But the stress of my illness had separated us too far. We spent a year like this, with me working on my health and seeing a counsellor for help with all the trauma and him working on his various practical projects.

Avalon, 1984–1987

The Arab-Egyptian Dance Class

Fifty women round and skinny
Dancing their passion dancing their dreams
In bright satins, silks, sequins and veils
Revealing what they may not seem
Arms aflutter hips ashimmy
Exposing midriffs, cleavage, bellies,
Office workers, housewives, mothers
Sensuous goddesses for the hour
Erotic priestesses with power
Dancing their passion dancing their dreams

When the class is over
They walk out buttoned up against winter
Drab in black and grey
Pale under their dancing glow
Homeward they go
Holding themselves a little taller
Carrying scarves and silks
Like packages of summer

Some friends told me about summer camps being held on the rolling hills a few miles outside the Somerset town of Glastonbury, very near where I had gone to that first festival. There was to be a dance camp followed by an astrology camp on the same site. Pete had no interest in either of these so I set off alone in my old Ford Escort, stacked with a tent, plenty of bedding and food. Luckily it was a hot summer and I pitched my dome tent with a circle of others near a protective hedge with a view of the Vale of Avalon and the distant Tor.

It was all light and colour again. I had survived the nightmare. It was as if I had been holding my breath since those searing words in the hospital and now I could breathe again. Glastonbury Tor felt like a beacon of hope, surrounded with a halo of golden clouds. As I set up my tent that night I felt a magic entering me as if the Tor was beaming invisible strength to me from afar.

'Have you been to these camps before?' I asked the girl with bright hennaed hair camped beside me.

'Yes, I came last year when they started. It was so great I decided to come again this year, and I've moved to Glastonbury as well. It's such an amazing scene here, lots of freaks and we all know each other. It's a real community. Loads happening,' she replied enthusiastically pulling on her poncho as the sun was setting.

That evening around the fire I met some of the others camping in my circle. One guy had just returned from Nepal and had that far away sadhu vibration. He was barefoot and wore the typical homespun Nepali shirt and waistcoat. Then there was a small dark gypsy-looking woman with her four-year-old son. She'd just split up with her partner and seemed enthusiastic but disturbed. They were all friendly and welcoming. This group felt familiar, my tribe. They were like characters from my sixties travelling days who had moved on and who were trying to create a new way of life.

The first morning I woke to the sound of a distant gong. Dance workshops would be held in a couple of hours and this was a wake up call. I wandered up the hill to take a shower in a shack with a solar panel on top. There were pallets on the floor and curtained compartments with shower heads suspended from the roof. Then I found the marquee where women in peasant skirts and dresses, men in Indian gear or jeans and half dressed kids were milling around or sitting at wooden tables eating, chatting and laughing. I helped myself to porridge and fruit and sat on a straw bale seat.

I looked enviously at these women of my age suckling babies, and at the wild free children running around. It felt like these families were living the life that was meant for me but was shattered. I couldn't accept that I wouldn't be able to have children and that my health was seriously impaired, so I decided not to believe it. After all, the doctors had often been wrong about other diagnoses. I would live for the moment. I was in the aura of Glastonbury—I would believe in miracles.

That week the camp was dedicated to different forms of dance and I danced as I hadn't done for years. I tired easily and had to rest frequently and go to bed long before the others. I had to pace myself and drop out of workshops half way through, but I was enjoying my body again and there was hope.

We danced circle dances from all over the world, holding hands and forming a community of movement, accompanied by musicians playing haunting folk melodies. I learnt how to shimmy my hips, draped in silky scarves, to the Arab Egyptian beat of a drum. I was enchanted by learning some hand *mudras* and foot beats of Baharat Natyam, classical Indian dance, as a young man strummed a gentle sitar. I woke up at night dreaming of a lifetime in India where I was a professional dancer always pushing myself further and further towards perfection. A lifetime so different from this, one where I had a strong physical body which brought me fame and wealth. It was a shock to wake up from these dreams to find myself in a tent feeling exhausted and with aching limbs. My spirit was strong, and I vowed to re-make my life. I was alive against the odds, and life was a gift to be lived to the full.

In the mornings my path crossed with a man called Patrick. Each day as I walked towards the showers and he towards the compost toilets we would say good morning. After a few days it became a hug and I would say, 'Here's my lovely man!' He was tall, with a beautiful open face, rather scruffy and I knew he was staying in a tipi. I was curious to know who he was.

After the dance camp the Astrology camp was restful and gave me time to think. The dance had changed me and I wanted to change my life. I wanted to live here! I felt at home for the first time in years, but how was I going to find somewhere to live, and what about Pete? Fate gave me a helping hand again, just as it had when I'd needed to leave Jeremy and Ickwell Bury turned up. Having made the decision to move I re-met an old friend who was visiting the dance camp for a day. I had met Ros on a self-development holiday on a Greek island called Skyros, where we had ended up on a beach one night celebrating the full moon together. Here she was again, as if on cue, inviting me to rent a room and share her house a few miles from Glastonbury. I said yes without even thinking about it and returned to Cambridge.

'How can you just leave?' I was surprised that Pete seemed upset as I was packing up my flat.

'I've wanted to make our relationship work for months,' I replied indignantly. 'I spent whole weekends alone without you even bothering to phone me. You haven't been really interested in me for months. I don't even

With my father, Harold

Patrick and I in the roundhouse

see Ishta any more. I don't want to be a backdrop to your life so it's better I get my own life together. We can still visit each other.' I felt a confused rage rising inside me. Why was he saying he cared now that it was too late, after months of seeming indifference?

'I didn't know you saw it like that. I've just been busy,' he replied sadly. 'I'll go and check your car out.'

In Glastonbury I felt myself part of an alternative community again, after years of feeling alone. I had been part of the hippy traveling scene, but this was different. Although there were many transient seekers who visited, there was also a large core group of people who had moved there because of the special mystical energy of the place and the feeling of community.

Glastonbury and its surroundings have long been called Avalon. In Celtic mythology, this was a mysterious and mystical island, an earthly paradise where eternal spring, health and harmony reigned. It was also said to be the island where the legendary King Arthur was taken when he was mortally wounded and where he was healed.

I was also coming there for healing, healing of my wounds of illness and childlessness. It was a place of mystic goddess energy where I could re-find my feminine self and the powerful priestess within me. In some New Age circles Glastonbury is even called the heart centre of the world, and immediately I moved there I felt a sense of the home I had been longing for. I had no money left to buy a house of my own, but at least I felt I was in the right spiritual and emotional home.

My life was full, I was healthier than I had been for years and had no time to miss Pete. I was soon seeing a few clients for acupuncture at the local complementary health clinic and started teaching a couple of evening yoga classes. Glastonbury opened itself to me like a flower. I met a lovely guy called Adam who became my lover, which was good but not all-important, because I was here to explore myself.

When I wasn't working I often went to Chalice Well, a sacred oasis of tranquillity on the edge of town, a beautiful garden surrounding a well whose iron-rich waters are said to represent the blood of Christ. According to legend the Holy Grail is hidden here and people come from all over the world to take the healing waters. I loved to sit by the lion's head, where the red water comes out in a stream, watching the robins darting among the flowers and shrubs. Birds are always so tame within the sacred space of these gardens.

Another place I liked to go was the Assembly Rooms café and hall, which was the heart of the community. In that echoey high ceilinged hall we shared ceremonies to celebrate the full moons and changing seasons, spent evenings circle dancing accompanied by musicians, and afternoons of talking circles. Saturday nights were like parties, where we danced to bands in bright wacky clothes. It was there that we exhibited our arts and crafts, and performed mythological plays. But the real heart of the Assembly Rooms was in the vegetarian community café, where synchronistic meetings would happen and where we would sit and chat with fellow Glastafarians.

Every kind of training course seemed to be available in that small town and I devoured as many as my income would allow. Illness had been such a major part of my life and now my greatest passion was to learn the best techniques for healing myself and others. I was initiated into Reiki, where we learned to channel healing energy through the chakras, the subtle energy centres along the spine. I did a course on the healing energy of plants using the now famous Bach flower remedies, and learned about the power of colour in Aura Soma, a blend of naturally coloured oils and herbs massaged into the chakras. I went to weekly healing circles with a healer called Tony Paine. He would come out with sudden loud channelled healing sounds, then we would pair up to give each other spiritual healing. I was always out doing some workshop or other, enthusiastically absorbing all there is to know about healing and self development.

It was early January when Adam and I went to the Assembly Rooms to watch the annual play. This year it was Antigone and the hall was decorated with huge hand painted banners depicting a panoply of Greek goddesses. As we went in I felt as if I had entered a Greek temple, and when the play began I was awed by the quality of the performance and the feeling of community in the audience. I had one of those moments when I felt my life as a play, where I was an actor, given the part which I was now playing: sitting in the Assembly Rooms. Everything in my life seemed to be moving with it's own momentum. Even though I made decisions and was proactive, it was as if my decisions had already been written in a cosmic script.

Afterwards, I invited Adam to come and have supper with me. We cooked together in Ros' airy open plan kitchen and were eating when the phone rang.

'It's me—Pete. I'm in Glastonbury. Can I come and visit tonight?.

'No! I'm in the middle of supper with a friend.' I was shocked. I hadn't expected this to be part of my drama tonight and didn't want to be reminded of my past. 'Come over tomorrow if you like,' I said reluctantly. The evening was broken, yet part of me still wanted to see Pete again.

'Don't you care about me any more?' he asked as we made lunch together the following day.

'Yes of course I do,' I replied cutting up the salad. 'But I've got a new boyfriend and I've started again. We tried for two years, Pete.'

'But we weren't really committed were we, with all the illness and everything?'

'I was committed,' I muttered sadly. 'But everything went wrong.'

'Why don't we get married and really try again?' He looked at me earnestly. I didn't know whether to laugh or cry. I felt like I was in my own Greek tragedy.

'It's too late, Pete. It wouldn't work.' I sat down, shaken, as he gazed out at the frosty garden.

'I think I'm going to come and live here anyway. Things aren't working out in Cambridge any more. I can't see Ishta so what's the point?'

I thought nostalgically of his little girl. I'd felt so much love for her when I lived in his home but I'd hardly seen her since.

'You mean Rita won't let you see her?' I asked shocked.

'No. We're fighting over her, like I never thought I'd do. I can't really talk about it, it's such a nightmare.'

'Let's walk up the Tor after lunch,' I suggested to break the icy sadness that had entered the room.

Chalice Well epitomised a gentle female healing energy for me, but climbing up the Tor in the depths of a freezing winter I was struck by a fierce male energy held within that sudden steep hill. We could hear the sound of drumming and didgeridoo coming from the top, and reaching there we found a group of young hippies making music. They were huddled in blankets, sitting around a couple of candles inside the the little hollow tower which had once been part of St Michael's church. We walked outside, the freezing wind whipping our faces.

'So you're thinking of coming here to live?' I asked, gazing out over the patchwork of the Somerset Levels beneath us.

'I'd like to, but I've got to sort out things at home first.' Pete looked pale and strained.

'Even if we're not together?'

'Maybe. You mean you're serious about your new boyfriend?'

'Maybe . . . ' With Pete my dreams of having a family had been shattered. The idea of rekindling my love for him was like trying to walk with no limbs.

After that there were difficult days. Days when I would watch mothers meeting their children from school and have to go away privately to weep. Days when I would feel I could no longer teach yoga, and that I wasn't strong enough to be an acupuncture practitioner.

'Why don't you go and see Geoff Boltwood?' a friend suggested when I told her about my sadness. 'He's doing something called Blessings from the Source tomorrow in Chalice Well house. It's free and anyone can go. I've heard he's the most amazing healer. You know that Indian saint, Sai Baba, who manifests healing ash? Well Geoff Boltwood does the same thing with healing oils.'

I had been to see Sai Baba in Bangalore, taking a few days off from the yoga ashram in Pondicherry. I remembered my consciousness ascending as he walked through the crowds of devotees with his afro hair and saffron robes. He would bend down and rub his hands together until a little grey healing ash would fall from his palms into ours. I remembered the sensation of the ash which seemed to be alive in my palms, emanating a powerful healing energy which spread though my body. I felt so comforted and happy being in his light and peaceful presence.

About twenty of us sit and meditate together. Geoff plays a tape of strange sounds which he says come from the voice of the Earth. He invites us to send healing to the Earth and to receive healing from her in the cyclical wave of our breath, knowing that we and the Earth are inseparable. At first it's hard to still the chatter of my mind, and I feel a great sadness about the pain we are inflicting on Mother Gaia with our pillaging and abuse. But gradually I become mentally quiet and feel myself surrounded by the high frequency energies of love and light. Then with my inner eye I perceive a Madonna-like woman dressed in vivid blue, surrounding me with her beautiful loving comforting energy. She tells me that she is always there for me, that all is well and that I too play my part in angelic work, in what I do for others.

I open my eyes to find a young woman standing in front of me beckoning me to come forward for healing. She's one of Geoff's helpers. I walk towards Geoff and he offers me a chair as he gets up to give me healing. As he raises his hands above the crown of my head and clears my aura, I feel a great sense of warmth and comfort flowing down my body, as if I'm being immersed in a bath of love. He takes my hands in his. 'Gently cup your hands,' he says, gazing inwardly. His hands are quite dry as he gently rubs mine, until a few seconds later I feel warm perfumed oil streaming out of his palms into mine.

As I am given the gift of healing oil, my consciousness rises like a bird freed from its cage. I feel as if I'm flying through the cosmos beyond time and space, tasting the true nature of my Being again. Thoughts are gone, and only a sense of Presence and love remain. I look into his eyes and see deep compassion. He gently raises me up from the chair. 'Share the healing oil with others,' he says serenely. Then his young helper guides me back towards the others and he calls someone else for healing. Dazed, I reach down to some people in the front who are sitting in meditation and, holding their hands, I share the oil. I find myself anointing their foreheads and third eyes with this blessed substance. I feel transformed, bathed in light and bliss. This is the nature of miracles I think. Miracles are none other than living in our wider truer state of Being.

I walk out of there renewed and elated. I may not have good health, my own home, or children, but I am being given gifts from Spirit. The high of the healing lasted for a week but I didn't return to the low I had sunk into before. It was another small step towards my true nature. I think spiritual growth is like this, like a seed which takes earth and time to grow, with peak experiences being like nourishing water.

One hot day that summer I was dancing in the Abbey Park. We were a circle of hippies, wearing flimsy colourful clothes, holding hands and moving to taped music from the Balkans and Brittany. Our teacher talked us through each dance slowly and then we practised it to music. The group met regularly but today was special for me as Harold was sitting on a bench watching, on one of his now frequent visits to the town. Afterwards we walked around the ruins of the famous Glastonbury Abbey, the seat of Christianity in England.

'You certainly seem to have found your place in Glastonbury,' Harold remarked as we sat in the shade of a giant copper beech tree watching the towering stone ruins shimmering in the sunlight. 'You always loved dancing, even as a little girl. Do you remember I took you to those ballet classes in Hampstead and you wanted to be a ballerina?'

'Yes. One of my happiest childhood memories is being taken to see a ballet with Margot Fonteyn and Nuryev. Perhaps wanting to dance was a memory of a former dancing life,' I added. 'I've heard that children are the best at remembering their past lives.'

'Do you believe that we've had other lives then?' Harold asked curiously.

'Yes, I'm becoming more and more convinced of it. It explains geniuses like Mozart being able to write sonatas when he was just a kid. He must have mastered music in a previous life. And it's the only thing that seems to make any sense of innocent people suffering.'

'That's not remembered from other lives, surely,' said Harold.

'No, I think that's to do with the law of karma, the law of cause and effect—as you sow so shall you reap. It doesn't just apply to one life but goes on from life to life. So perhaps if you were cruel in a previous life your soul decides to learn the lesson of how it feels to be treated badly and puts you in a position to experience cruelty in this life.'

'So you're saying that you think we have a soul which decides things before we are born?' Harold looked like an archetypal beautiful elder, staring into the distance.

'Yes, so that we can learn and evolve. And it seems we do most of our learning through suffering, until we become truly integrated, enlightened.'

'Maybe. It all seems a bit far fetched to me, I've always been an agnostic. I don't have any definite beliefs.' He smiled good naturedly.

'Did I tell you Pete moved down here a couple of months ago? But it's not working out very well. He's living in a shared house in the centre of town.'

'And you're seeing him again?'

'Yes, we'll see him tonight at the party. I ended it with that man Adam, although he was lovely. Pete wanted me to go back to him, try again. He even asked me to marry him. Now I wonder if I've made a big mistake getting close to him again. We just don't seem to be able to talk about things or get on any more. Do you think these difficult relationships are to do with you leaving when I was three?'

'Perhaps,' he replied uneasily. 'You know I never wanted to break up the family. It's just that your mother and I were always the best of friends, but there was no passion. At least on my part.' I thought of my mother's cool Swedish reserve and could understand this.

'I think it's probably as much to do with Terence.' I remembered the feelings of disgust I had towards my stepfather. 'I just don't trust men, so I choose ones who I can't love properly or who can't love me.'

'I think you can love all right,' he replied thoughtfully. 'Perhaps you just aren't the marrying kind.'

Harold went back to my friend Emma's small Bed and Breakfast where he was staying, as I had no room for guests. I felt unexpectedly nervous that night as I changed into my long party frock before meeting Pete. As we approached the circular marquee where the party was being held, a beautiful butterfly pendant I was wearing fell off onto the dark stony path. The pendant was important to me. It was one of the few things my mother had given me and I felt that the butterfly was my power creature. It symbolised my struggle to move from the disintegration of the pupa to the beauty of wings. Pete and Harold soon tired of looking for it and went ahead into the party, while I continued searching. Then I saw someone coming out. It was the man called Patrick who I'd had hugs with at that dance camp and had seen around town since then.

'What are you doing crouched out here in the dark?' he asked, sounding amused.

I stood up, hoping to appear nonchalant. 'Oh just looking for a bit of jewellery which fell off,' I replied vaguely, trying to cover up my embarrassment.

'Let me help you,' he said, and within minutes we had found the pendant.

'Thanks so much,' I said, greatly relieved.

'You're welcome,' he replied, walking off into the darkness.

I went into the hubbub of the party and sat down next to Pete. I looked at the dirt-splattered pendant in my hand and swallowed as I saw the butterfly was cracked right down the middle.

'You found it then,' said Pete, as Harold looked on benignly.

'Yes, but it's broken,' I replied looking down at the nasty mud spattered crack. We sat with our drinks, watching the dancing. I noticed Patrick dancing with a beautiful dark-haired woman. He looked very handsome out of his normal scruffy clothes. And there was Adam also looking very attractive as he danced with his new partner. I got up and went to the dance area. Pete seemed distant from me, engrossed in talking to a slim blonde woman who had been sitting beside him. My dad was happily chatting with a group by the makeshift bar. The hours went on and I danced alone and chatted to friends as Pete continued to ignore me. I knew something was going on between him and the blonde and felt sick. But I didn't feel able to approach him or speak to him. He had offered me the chance of marriage and I had turned him down. Why shouldn't he chat up another woman? I left at midnight and Pete stayed, although we'd arranged to spend the night together. I lay in bed feeling as if my body was being severed from his, and although I knew this had to be, it was still agony. I was the broken butterfly. He turned up at four in the morning to find me curled up in bed, my face swollen with tears.

'You should have come back earlier,' I said, hoarse with emotion.

'I'm sorry. I just didn't want to leave.' I knew he was afraid to tell me the truth.

'Because you've fallen in love with that blonde.'

'Amy,' he said, looking surprised as if I wouldn't have guessed.

'You made it pretty obvious, in front of Harold as well.'

'I'm sorry. It just sort of happened.' I could see he was trying to hide his elation.

'There's nothing really to say is there?' I felt emptied out with the inevitability of it all.

'I'm sorry, he said as he left, 'Maybe in another lifetime . . . '

'I don't understand how I can have done all these healing workshops and had these spiritual experiences and still feel so bad about my life,' I told my counsellor a few months later. 'Pete's getting married and going to have a baby with Amy and I just hate them. I feel like I was the one meant to have the baby and now it's her. And I can't look at babies any more. If I do, I just want to cry or steal one. So I just walk away.'

'You haven't completed your grieving process about not having children,' she reminded me gently. 'And that's nothing to do with your spiritual experiences, it's to do with you as a woman in this body. You seeing Amy getting what you thought you would have with him is bringing it all to the surface again.'

'I know, but I don't know what to do. It just makes me feel like leaving Glastonbury, seeing them walking around town hand in hand, her with her smug bump. Neither of them even talk to me. It's as if I never existed. At least Pete could try to be friends, but now he's got her, he can't be bothered.'

'You need to be gentle with yourself, nurture that wounded part of yourself, speak to it as if it was your own little child, with absolute compassion. Stop being so hard on yourself. You've had a difficult time.'

'I know,' I sighed. 'And it just seems so unfair. I felt as if my life was starting again here in Glastonbury. Within nine months I've gone from being happy and optimistic, with two men caring for me, to having no-one and feel empty and desolate again. The time it would have taken to have a baby,' I said bitterly. 'And now the weather's getting cold again and I'm frightened of getting ill. I know I should winter in a warmer climate but I don't know how to do it.'

'Be patient with yourself,' the counsellor replied, looking concerned. 'If you can express your grief your immune system will grow stronger and you'll be less likely to get ill.' I walked home alone with my familiar emptiness.

Sunny Summers, 1987–1988

Beloved

Beloved
I want to dance with you again
Dance out of my broken past
Into togetherness
Beloved under the flowering full moon
Let me touch your heart
And know
There is nothing to fear or part
The breathing blue air
Of Love

Welcome to the path of the heart! This path of love doesn't go anywhere. It just brings you more here, into the present moment, into the reality of who you already are.

Ram Dass

A week before Summer Solstice my dear friend Emma and I packed up my car with tents, bedding, supplies of flower remedies, massage oils, homoeopathic remedies and a first aid kit to go and work at the Glastonbury festival. I had met Emma when I first arrived in Glastonbury. She was the same age as me and, although she had had a conventional working life, we found we had much in common. Now we were off to run a welfare dome at the festival. I wouldn't use my acupuncture needles, but would still be able to massage the appropriate points if people needed treatment. In fact, my acupuncture practice wasn't thriving, as I was beginning to realise I wasn't at all suited to needles! But I could also use my counselling and healing skills. Emma was also an excellent and empathic therapist.

We arrived a few days before the mass of people and watched as some one hundred acres of quiet fields turned into a vibrant city of wide stages and expanses of tents.

'It's so huge these days,' I exclaimed to Emma, watching the site fill up and remembering the modest gathering of hippies I had joined all those years ago.

'About 150,000 they say, and it's still growing. Look at that beautiful yurt they're putting up over there.' She pointed towards a large circular wooden framework a few bare chested men were assembling on the other side of the field.

'Nice looking guys,' I commented laughing.

'Yeah, but too young for you!'

'Don't I know it!' I shook my head mock sadly.

The festival site was beginning to look like some exotic movie, with characters dressed in all sorts of costumes wandering around setting up stages and building different structures. There was a field of tipis which emerged from the morning mists with timeless beauty. There was the Green Field, where alternative methods of building and crafts were demonstrated. There was the Healing Field where we were camped, with wind chimes and Tibetan flags dancing in the breeze, and a miniature healing garden with pots of herbs and flowers.

Many of our friends were setting up massage and complementary healing venues in their own tents, where they would work and earn good money. The fields lower down, about 80 per cent of the site, was what we called Babylon: areas which soon would become almost impassible with crowds on a hedonistic music, alcohol and drug binge. There were avenues of cafés and food stalls where you could buy anything from hot dogs to tofu burgers. There were funky clothes and ethnic fabric stalls, alongside music stages and dance marquees. Overlooking all was the Pyramid, the main stage where Van Morrison was to perform this year.

By Saturday night we could hear at least four bands playing from different corners of the neighbouring fields. An array of distressed youngsters were lounging on strips of foam in the big dome tent we'd borrowed for our welfare haven.

'I can't hear myself think,' Emma muttered as she looked through the boxes of remedies in our medicine chest.

'What's wrong with the girl you're treating? She looks in a terrible state,' I asked as she rummaged around.

'Her boyfriend's disappeared with her best friend,' she answered not turning around as she continued to look though a box of homoeopathic remedies

'Sounds familiar, poor girl. Try some arnica. It might calm her down— the shock.'

'That's what I'm looking for. God, I don't know how long I'll be able to keep this up. I'm exhausted already,' she muttered wearily.

'So am I. But we said we'd go on till midnight, and anyone who needs to can just crash on the foam after that. Tomorrow afternoon we can go out and catch Van Morrison wailing on the main stage.'

When we got to see Van the Man I was disappointed. I loved his music but it was weird seeing him there, in his white stay-pressed trousers, playing like an automaton as though he was only doing it for the money. Always the romantic, I had expected the reality of seeing him to match up to the poetry of his lyrics.

After the Glastonbury festival we ran the welfare dome at the Oak Dragon Camps, a series of small family orientated events inspired by the original camps which had first drawn me to Glastonbury. About two hundred and fifty people came to these camps, which were a week to ten days long, each one on a different theme. This year there there was a healing camp and a

Sunny summers

An Oak Dragon camp

dance camp run back to back. They were held at Nanteos, the very same mansion in Wales where I had gone to recover from my miscarriage in 1971. Now it was 1987 but the old mansion looked much the same as we pitched our tent in the rolling grounds.

We unpacked our remedies and put them on the carved wooden box covered with a white cloth. We laid sheepskins on the floor and covered some mattresses with Indian bedspreads. Lily, Emma's ten-year-old, went off to find out what the children were up to.

'I've brought these materials to decorate the place with,' Emma was unpacking and hanging up a pile of brightly coloured silk saris and throws. We had both led nomadic lives and knew how to make a place feel special with a few easy touches of exotic materials. When we had finished the tent looked like an oriental casbah, feminine, comfortable and colourful.

'The Welfare Tent is open now!' I wandered around calling out to the camp crew working outside. They were busy erecting different structures. A group were putting up a tipi. The cone of wooden poles pointed into the sky as the guys began to lift a great sail of white canvas, the skin of the tipi, and manoeuvre it on top of the poles. Men in bedraggled jeans, boots and jackets were digging a trench for a set of earth toilets. These would be topped by wooden cubicles with a toilet seat in each above the trench below. There were men and women stacking firewood, for use both on individual fires in each camping circle and for the large central one, which was already alight. Women sat around the fire preparing vegetables and cooking while their little children ran around nearby.

'I'm making tea,' said Emma when I returned from my wanderings. 'Have you seen Lily?'

'Yes she's playing with some other girls outside one of the domes over the other side. They seemed to be dressing up in some fairy outfits. She looked fine.'

'Yeah, I know she's happy here, free from her dad and the boys,' Emma replied wistfully. She had lost custody of her children after she had taken her young son to India to be with the Dalai Lama. Her husband had willingly consented, but later, in court, accused her of abandoning her children to go on the hippy trail. She was constantly devastated by this injustice and now she only had Lily for three weeks, half the summer holidays.

The healing camp passed quietly. People wandered into our welfare tent for counselling and comfort more than anything else. We spent a large part of the time outside around our camp fire, which constantly had a kettle perched on the trivet. The dance camp was much noisier, with a strong fiery energy and passion. As always, I enjoyed listening to the live music which went on all day.

'I've met this really interesting guy,' Emma looked flushed. 'He was at the creative dance workshop this morning. He's called River, usually lives in the States but he's been travelling around Europe for a few months and ended up here. He said he's never experienced anything like this before, this feeling of sharing in a creative community. I've invited him round for tea.'

'Great!' I replied. 'It's high time you had a bit of romance in your life.'

'I don't know about that, but at least he's good to talk to.' But I knew her well enough to see the signs.

In the evening I was struggling with my usual weakness and exhaustion as I put on my orange and red swirly dress to go to the big party. The high point of the dance camp coincided with the full moon and we were all celebrating with a party in the biggest marquee, accompanied by the Funky Soul band. That night River stayed in our little camp circle, and soon he was part of the family.

'He's invited me to stay at his place in California when we leave,' said Emma excitedly a couple of days later. And I'm going to go—kidnap Lily and just leave the country. I can't stand any more of this.'

'But Em, are you serious? You'll be wanted by the police, hunted for. You can't just take her.'

'I can,' she replied smiling to herself. 'I can and I'm going to. I've decided!'

Within the week she had sold her car and her tent and had given away her bits and pieces. With the money she booked a plane ticket to San Francisco. I was amazed and could hardly believe this was really happening. She was my closest friend but there was nothing I could say or do to stop her. A couple of days later we hugged goodbye, tears streaming down our faces. Lily looked quite unfazed by it all, quite ready to start a big adventure with her mum. For me it was the end of the summer. It would soon be the first of September. The dance camp ended and I went back to Glastonbury to struggle through winter, maintain my acupuncture practice as best I could and teach some yoga.

Summer came again and another friend, Ella, and I decided we would have a holiday from Glastonbury and go to a retreat in southern France. We took her car and drove to a château near Toulouse to be with the American hippy guru of the sixties, Ram Dass.

We arrived in the gentle hills and put our tents up in a field purified with the gentle scent of lavender and loud with the trill of cicadas. As evening fell we all gathered in a sunny hall with bay windows overlooking a patio bordered by pots of geraniums and roses. Ram Dass started the retreat by telling us his story:

> Years ago in India I was sitting in the courtyard of a small temple in the Himalayan foothills. Thirty or forty of us were there around my guru, Maharaji. This little old man, wrapped in a plaid blanket, was sitting on a plank bed and for a brief uncommon interval everyone had fallen silent. It was a meditative quiet, like an open field on a windless day or a deep clear lake without a ripple. I felt waves of love radiating toward me, washing over me like a gentle surf on a tropical shore, immersing me, rocking me, caressing my soul, infinitely accepting and open.
>
> I was nearly overcome, on the verge of tears, so grateful and so full of joy it was hard to believe it was happening. I opened my eyes and looked around, and I could feel that everyone else around me was experiencing the same thing. I looked over at my guru. He was just sitting there, looking around, not doing anything. It was just his being, shining like the sun equally on everyone. It wasn't directed at anyone in particular. For him it was nothing special, just his own nature. When Maharaji was near me I was bathed in love. Then he turned to me and said, 'Give me the medicine.'
>
> 'What medicine?' I asked. 'I don't have any medicine with me.'
>
> 'Yes, you have, in your pocket.' Then I realised he meant the LSD

I had on me. It was several trips. I handed him the LSD and watched him swallow the whole lot at once. I was nervous seeing him take so much and felt responsible for a potentially dangerous situation. But after some time I realized it was having no effect on him whatsoever. His consciousness was already higher than the drug, so it made no difference. Maharaji changed my life.

Now Ram Dass was our teacher. He taught us to have compassion for ourselves and helped us learn to witness our 'monkey mind,' the mind which we are so identified with and which causes us so much suffering.

'Love is like sunshine. It permeates everything and is the bliss-consciousness of existence,' he told us laughingly as we chanted and meditated together.

He showed us a horrific video of a war zone. 'Keep your hearts open and have as much compassion for the perpetrator of suffering as the one who is suffering,' he said. 'You need to be able to keep your hearts open even in hell, and that's not easy!'

I hoped that by doing this retreat I would become more balanced and change on a deeper level. I was tired of having the highs of spiritual experiences and then falling low again. But instead of falling in love with my deeper Self, I soon found myself falling in love—or lust—with the guy who meditated in front of me! How did he manage to keep his back so perfectly straight and still when I was squirming around in agony after half an hour? How did his Indian clothes always look so perfect when we were all camping? When he turned round to smile seductively at me after the session, I got goose bumps all over. I came here to experience unconditional inner love and peace. Why did he have to be the most gorgeous man in the room sitting there in front of me, an immediate distraction if I dared to open my eyes?

Ram Dass didn't call himself a guru but was one in the true sense of the word, which simply means one who leads us from darkness to the light. When someone asked him the cynical question about it no longer being the time for gurus, he said:

Some gurus have got into ego and power trips, and given all gurus a bad name. But do we throw away a bag of apples because of one rotten one? We have teachers in all other fields, so why not have someone who can guide us on our spiritual journey, the most important journey of all. They can save you a lot of time and show you possible pitfalls, although it's always up to you what decisions you make. You have to use your own discrimination when choosing a guru. You can recognise a true guru by their lack of ego, by their not asking for money or unquestioning allegiance, and their detachment about whether or not you become their follower.

Every morning, before the real heat set in, there was an optional yoga session, followed by a breakfast of fruit and yoghurt. Then we had long meditations followed by discourses in which Ram Dass told us more about unconditional love.

Unconditional love really exists in each of us. It's part of our deep inner being. It's not so much an active emotion as a state of being. It's not, 'I love you for this or that reason,' not 'I love you if you love me.' It's love for no reason, love without object. It's just sitting in love, a love that incorporates the chair and the room and permeates everything around. The thinking mind is extinguished in love.

He encouraged us to enjoy the weather when we weren't in sessions with him. We would walk half a kilometre through sunflower fields to a small waterfall and pool in the river, where we stripped off and skinny dipped like children released from school. And of course there was The Man. How could I be detached when he started fooling with me flirtatiously in the water. 'You'd make a good mermaid,' he said playfully diving between my legs under the water.

He would lead me on when we were out of the meditation area and then be completely cool and detached once we entered the hall again. I was becoming obsessed and I was watching my mind and emotions with about as much detachment as a fly. Falling in love was my addiction. I had always prided myself at being the non addictive type. I'd never been addicted to smoking, although I'd smoked a bit in my youth, and I'd never been able to drink. I loved chocolate, coffee and tea but when I found they did me no good I gave them up without much difficulty. But here I was on retreat facing my biggest addiction: the need to have a love object to fill my mind with, to distract me from facing myself, to give me the illusion that a perfect romance would bring me my ultimate fulfilment.

Then I saw *his* addiction. He was flirting and leading several women on at the same time. This was obviously his pattern. He knew he was gorgeous and was subtly playing the field. But that was not my problem. My problem was trying to extricate myself from distraction and drop my romantic illusions. Again detachment was the name of the game.

I don't know how well I succeeded but at least I became really conscious of my addictive pattern. I knew I wanted peace above all else, that once I was anchored in Divine Love my outer relationships would improve. As time went on my mind quietened and my desire cooled. I appreciated breathing the fragrant air when I woke at dawn and I appreciated the sudden beauty of a butterfly, a tree or a stone. I felt gratitude for the vivid colours of sunrise and sunset, smiles with other participants over silent meals, and the wafting scent of Mediterranean vegetables cooking as we meditated. Mostly I appreciated Ram Dass's presence and humour which enfolded me like the cloak of unconditional love I had always longed for. This was the greatest healing for me. All too soon the holiday retreat was over. Ella and I travelled back slowly by car, giving ourselves time to adjust to the world outside the magic bubble of the retreat, and enjoying the pastoral scenery and the gold of southern sunshine.

Marriage, 1988–2000

The Rainbow

It was a special day unlike any other
With hardly a moment to gaze outside
When just before dusk I opened the door
To a rainbow painting the sky
She tinted the air and bridged the valley
With a wing of vivid pulsing colour
Like a perfect ethereal butterfly
I wanted to reach out and dissolve in her beauty
Roll in her light and touch her colour
Or draw her down and keep her forever
Preserve her like nectar
Or sweet summer wine
But she was already fraying and fading
Ephemeral as dreams
In the night
Fraying and trailing her tendrils of colour
Like hopes
In the arch of the sky

A couple of months later at a friend's party I met Patrick, the man who had helped me find my butterfly pendant on the night I had split up with Pete. We had known each other as acquaintances since we first met at the dance camp which brought me to Glastonbury. He looked like a handsome farm worker with his red spotted neckerchief, beard and tanned muscled arms showing beneath his rolled up sleeves. He had style and an intelligent open face with large warm blue-grey eyes. Although he was tall and well built, he wasn't in fact very well. I knew he had a chronic illness, although I didn't know what it was. But I also knew it wasn't totally debilitating because he made his living making tipis.

We felt a sudden strong attraction to each other at that party and arranged to meet again soon. Our first date was to be supper at the old stone cottage where I was living at the time. The relationship nearly ended before it began when he failed to turn up.

'The bastard is standing me up!' I yelled to myself after an anxious hour turning the oven down and rescuing the rice. 'I'm damn well not going to get involved with another unreliable man.'

But next morning I knew I had to phone him. 'So what happened to you last night?' I was trying not to sound irate.

'Oh God, I'm so sorry,' he replied sounding embarrassed. 'I'm in bed with a fever—my brucellosis. I get these bad bouts from time to time. I thought we left it that I would phone you if I *was* coming, not if I wasn't. This illness affects my mind and sometimes I get forgetful. Lets go for a walk together as soon as I'm well again.' I put the phone down surprisingly elated.

A week later we went to Cadbury Castle, the site of Camelot, the seat of King Arthur's dreams and legends and a suitable place for the possible start of a romance! We walked up the steep hill while Patrick pointed out landmarks and field patterns, reading the landscape like others would read a book. He took my arm protectively as we walked around the remains of the hill fort. We found a good view point and sat side by side on an ancient rampart gazing down at the rolling Somerset hills in companionable silence.

'I love Somerset,' he said. 'I was brought up here. I travelled a lot after I left agricultural college, spent several years in Africa and a year in Israel, but Glastonbury is the first place I've lived for more than a year or two in my adult life. I came here to spend the winter and it felt like home immediately, it was the landscape at first but now I feel part of a real community and that's important.'

'Yes, it's important to me too. What were you doing in Africa?'

'Oh I was working for VSO and later became a farm manager. That's where I got my illness—from infected cattle,' he said nonchalantly. 'I know you've had an illness too, but you look really well now.' He turned smiling towards me appreciatively.

'I am at the moment. I often get bad in winter, though. Then my bones hurt and it's like having flu for weeks on end. I had very bad TB when I was young and I've never really got my strength back.'

'Sounds like me. I'm usually fine in summer but in winter my brucellosis recurs. It's a fever, a bit like malaria,' he added, completely without self pity.

I was fascinated by the synchronicity of our illnesses, mine from milk, his from cattle and both recurring in winter. 'It's good you understand,' I said and I found myself leaning back towards his outstretched arm. 'It seems that almost no one understands chronic illness unless they've experienced it themselves or been close to someone going through it.'

'I know, and for us who look big and healthy it's even harder. Some people just don't believe I'm ill.'

'Yes,' I said. 'I can have a little bandage on a finger and people ask what's happened to me and seem concerned. Yet I can spend weeks in bed and no one notices or cares, because by the time I'm able to go out again I look quite well. But I like looking good too, so I suppose I do hide it to some extent.'

The conversation drifted to our recent relationships. Patrick already knew how I had suffered in a painful one that had ended not so long before.

'I've just got out of a bad one, too,' he said. 'I split up with this woman, Mary, a few months ago, but . . .' he looked away hesitantly, 'but she's going to have my baby in a month.' He picked angrily at the grass and looked towards the distant hills. I felt my throat contracting, swallowing down the familiar pain of childlessness. This was exactly what I didn't want to hear.

'It was incredibly painful,' he said, wiping his eyes. 'It started last winter when she came to help make her own tipi with me. From there it became a postal romance—she lives in Scotland—and by the time we met up again we had each built up a fantasy of who the other was. We only had a few passionate weekends together, but we were so in love that we thought whatever happened between us, even a child, it would be perfect. But then she got pregnant and immediately ended the relationship. I wanted to talk about it but she refused to communicate. Now it seems she didn't really want me at all, she only wanted another child. I feel like I've just been used as a sperm bank.' I could see the bitterness rising in him as he spoke. I took his hand.

'It's a horrible situation but I do want to be some kind of a father to my child.' I put my arm around him and felt a huge wave of compassionate love. Maybe a relationship with him wouldn't be a matter of getting what I wanted but of helping him in his own pain.

The afternoon turned cloudy and we went back to the caravan where he lived in winter—in summer he lived in a tipi in the fields. He lit his wood burner and made me tea. We sat opposite each other in his tiny space.

'I don't think I'm ready for another physical relationship at the moment,' he said drawing the velvet curtains against the dusk, 'Although I'm really attracted to you.' The caravan became warm quickly and he took off his old cable knit sweater.

'I feel the same. I'm feeling quite vulnerable after what I've just been through,' I said. We hugged and cuddled and decided to be no more than good friends for at least three months.

Three days later Patrick visited me in my cottage. He split some firewood and brought it inside to the hearth. I watched as he casually picked up a piece of wood and deftly reduced it to a handful of kindling as though the hatchet was as extension of his arm. He lit the fire and tended it like he was absent-mindedly stroking a well-loved pet. We drank tea and chatted.

'I really need to go upstairs for a little rest,' I said after a while. What a relief it was to feel OK about revealing my physical weakness to a man.

'That's fine,' he said. 'I need a rest too.'

'Would you like to rest here on the sofa or upstairs?'

'Hmm. Upstairs I think.'

So much for waiting three months!

Patrick's son, Caleb, was born a month later in mid November and Patrick went up to visit just after his birth.

'How is he?' I asked brightly on the phone, trying to disguise my anguish.

'He's fine,' I could hear the stress in his voice. 'But it's really hard being here with Mary. I don't feel like his father, and I hate this village and these lowering mountains.'

'I'm missing you, but it won't be long.' I swallowed back the tears.—Who is this other woman who has Patrick's child when she doesn't even want *him*? She already has four! She should give Caleb to me, I deserve him, I love his father, and I can't have children.—My heart felt squeezed dry. There was a vice of pain tight around my temples, affecting my eyes, which just didn't want to see this childlessness any more.

That night I had a vivid dream.

> I'm a young Tibetan Buddhist monk. I'm in a stark temple overlooking a sparse dry landscape . . . vast rocky plains with snow capped mountains in the distance. I'm at the centre of a ceremony, being initiated into the order. I'm being given maroon robes. A sleeveless saffron top. A dorje and a bell. A smiling shaven monk gives me my new spiritual name. Afterwards musicians break out in a cacophony of strange sounds. A horn, some drums and cymbals. A white scarf is put around my shoulders. Later there is great feasting.

I woke up disturbed but comforted. The dream felt so real, like me in another lifetime. Seeing my life in the light of ongoing lifetimes, everything made sense, even the anguish of childlessness. Without karma the world would be a totally random and unjust place. But still I am a woman and I wanted my own family, I wanted babies to cherish and give my life meaning on a human plane, never mind karma and past lives.

I do believe that our soul chooses our major life experiences before we are born, to learn particular qualities or to reap karma from other times. Who knows what was the reason my soul chose that I should be unable to have children? I had to learn to accept the unacceptable.

Patrick returned and our relationship grew deeper. During the day he worked on his sewing machine in a workshop near his field, listening to Radio Four to occupy his mind. The field was a wild flower meadow that he'd been able to buy some years previously when he had inherited some money, in order to save it from being turned into a monoculture of ryegrass. I still had my part time jobs in town. But in the long summer evenings I'd spend the night out in the country with him, cooking outside or on the fire in the tipi, and sleeping protected by that circular white pyramid of canvas. I would glimpse the night sky and stars through the smoke hole as we lay together on sheepskins. We gardened a small vegetable patch, socialised with friends and went to events in Glastonbury. We had an ease of communication I had never experienced with a man before. He was my best friend and even when we did have disagreements we were usually able to sort them out with humour.

Some of the best times we had together were at festivals. We liked to meet old friends, go to workshops and enjoy ourselves, but at the same time always had to take care of our delicate health. So though we did some partying we would end up companionably in bed together early at night. Our favourite festival was the Green Gathering, held on an organic farm in Wiltshire.

The Green Gathering had started in 1980 and Patrick had been one of the founders. By 1990, it had become a large off grid eco festival where all us alternative types could meet up and share skills, workshops and fun. There was a craft area where you could learn anything from felt making to wood turning, a healing area where you could both receive healing and learn healing skills, a children's area, theatre and music stages, a permaculture garden, and vegetarian restaurants and cafés. All the venues were either outside or in big marquees, yurts, and other simple structures.

Patrick would spend hours sitting around chatting with old and new friends, making them tea on the tipi fire. For him making fires was an art form, and he reckoned he could boil a kettle on an open fire from scratch quicker than on a gas ring. Meanwhile visitors would peek in through the open door to see how tipi dwellers lived and I watched Patrick admiringly. He was as warm and open with strangers as he was with friends. Like me, he had the gift of making everyone feel at home.

In the second year we were together Patrick, with help from several friends, built a one-room roundhouse to replace the caravan as his winter quarters. I was then living in a bungalow in town and the roundhouse was a much more attractive place to be in summer, so I moved in there while Patrick was in his tipi on the White Field, just a short walk away from me. But still I wondered if we would ever make a life together. Patrick had never had a relationship lasting more than three months before, yet I couldn't imagine life without him.

When we went for walks together, he brought nature alive for me in a way I had never experienced before. He was always pointing out and explaining things, like how the landscape had been formed and why particular plants grew in certain places.

He was always open to listening to my problems and had the rare gift of really being able to hear me, especially where it concerned my health. But I felt I had to prepare myself for the possibility of another disappointment. Perhaps he would never want to live with me, although we were still in love. After all he had never lived with anyone before. I knew I needed a deeper commitment but I had no idea what he wanted.

One day when he was delivering tipi poles to someone in Devon he met a man who introduced himself as a teacher of permaculture, an ecological design system for sustainable living. In that moment something clicked inside him and he thought, 'This is it! This is why I'm here.'

Within a few days he was on a six month weekend course in Devon studying the basic permaculture principles. The following year he took an advanced course up in Lancashire, and was encouraged by friends to attend a follow-on course in teaching permaculture. It was on this teachers training course that he was told he had a real gift for teaching and he decided to give up the tipi making business and become a full time permaculture teacher.

While he was away I was haunted by sickening waves of uncertainty. I felt that my career as an acupuncturist was over. I just wasn't cut out for it and had in fact started a counselling course and group leadership training. I had always wanted to work with people but sticking needles into them felt distinctly unfriendly.

I also wanted to feel like a real family, but this was difficult living separately from Patrick and without children. He visited his son Caleb in Scotland twice a year, and I would usually go with him. I loved Caleb and wanted to have a close relationship with him, but as well as finding the situation extremely painful, neither of us could become really close to him as he lived so far away. I was still secretly hoping that by some miracle I would get pregnant. I wasn't menopausal yet and doctors could be wrong. Unfortunately, we weren't in any position to try adoption either, and Patrick had no desire to have another child except if it happened naturally. Now summer was drawing to an end and it was time for me to move back into town. This would mean moving further apart rather than closer together.

The day after Patrick returned from his course we went into Glastonbury together. We needed to talk and decided to have a picnic lunch after we'd done our shopping. I hadn't seen him for a couple of weeks, the longest we had been separated since we met, and we needed to clarify what we were going to do in the future. I was feeling nervous, but he seemed remarkably cheerful. He told me he was off to buy some seeds at the plant nursery cum flower shop while I got the groceries. I was wondering if we would get time for an intimate chat, as we only had a short while before an important meeting I had that afternoon about a relaxation tape I was in the process of recording.

'Shall we go up on Chalice Hill?' he asked me when we met up from shopping. I couldn't understand why he seemed so happy while I was feeling anxious about our future. He also seemed strangely secretive, holding something behind his back. He must be in a super good mood after his course, I thought, and has bought some goodies for the picnic.

'Yes let's have our picnic up there. It's one of my favourite places,' I answered quietly, looking forward to at least an hour of quality time together.

'What about under the old oak tree,' he suggested as we reached the sacred hill. 'Lets sit here,' he pointed to a patch of shade as we reached the gnarled old tree. He was smiling and still holding whatever it was behind his back. I sat down feeling tired and hungry, wondering what all his enthusiasm was about. Before I knew what was happening Patrick was kneeling in front of me, looking laughingly into my eyes and holding a bunch of red roses.

'Will you marry me?' he asked, looking so sweet and enthusiastic.

I gasped, my heart pounding. 'Yes!' I threw myself into his arms laughing, and we kissed to seal the pledge.

Afterwards he said he'd never seen anyone look so surprised in all his life.

It was 6 October 1990 and a blustery autumn day. I woke early in Patrick's little round house, my stomach dancing and my mouth dry. I dressed in a silk turquoise gypsy skirt, an antique cream blouse and an embroidered peasant jacket. My friend Caroline put flowers in my hair. Patrick wore a tweed jacket and a silk scarf. He always looked ruggedly handsome and rakish, and when he dressed up he looked positively dashing. After a brief civil ceremony at the Registry Office we drove to Chalice Well gardens where our closest friends and family were gathered waiting for us.

For me going to Chalice Well was always like stepping into a world beyond the veil. There I felt a sense of homecoming and the presence of the elementals, those magical nature spirits I had encountered in Wales years before. I felt soothed by the sound of water and the rustle of leaves above me. At the Well itself there is a holy thorn where people tie ribbons to take their prayers to the other world. A little further down the slope the well water emerges from the ground through a stone lion's head, which is where we now gathered for our wedding ceremony.

We stood in front of the holy spring as a dear friend garlanded our heads with wild flowers and ivy. Then she filled blue china chalices with water from the holy spring and handed one to each of us. We stood opposite each other surrounded by loving faces, looking into each others eyes. I drank a sip and and made this vow:

> With this water I pledge myself to this marriage,
> For the highest good of ourselves,
> Mother Earth and the Great Spirit

I handed the chalice to Patrick. He took a sip and repeated the same words, looking lovingly into my eyes and offering the chalice back to me. We kissed and our friends and family clapped in celebration. I felt a huge wave of love

Our wedding ceremony at the Chalice Well gardens

and joy enfolding me. Both my mother and father came into the centre of the circle to kiss us. I had never felt so close to them before and I realised at heart they had only wanted my happiness and had hated seeing me suffer so much. Patrick's mother Peggy also came and hugged us, delighted that her eldest son was marrying at last.

When the ceremony was over we all walked down to the lower gardens to do an Israeli wedding dance. We stood in the centre of our circle of friends as they danced around us, each one with their hand on the shoulder of the one in front of them. We were showered with love and blessings. I felt the blessings dancing all through my body as I stood with my beloved Patrick in the middle of that circle receiving more love than I had ever imagined possible.

From Chalice Well we drove back to the community where Patrick had his workshop and round house. The biggest workshop was decorated with garlands of autumn flowers, berries and leaves. It all looked welcoming, bright and festive, and soon the house was humming with a hundred guests.

Just before we started eating, a rainbow appeared in the sky. I felt it was a spiritual blessing from my Tibetan lineage, where rainbows are regarded as a deeply auspicious symbol of transformation. The afternoon and evening were spent eating, socialising and dancing, and by night time I fell into bed with Patrick totally exhausted and very happy. We had a short honeymoon in a little hotel in Cornwall, a gift from my always generous older brother Robbie.

Like many women I believed that marriage would be the fulfilment of all my dreams. The reality was more complex. We were very happy together to begin with but gradually I found that, like many men, most of his attention was devoted to his work.

Shortly after we got married we moved to Devon. For some time I had been saying how much I would like to move further west and be nearer the sea, and Patrick had the idea of forming a business partnership with some permaculturists in Devon—an idea that evaporated as soon as we arrived.

We spent our first winter there in a flat in a converted stable block on the edge of Dartmoor. It was beautiful, set among tall trees with a rushing stream nearby, but it was desperately damp. We had a few brief weeks of happiness until Patrick became ill with his brucellosis and was bedbound for weeks. I continued on, never feeling well but determined to be strong enough to look after him. Clothes grew mould in the cupboards and despite a dehumidifier and an Aga we both struggled with illness till spring. It was a hard beginning but by the next autumn we had found an idyllic warm dry cottage in a nearby hamlet, nestled between woods and the foothills of the moor. I loved it there and began to really feel at home.

Patrick started teaching permaculture and writing his first book. Meanwhile I completed my counselling training and got a job counselling students at Dartington College of Arts. I loved the work, as I could easily identify with the students and, unlike acupuncture, it felt totally right for me. But Patrick wanted to move back to Glastonbury. Living in Devon made him realise how deep his roots were in Somerset. When the landlords wanted the cottage back I reluctantly agreed to move, giving up my fulfilling work and leaving the house and landscape I had come to love.

Coming back to Glastonbury I found its spiritual energy was no longer enough for me. I didn't find work easily as the town is full of counsellors and I'd lost my niche teaching adult education classes which I had taught previously. Despite a good social life, I was becoming a bored housewife, supporting Patrick's career but not evolving my own.

We found a long term let in a bungalow, but although it was secure it was far from assuaging my longing to create a home of my own. In Devon our cottage was intrinsically beautiful but here, no matter how many small improvements I made with a coat of paint, ethnic rugs, exotic pictures and throws, the place was still an ugly seventies box with little soul. I often found myself depressed with the frustration of living somewhere that felt so wrong for me.

One thing we always had in common was our love of nature. We often visited Patrick's field, a wild flower meadow, bordered by a little wood he had planted many years before. It was on the edge of that wood on a cool November day that we started planting a small orchard of fruit and nut trees. The afternoon sun shone low and clear over the flat fields towards the distant Tor as we put in the apple and pear trees, bedding the delicate roots gently in the soil, mulching with manure and cardboard, and putting wire deer guards around their little stems. The following year we returned to plant hazel and walnut trees. It was at times like this that I felt closest to this nature-loving man I had married.

Another way we felt close to each other was when I started working with him on his permaculture courses. I became the group facilitator and taught the social and people-centred aspects of permaculture. Despite Patrick's initial reluctance to working together, our partnership flourished and from then until now people have often said how well we complement each other. I got satisfaction out of this work as I was doing what I'm best at, working with people and passing on some of the skills I have learnt to others. But I felt a sense of regret that I was contributing to Patrick's work rather than creating my own.

Something that really was my own was joining the Avalonian Free State Choir. This small town choir, consisting mostly of untrained singers, produced the most beautiful harmonies and sang to a truly professional standard. We performed world music both locally and at festivals. Our choir embodied the Avalonian myth, the ability to transform something ordinary into something transcendent and remarkable. Our most memorable performance was on the main stage of the Glastonbury Festival in 2000. It was so exciting preparing to be up on that huge pyramid stage where all the Greats had performed. We were given a Sunday morning slot, which the founder, Michael Eavis, had reserved for a few local groups.

As we walked up onto that famous stage a divine energy took over. We soared in harmonies which brought our audience to ecstasy. It was the most incredible feeling to be looking down on those waving appreciating crowds! Now all the rehearsals in the cold Assembly Rooms were worth while. Now all those Bulgarian words I had struggled to learn flowed fluently out of my mouth. We were flying high in the most pure sound, all personal differences forgotten as we merged into one. I knew Patrick was in the audience cheering us on, as were many friends and family of the choir. When we left the stage, friends came up to congratulate us and Patrick put his arm lovingly around me. 'You looked great up there,' he said. 'I felt so proud of you, knowing how hard it's been for you standing up through all those rehearsals when you felt weak, and keeping at it.' He was one of the very few people who understood how hard it still was for me to do what others regarded as normal.

Summer was over and I wasn't looking forward to another winter in England. Winters were still like endurance tests for me with repeated attacks of illness and debility. I'd already been through six winters in our bungalow since we'd returned to Glastonbury. Patrick's health had improved to the point where he was able to teach a ten week course away from home from January to March. There was no longer any reason for me to stay in Glastonbury while he was away.

I looked through some old copies of *Yoga Today* which I'd had lying around for a couple of years. A yoga centre in southern Spain caught my attention as I leafed through the magazine. That afternoon I was on the phone to Casa El Morisco. 'I'm a yoga teacher, living in England.' I tried to sound confident. 'I wondered if you had any openings for teaching with you this winter?'

'We are not actually open in winter,' a friendly male German voice replied. 'But we do maintenance work, and if you would like to work a few hours in the kitchen each day you could come and stay in exchange.' I felt the synchronicity working again.

Part Three: Spain

The Alpujarras, 2000–2001

Home in The Alpujarras

In the morning the mountains awake
Clothed in dreams of snow and slate
And with an eagle's silent flight
I watch the softly dawning light
Here in the Alpujarras
The spring sleepy with oleander
I walk with my little dog Luna
Collecting our silky drinking water
As it whispers like prayers from the hills
Soon the first rays of sun
Touch snowy peaks amber
As I follow the worn goat path down
Breathing scents of rosemary and lavender
Crossing the magical threshing *era*
Until I reach my land so familiar
Dusted with frost and the oranges of winter
Glowing like lanterns to welcome me home

By January I was in Spain with a woman friend. Casa el Morisco was an exotic white mansion, with a large circular yoga hall, lush tropical grounds, a swimming pool and little individual units for guests, where we were housed. The Costa Del Sol is one of the warmest places in Europe in winter. It was January and felt like a warm English summer. The kitchen work was gentle and we had time for sunbathing and walks to the nearby beach. My health improved immediately. It was idyllic staying there for a month.

Just when I was getting restless and feeling I would like to explore more of Spain, I met Frederik. He and his friends had come from a place called Órgiva to work on a creative building project in the grounds. 'We live in El Moreón,' he told me. 'It's a kind of community of houses and live-in trucks in a hidden valley in the hills, about an hour's drive inland from here.

'That sounds interesting,' I said.

'We'll be going back in about a week if you want a lift.' He seemed really open and friendly. I'd heard about Órgiva back in England. It had a reputation as a lively beautiful area where many foreigners were living alternative and sustainable lifestyles, renovating old farmhouses and building their own simple homes. There was also a family I had known in Devon living near there, Aspen, David and their son Samuel, and I had an open invitation to visit.

David met the two of us in the bustling little market town. We drank coffee outside a café and then set off for their smallholding. They had an old Land Rover. 'You need one of these if you live up where we do,' he explained pointing to the rugged slopes which rose above us and led on to the snow capped peaks of the Sierra Nevada. It took half an hour to drive from the nearest tar road, up a zigzag track with frightening drops down steep slopes. At thirteen hundred metres, their farm was on the same level as Ben Nevis, but it's only considered a foothill. The landscape on the way up was vast and spacious, with rocky outcrops and sparse vegetation. Only little Mediterranean pines, olives and almond trees punctuated the land with green. This region, the southern side of the Sierra Nevada and its foothills, is called the Alpujarras. It felt more like Tibet than Spain.

David and Aspen's place was called Semilla Besada, the seed that was kissed. It certainly felt kissed, with an abundance of food growing in its soil. There were raised beds full of annual and perennial vegetables, interspersed with companion plants of bright calendula, borage, and nasturtiums, a herb spiral of sage, rosemary, thyme, lavender and wormwood nearer the house, and a newly planted orchard of apple and nut trees.

My friend left after a few days but I stayed a fortnight. I learnt how the family organised their permaculture smallholding, growing vegetables, living with solar electricity, and keeping goats and chickens. At that time they were building a huge water storage tank out of disused tyres, and David went down to the local garages to pick them up. He was also teaching Qui Gong, an ancient Chinese system of health care that integrates postures and breath, and we practised it against a backdrop of distant mountains. I loved the fine air, the vast skies, the quality of blue light and the sunshine. Although I had enjoyed the coast, I felt more at home in this area. Apart from being exquisitely beautiful it was pervaded by a strong spiritual energy. I felt high just being there!

'I'd love to come to the Alpujarras again next winter,' I told the family when I was due to leave. 'But I'd like to stay a bit nearer the town, so I could be more independent.' I couldn't manage driving that precipitous track on my own.

'I'll take you to see a house for rent on the edge of Órgiva,' said David, always willing to help. The *casita* belonged to an English couple who had bought cheap farm buildings and done them up for rent. I booked it for a month the following January.

So it was that I returned to the UK happy to be with Patrick through the summer, helping facilitate our permaculture courses but knowing I would be in Spain for at least a month the next winter. I was excited, and prepared myself for my new life by doing an intensive course in Teaching English as a Foreign Language.

The following January I was back with another friend and began getting to know the area. Every Thursday there's a market in Órgiva. The whole town comes out to buy cheap food and clothes, to socialise and sit outside the open air cafés. It was at a colourful vegetable stall where they also sold seedlings that I bumped into Layla, who had been a permaculture student on one of our courses. 'What are you doing here?' I asked, surprised at what a small world it is.

'I'm helping on a smallholding,' she gave me a hug, laughing. 'Why don't you come and visit me? It's a beautiful place. We're having an Imbolc celebration next week with a bonfire. Do come.' She gave me her bright smile. Imbolc is one of the Celtic festivals we used to celebrate in the Glastonbury Assembly Rooms. This place was beginning to feel like home from home.

Thus I found myself sitting round a bonfire on an old circular stone threshing floor on a full moon night in February. Layla introduced me to her group of English friends who lived in the hamlet nearby and we chatted and ate charcoal baked potatoes as the fire glowed and spat in the centre of the circle. A few dogs sniffed around for scraps. Venus was just beginning to rise above us and the distant white mountains glowed enticingly in the distance.

'This would be a wonderful place to live in winter,' I said turning to Layla. 'It's amazing sitting outside in February.'

'There's a farm house for sale just a couple of minutes walk away,' she replied. 'I don't know if you'd be interested . . . We could go and see it.'

We crossed a small irrigation channel in the growing dusk and entered the land that went with the house. I looked around almost reverently. Oranges glowed on the trees like lanterns and the earth itself seemed friendly and familiar. I stood completely still. It felt as if the air was being sucked from my body as the outside world went silent and a voice in my head said loud and clear: 'This is your home, this is your land!' I breathed deeply.

'I'll show you the house,' said Layla. We walked round the front of the house and entered a wide verandah scattered with old newspapers, broken planks and pictures, with a fireplace full of rubbish in one corner. I had an unnerving sense of deja vu.

Back at the bonfire Andy, who lived in a neighbouring house, told me about the old man who had lived in the house before. 'Juan was one of the best orange growers in this area. Even when he was old and ill and had to live with his family across the river, he'd come over every day to look after his trees.' Andy smiled at me. He looked like a wiry Spanish farmer, although he was English and had been a school teacher in his former life. Now he and his partner Carol were living the peasants' life on their smallholding. 'I can phone his sister Amparo tomorrow and ask her when she could show you the place,' he added helpfully.

The next day I phoned Patrick. I was sure that with his earthy common sense he would be against any impulsive decision to buy an unknown house in Spain. But he said, 'If you still feel the same about it when you've seen the inside, go for it! You've always wanted a home of your own. Twenty five thousand pounds? It's just what we've got in the bank. We've never had so much before and probably never will again. We couldn't do anything meaningful with that money here. This is your chance.'

A month later the deeds were handed over to me. Amparo and I must have looked a strange couple as we sat in the lawyer's office, she a typical dark Alpujarran widow, small and squat, dressed all in black, and I a tall foreign alternative type. I could see her mind working as we sat together with our interpreter, happy at a sale but wondering why on earth I would choose to buy such a primitive house in the wilds of Spain. Soon I had the old fashioned brass key in my hands. It looked like something out of Harry Potter, a key that would open a treasure chest. And it did!

I was due to go back to England a few days later but I wanted to spend at least one day and night in my own home before I left. It just so happened that the Dragon Festival was just starting then. I'd been told about the festival but I had no real idea what it would be like, although I knew it was one reason for the house being sold so cheap. It was an annual gathering which had started as a small local event to celebrate the spring equinox but had now escalated into something huge and noisy, where thousands of travellers from all over Europe met up and played loud techno music. It was held in the wide dry riverbed about a hundred metres down from my house!

Normally there were a few travellers in live-in trucks parked up there, but as I drove down the riverbed I was shocked to see the numbers of new ones arriving. But once I got used to the idea I decided I might as well join in and enjoy the revelry rather than fight it. I spent the warm afternoon picking and juicing my oranges and lemons with a neighbour, then wandering around the festival selling paper beakers of fruit juice.

By evening no one wanted juice—it was all drugs and alcohol—so I went back to my shell of a home to sleep. Even with ear plugs the noise was too loud to sleep but still I had no misgivings. This festival would only last a few days and I loved my new home. I needed to be up at five in the morning anyway, so what did it matter?

The air was warm and dry and I felt the benign presence of Juan's ghost looking down on me. I felt he was happy that someone would take care of his land. My eyes grew heavy from gazing up at the knobbly black beams, my mind was soothed by an old lace curtain which swayed softly in the night breeze, and despite the noise I fell asleep. I slept for a few hours with the murmur of water in the irrigation channel outside my window just audible, like a delicate pulse of life beneath the deathly thump of techno music.

In the morning I pulled on my jeans, wheeled my suitcase down the path by starlight and set off in my hire car for the airport. But I had to drive through the festival first. It was mayhem, with marquees of loud music everywhere and people staggering around in the dark completely out of their heads. Just follow the pale track, I kept telling myself, and keep focused. But I didn't know the track, and the place bore no resemblance to the daytime riverbed. I became completely disorientated and suddenly I wasn't on a track any more but stuck in sand. Don't panic! I told myself, there are plenty of people around. But these weren't people interested in helping push or dig out a car in the middle of the night. I asked a likely looking guy if he could give me a push. 'You selling drugs?' he replied blearily feeling in his pockets. I began to panic, I had a plane to catch.

I went back to the stranded car, took a few deep breaths and prayed for guidance. There had to be a solution. Then it came to me. Layla's friend Tony sometimes parked down here in his live-in van. He would help me if I could find him in this chaos.

OK, I told my intuition, you have to guide me now. Bring me to Tony's van because in this darkness I really don't know where it is. My feet took me there of their own accord. I knocked nervously at the wooden back door. He appeared rubbing his eyes and putting on his small round glasses, looking like a dishevelled young Gandhi.

'Don't worry,' he said amiably, apparently unfazed by being woken up at dawn by a relative stranger. 'I'll just get some cardboard and a spade and be right with you.' I nearly cried with relief. 'We'll put the cardboard just in front of each wheel and I'll dig out the back ones,' he said efficiently as we reached the car. 'Now just drive out slowly,' he said when it was done. The car emerged, from the sand like a beached whale back in the water. 'Don't forget—keep following the left hand track,' he shouted after me.

'Thank you so much,' I shouted back as I drove off. You must be my guardian angel, I thought to myself.

Casa Alma, 2001–2002

The Olive Tree

This ancient olive is the guardian of my home
With silvery green fingers pointing to the sun
His gnarled grey trunk reaching deep into the earth
With old man's roots
While bitter black fruits are weathered by winds
And kissed to ripeness by ebbing October sun
In January we will lay green nets
And rake dark fruits to the ground
Liquid gold to feed the coming year
Here I feel the sap rise in spring
And in summer seek shade from the fierce sun
At night I taste the magic of the moon
Framed in silver leaf
Until at dawn the tree emerges
Like a trusted friend again and again
Through seasons turning

I returned to my house in October with Patrick. 'This is amazing,' he
said, scooping up a handful of fertile earth from what had clearly been the

vegetable patch and looking around at the warm orchard of orange and olive trees. 'It feels like an oasis, with all this water around. But those hills look pretty burnt out and arid,' he pointed across the valley.

'Yes, but in springtime the hills looked much greener, and there was always snow on the mountains,' I answered happily. 'It looked less like moorland, and you can see the green of the pine trees on those lower slopes.'

The house was indeed in a small lush oasis fed by an *acequia* which ran along the top boundary of the land. The *acequias* are an ancient Moorish system of water channels which run all through the Alpujarras, bringing water down from the high Sierra Nevada to feed the valleys below. 'They're the life blood of this area,' my neighbour Andy had told me enthusiastically when I was about to buy the house. 'They keep it green and fertile even in summer. Our hamlet is particularly fertile,' he added proudly, 'As we've got two *acequias* coming straight to us from the river.'

I decided to call the house Casa Alma, The House of the Soul, and I had a vision of it becoming a centre for spiritual retreats and healing. It was made of whitewashed stone, with a flat roof, massive walls and a big wooden metal studded door, in traditional Alpujarran style. The roof was made with beams of eucalyptus trees, supporting a layer of cane and a top coating of a special clay called *launa*. There were still old hooks on the beams with the remains of onion and garlic strings, and a huge tin barrel filled with some viscous olive oil. There was no bathroom or toilet, and the kitchen was a tiny sooty room which you could only reach from the outside.

Patrick and I cleared out the old junk, cleaned windows and made ourselves a little bedroom nest with things that had been left there: an ornate black metal bedstead with a mattress filled with sheep's wool and a huge old wooden wardrobe. We cleaned the gas cooker and moved it to an inside room which thus became the kitchen. We found a round wooden table and a couple of rope seated chairs and put them in the *tinao*, a large verandah, to make it our dining area.

We didn't know until we looked underneath it that the round table had a metal brazier attached to the legs near the floor, a traditional Alpujarran *mesa camilla*. When cooking was over the peasants would put the remains of the fire in the brazier. The top of the table would be covered with a large woollen table cloth which went down to the floor, creating a kind of tent where the family would sit on cold winter nights warming their lower halves. This is the only heating that some traditional Alpujarrans have even today.

Patrick and I were at this round table one day sharing lunch with a friend when we heard sniffling and scratching sounds coming from below. We looked and there curled up in the empty brazier of the *mesa camilla* was a little black shaggy dog. She looked up with beseeching eyes and wagged her tail. She was clearly asking, 'Can I come and live here?' I scooped her out of her hiding place. She was dirty and trembling and I noticed a terrible smell coming from one of her ears. But she looked at me so imploringly and wagged her tail so fervently when I stroked her that I knew she was mine.

'She must be one of Tony and Lil's strays,' I said to the others. 'Come up to escape from those other bigger barking dogs.' As if in agreement the little dog wagged her tail like a helicopter and looked at us longingly. Later that day I went round to my neighbours and sure enough she turned out to be one of their rescued strays. They'd seen her wandering around near the internet shop in town on several occasions over the last couple of weeks, as if someone had just left her there to fend for herself. So they picked her up and brought her home. They were delighted to have found a good home for her. It was full moon the day she came to me so I decided to call her Luna.

We began to turn what was a shell of a house into a home, helped by a pair of local builders, a tall dark Englishman and a blond Spaniard with a pony tail. The Englishman, Neil, was a neighbour, who was always supportive to me throughout the time I lived there. They brought the materials up to the house on his mule Capitana because no vehicle could get up the narrow stony path.

By mid November wild freezing winds swept around the house like hungry ghosts, and the time approached when Patrick had to leave for England to teach. Aspen and David offered to drive us to Granada, so that once Patrick was on his train I wouldn't have to return alone. My stomach was a knot of nerves and fear at the prospect of being left alone in Spain for months on end. As we sat in the back of their four by four he chatted gaily with them while I felt increasingly overwhelmed. Would this be the end of our marriage I wondered? He had seemed unduly pleased to be returning to the UK, saying that he was really looking forward to time alone. As the three of them chatted, I sat there going through my own inner nightmare, not wanting to talk about it in front of Aspen and David.

As we drove into Granada we could see the snow capped Sierra Nevada glowing like angelic guardians in the distance. The sight of them brought on my familiar longing to be free of emotional fear and trauma. We drove through the outskirts, a mess of industrial estates and utilitarian flats, like so many modern cities. We had some to kill before Patrick's train left, so we parked in the central car park near the beautiful fountain of pomegranates (Granada means pomegranate), amidst the grand eighteenth century architecture. I could see this was a beautiful city, lit up by the wonderful light of the Andalucían sky, but I was too tense to enjoy it.

'Let's have some tapas,' said Patrick, completely oblivious of my inner turmoil. Tapas is the most generous aspect of Spanish cafés. Even if you only have a beer or grape juice you are brought a little snack, maybe a small plate of potato salad, barbecued meat, bread with a slice of sausage or cheese, or perhaps a piece of Spanish omelette, all for free.

'I'll take you to a good tapas place,' said David, leading us through a labyrinth of narrow cobbled streets until we entered a noisy dark bar where a crowd of men were drinking and eating, although it was only mid morning. I ordered a mosto, a non alcoholic grape juice, although it was at times like this that I wished I could drink.

Coming out of the dark bar we were momentarily blinded by the clear light and found ourselves on crowded pavements passing the superstore of Corte Inglés and surrounded by elegant cosmopolitan townspeople. We walked on pavements of marble and strolled through cobbled passageways to a picturesque square with ancient walls, ornate fountains and jacaranda trees. But now it was time to get back to the car and drive to the station.

I hugged Patrick hurriedly trying to hold back the tears as Aspen and David waited, looking away. Then he was gone through the glass doors of the station. I felt myself space out and away from my body with shock. I wanted this new life, but somehow I hadn't really taken on that I would be doing it alone.

What am I doing in this semi-ruin? I wondered forlornly when I returned from Granada. Everything felt different when I was on my own. There wasn't much sun and I hadn't computed that it could be this cold. With no bathroom or toilet I had to squat over a hole in the ground outside. No running hot water. A cold concrete floor and no proper wood burner, only the open fire outside on the *tinao*.

I was in my fifties now and my health hadn't fundamentally changed. The house needed so much renovating, and with Patrick gone it hit me that I was responsible for everything. I had to be the one to decide what the builders would do next, the one who had to go and choose the building materials, driving down the riverbed to town, not speaking a word of Spanish or knowing the first thing about building. But I had fallen in love with this fiercely beautiful place. My inner voice had led me here and I had a dream that one day it would be a sanctuary, where I would run groups and people would come for individual retreats and healing. I just had to make it work.

And then the universe sent me Romany and John. I'd known them for years on the UK healing circuit and had heard they were heading for southern Spain. A couple of weeks after Patrick left I went to the Thursday market in town. As ever it was alive with stalls of colourful fruit, vegetables, spices and the usual cheap shoes and clothes you see in markets everywhere. When I'd bought my food I walked past the cafe where most of the foreigners congregate and there they were, sipping tea in the sun. Romany looked like a harlequin with her cropped fair hair, colourful jacket and leggings and John, with his bushy eyebrows and grey beard, like a wise old sage.

'How's it all going?' Romany asked excitedly after hugs and exclamations of surprise and delight.

'It's wonderful, but since Patrick left I do feel alone and overwhelmed.' I swallowed down the tears. 'What about you? What are your plans?'

'We've been staying in a rented *casita* near Torvizcon for the last two weeks, but we can't afford that any more and we'd like to do some sort of exchange—work in return for rent.'

'Well you'd be very welcome to stay with me,' I replied hesitantly. 'But I warn you it's incredibly basic at the moment, a bit of a building site.'

'No problem,' said Romany enthusiastically, and John nodded in agreement. 'It sounds like a win-win situation!'

John was a great gardener and once they were installed he started clearing the land and making sure all the water channels were running, the little channels within the garden which take water from the communal *acequia* to individual fruit trees and the vegetable patch. Romany and I did what we could to make the bedrooms liveable with a coat of paint, bright rugs and second hand furniture. The builders put a glass fronted wood burner in the corner of the sitting room and soon we were having baths in a tin tub beside the fire. Nevertheless by mid December we all had terrible colds and Romany and John decided to house-sit a nearby house whose owner was away.

In quieter moments I would sit on the *tinao* gazing at the distant snow capped peaks against the wide blue skies. It took me back to India, before my heartbreak and illness. It could feel so timeless, just sitting there gazing at the changing light and the feathery clouds which cloaked the mountains. I loved the spaciousness and the vast scale of the landscape, which healed and fed a hungry part of my soul.

Building with Neil

There were no electric cables in sight and no roads within earshot, only the sound of birdsong, goat bells and bubbling water flowing through the *acequias*. I could walk out of the back of my house in my pyjamas onto moorland dotted with broom, wild thyme and rosemary. Usually I only met the local children playing on the hills or neighbours collecting drinking water from the spring. Occasionally I would meet the shepherd with his three dogs and mottled flock.

Olive harvest

One day in early January, I went round to Romany and John's and saw a white horse tied up outside their house. On the patio was a Spanish guy with smouldering eyes and dark curly hair, talking and laughing with Romany and John in garbled Spanglish and sign language. 'She needs help,' Romany pointed to me as I appeared on their patio.

'I certainly do,' I smiled, wondering where on earth this person came from as I pointed towards the olive trees which were just ready for harvest.

With very few words Chucha and I seemed to come to an understanding: He would come and stay with me, and his white Arabian horse Blanco would graze and manure my land. 'No me gusta vivir in house,' he smiled widely. 'Eat solo cruda tambien.' I didn't really know what he was talking about, but much to my relief he put a tent up outside and ate only raw food.

Next day we started on the olive harvest, with Romany and John helping. 'Put down así,' Chucha demonstrated as we laid wide green nets under the trees. 'Así,' he instructed as he shook the branches with poles or clawed off the olives with long finger-like rakes. 'I go up,' he gave his wide grin, shimmying up a tree like a monkey and hitting the branches which were inaccessible from underneath. Olives showered down all around us and soon we felt as if we'd been olive picking peasants all our lives! These olives were small black ones which would be taken to the mill for oil. The larger plump green and purple ones we kept and preserved in salty water for eating.

After about an hour of harvesting I felt weak, and dizzy from looking up. So I went into the house and squeezed oranges and came out with a jug of fresh juice. I'd never liked oranges in England but these were sweet and succulent, like a completely different fruit. At the end of the day I looked around my trees appreciatively. I only had an acre of land but what abundance! I had about a hundred trees altogether, mostly oranges but also tangerines, lemons, pomegranates, olives, figs, quince, medlars, loquats, grapes and a special almond tree.

Chucha left contentedly with his share of oil after the harvest and now I had a new young wwoofer Anika, a recent arrival from Sweden [wwoofer is an acronym for 'Willing Workers On Organic Farms', an organisation started in the UK to enable those who want to learn more about organic agriculture to do so on an exchange basis, in return for food and board. Now it has become a more flexible arrangement with lots of wwoofers working in all sorts of ways from building to cooking].

'Let's have a day out,' I said to Anika one morning after a hard day of cleaning the kitchen in preparation for painting. 'We'll go to the hot springs at Alhama de Granada. It's an ideal place to relax and chill out,' I told her as we chatted in the kitchen, cutting up home made bread and boiling eggs for a picnic.

'Is Romany coming?' she asked nervously. She was twenty-five but always looked like a lost child. 'She said she'd give me a healing today and I don't want to miss that.' Romany was fast becoming the local barefoot healer and guide. She did a lot of treatments for the travellers who lived in vans and buses on the riverbed, some of whom were becoming our friends.

'Yes she'll be here any minute. She can give you your balance when we get there. John's staying at home—he needs a bit of space,' I added, as Romany bounced in wearing her baggy trousers.

Half way down the track we met a herd of goats. I drove slowly but suddenly a kid was in front of me and I swerved. Before I knew it our front wheels were down in the *acequia*. 'Dammit, that's just what we need!' I swore as the car perched precipitously halfway down the ditch.

'I'll squeeze out,' said Romany brightly from the back. 'You get out first, Anika, and I'll follow.' The goats had disappeared down the riverbed. 'I'm sure nice Nick who lives in that caravan has got a tow rope with his four by four.' She seemed to be enjoying the drama.

'And what about me?' I said petulantly from my angled seat. 'I can't even move from here without unbalancing the car.

'Don't worry, I'm sure there's a win-win here somewhere, said Romany. 'We'll be right back.' And she strode off, with Anika trying to keep up like a little dog.

'Fuck it, I don't I even get one day off this Alpujarran madness,' I muttered to myself.

An hour later we were on our way. I was feeling weak and irritable and let the others' conversation wash over me as I drove north towards Granada. As we neared Alhama we passed through wide groves of almond trees covering the rolling hills. Descending a steep valley we were enveloped in a healing pink haze of gauzy almond blossom. All my irritability lifted and I felt transported into a delicate soft world of pink, as if I was surrounded by hundreds of ballet dancers in frilly tutus. I started singing and the others joined in as we drove through a gorge where ochre rocks towered above us and ferns and poplar trees grew from the river below. At the end of the gorge is a hotel where visitors come to take the healing waters from the hot mineral spring. Outside it the surplus water flows into three hot pools which lead down to the cold flowing river, and here anyone can bathe for free.

I floated in the warmth, feeling as if my body was melting and my hair transforming into water weed, gently undulating with the flow of water. I looked up at the cool winter skies and the bare poplars swaying in a gentle breeze. I felt utterly content and relaxed as if I had found my element, immersed in this rocky womb of water.

On the second weekend in February the weather turned cold and wet. We placed buckets strategically under the drips from the roof. This was apparently all quite normal for the Alpujarras. The old peasant houses were built for sun, not rain. It reached the limit when I had to move my bed in the middle of the night to avoid a new shower of drips! I was feeling ill with the damp and Anika was leaving the following day. I clutched my hot water bottle to my chest and lay there almost fully dressed with a woolly hat over my head listening to the wind howling around my house and the rain on the roof.

My closest companion at this time was Luna, and she was such a sweet and easy little dog. She was always so happy to snuggle up for a cuddle when I was lonely, and quite happy taking herself out for a short walk on the land when I was too weak to take her. She hated the cold wet weather as much as I did and slept on a sheepskin on the floor near my bed. I'd never had my own dog before and hadn't realised what an intimate relationship one could have with an animal.

Her right ear was severely infected when I first got her and she had to have an operation. The vets removed a spiky bit of dried grass which was stuck in her middle ear. 'She will be fine but probably about 80 per cent deaf in her right ear now,' said the kindly woman vet, as she handed me the sleeping bundle. 'She also has an immune disease called leishmaniasis, which will make her weak,' she added sympathetically. 'It is very common here and she will probably survive for years yet, but bring her back if she seems really ill and feverish and we will give her some medicine to take.'

As I carried her back to my car I felt such love and tenderness for this little creature. She was like an aspect of myself that needed to be cared for. With a strange synchronicity we both had 80 per cent deafness in our right ears and chronic debilitating low immune systems.

I stayed in bed all that weekend but at last the sun came out. I could see it through a crack in the shutters. It was a fine morning and about ten o'clock when there was a knock at my front door.

'Hello,' I yelled blearily getting out from my cocoon. 'Who's that?'

'Hello. It's Leonardo,' came the deep voice. He was a young Colombian guy who had been on one of our courses that summer and had arranged to come and help me in part payment. I pulled on my poncho and rushed to the door. 'Leonardo, it's so good to see you!' He opened his arms and I fell into a great big bear hug and burst into tears.

'You don't look very well,' he said, looking concerned as we sat drinking tea and eating porridge by the fire.

'If I'd known how hard it would be, I don't think I'd have had the courage to buy this place.' Leonardo looked at me sympathetically with his deep brown eyes. 'But I love it here and generally my health is better than in England.'

Next day a couple of girls came by. 'Is Leonardo living here'? They blushed coyly. 'We met him hitch hiking out of Granada yesterday.' Leonardo appeared, smiling nonchalantly.

The stream of girls continued throughout his stay. He looked like a Greek god and was easy going, intelligent, sensitive and practical. I had to remind myself that he would see me as a mother. I was missing Patrick and our intimacy, and was certainly not about to fall in love with a much younger man, but we soon became great friends.

He cleared the water channels, which had got clogged up with leaves and twigs from the winter winds. He made raised beds and composted them with manure from the local mules. As a Spanish speaker he was able to help me with all the buying of building materials and bureaucratic transactions. Together we weeded overgrown areas and planted up a good vegetable garden.

We went to the *rastros*, second hand warehouses where you can pick up amazing bargains from beds and baths to little ornate shelves and crockery. One famous day we managed to find a whole bathroom suite in pale blue for a knock-down price. He drove me to the municipal dumps where we found time-stained wooden doors with large metal studs, second hand window frames, shelving units embossed with traditional patterns and a grand old sofa with miscellaneous non-matching chairs. We visited the local marble cutters' yard where we helped ourselves to offcuts of fine local marble available for free. We made these into outdoor coffee tables and indoor work surfaces. It was fun making creative use of recycled and local materials, and fitted in with our eco values.

Living with solar electricity also fitted in with my ideals, but I had no idea how hard it would be. I had a poor system that had been installed haphazardly. During winter, when there were often days when we had little sun, I had little or no electricity. That was the very time we most needed light but after a few cloudy days in a row the batteries would be exhausted. Other people used generators when their electricity went down. I bought one which immediately broke down and, after changing it a couple of times, I gave up on even trying to get it fixed.

But with the lovely Leonardo there, I didn't need electricity. We sat around telling stories by candle and fire light. He felt like family and I imagined him to be like the son I'd miscarried. Strange to think my son would have been about the same age, in his early thirties.

By the end of that first winter the house was quite habitable. My neighbour Andy had tiled part of the house, though there was more left to do. The trees were pruned and the land looked cared for. Another wwoofer was living with us by then and we all decided to go to the beach in my van for a few days before Leonardo had to leave.

Luna watched nervously as we packed provisions in the van, and made sure she jumped into the front long before we actually set off. At this stage she was still terrified of me leaving her. One day, when I had left her at home to go shopping, she'd raced after the van and even with her tiny little legs managed to keep up for the first couple of kilometres. I had no idea she would do such a thing and was completely oblivious until my neighbour Neil, who was following us, picked her up, flagged us down and gave her back to me.

On the beach we meditated, watching the sun rise and set, swam and made food on my little gas burner. I watched Leonardo strolling around half naked and helped him build a shade for Luna. He was such a beautiful young man in every way. We had spent two months sharing our lives together and there had never been a cross word or a bad feeling between us. We hugged goodbye on a clifftop road overlooking the sea. I felt a tight band of grief around my lungs as I watched while he put his thumb out to start hitching to Malaga. I was sure someone would stop very soon for him and his journey would unfold magically. He was that kind of a guy.

Journeys, Inner and Outer, 2002–2004

Qi Gong or War

Here I am holding up the sky
While bees drink pink almond nectar
A fingers touch away
From my flat Moorish roof
Here I am shooting an arrow for peace
Into clear opal skies
While troops amass arms against Iraq
And distant snow capped peaks
Keep silent vigil
Here I am bridged between heaven and earth
My very breath sucked away by beauty
While fear prepares
To tear the fabric of lives
Missiles of fire cutting the sky
Here I am weeping
With a thousand bereaved mothers
Sharing breath with wounded displaced others
Heaven and earth meeting softly on this roof

When I came back to Glastonbury I suffered from culture shock. Not only did I have to get used to being back with Patrick and living in a small bungalow, but I missed the anarchy and spaciousness of my new home, the canopy of unbelievably blue skies and the healing sunshine. It was like contracting into a smaller skin. But, although it was difficult to readjust to Patrick when I first arrived back, my fear of our marriage dissolving seemed unfounded.

I was offered a weekend job as a counsellor at a holistic centre in north Cornwall. I worked with the clients using yoga, relaxation, counselling, visualisation and guidance. Some of them were seriously depressed and others were practically bed bound with various illnesses. It was very rewarding work. I found I was a great help to my clients, most of whom had never experienced anything like what I offered before. It felt good to be using the skills that I had spent so long acquiring over my life. It also made me feel my suffering had been worthwhile as I was better able to understand others who suffered.

I also loved simply having the strength to work there, including driving all the way there and back. Living in Spain in winter was definitely helping me have more energy throughout the year. Previously, winters had been full of illness and I'd spend summer gradually recovering before crashing again as the next winter came on. Now I could actually build up my energy.

Paramahansa Yogananda

Since I had returned to Glastonbury from Devon I had been part of a meditation group. It was based on the teachings of that same guru whose book, *Autobiography of a Yogi*, had jumped out at me from a bookshelf in Pondicherry all those years ago. Paramahansa Yogananda was his name and he was the one who brought yoga and meditation to the west. This year our meditation group was visited by a woman teacher from Italy, Kirtani, who was empowered to give an initiation into Kriya Yoga. This is a meditation which helps raise the vital kundalini energy and opens the higher energy centres. It has been passed down through an ancient Indian lineage of enlightened gurus, of whom Yogananda was one. Another of these teachers is a certain Babaji who is said to be immortal and still living secretly somewhere in the Himalayas with his band of followers. As soon as I heard about the possibility of taking this initiation I felt drawn to it.

The day before I was initiated into Kriya I wondered if I was doing the right thing. It involved me pledging my allegiance to Yogananda and his lineage, but I am such an eclectic spiritual seeker that I had my doubts. That night Yogananda appeared to me in a dream saying, 'Do not worry about making this decision. It is already made. I have been watching over you all these years. You do not have to decide to take me on as your guru as I already am with you. And if I and my lineage are not right for you at any time, I will lead you to the ones who are.'

I was reminded of a Lama Govinda's definition of a guru:

A guru is far more than a teacher in the ordinary sense. A teacher gives knowledge, but a guru gives himself [herself]. The real teachings of a guru are not his [her] words but what remains unspoken, because it goes beyond the power of human speech. The guru is an inspirer in the truest sense of the word, i.e. one who infuses us with his [her] own living spirit.

It is said that a guru does not need to be present in a human body, especially if there is someone present who has a direct link with the lineage they represent. Kirtani had been initiated by a direct disciple of Yogananda, so I was happy to be initiated into the Yogananda lineage by her. The initiation was a great blessing and I felt renewed with spiritual energy.

'What's it like, living in both Glastonbury and Spain?' asked a friend, as we sat having lunch in the Glastonbury courtyard café, surrounded by alternative-looking tourists.

'I don't live a double life,' I replied, trying to find words to describe my experience. 'I live two completely different ones. In Spain I'm this brave wacky single woman living a back-to-the-land life, where hardly anyone even knows I have a husband. And here I'm very much half of a whole, Patrick Whitefield's wife, who helps him on his courses and does a bit of work of her own.'

'At least you have Luna now, doesn't she give you some sense continuity,' said my friend.

'Yes, Luna is the one constant between my lives.' I sighed, looking around the café for Luna. There she was as always, 'doing the tables'—seducing people with her eyes, asking for scraps. Her top canines were missing which made her bottom teeth stick out endearingly and she wagged her tail like a helicopter as she begged for food with liquid black eyes which seemed to look into your heart. Patrick called her 'the dog for whom the word "sweet" was invented.' This was how she'd made her living in her street dog days and now she simply couldn't resist the habit even though she was well fed.

That autumn Patrick and I took her back to Spain on the Santander ferry. She was booked into the kennels up on the dog deck. 'She looks terrified,' I said to Patrick as she looked at us with disbelieving eyes when we shut her into the metal kennel. She was surrounded by big barking dogs in a structure like a chicken battery.

'Let's just go to the café for food and hope that she's settled by the time we come back.' Patrick took my hand reassuringly. An hour later we returned to give her a walk and found her curled up and trembling. We took her for a stroll outside on the deck and she looked around at the other dogs nervously. I couldn't bear the thought of putting her back into that kennel to suffer all night.

'Come on, let's put her in my Spanish basket,' I whispered. 'We can cover her up with my jacket and smuggle her down to our cabin.' We looked around the dog deck furtively and when no one was looking our way Patrick quickly lifted her into my big basket and covered her up leaving a tiny hole for her little black nose.

This is what I did on all future trips. I was always afraid of getting caught, carrying her up and down from my cabin to the dog deck to pee.

Sometimes she would peek her little nose and button eyes out from the top of the basket and it was only that no one would have believed I was carrying a dog around that made her invisible. The worst time was one morning when we were arriving in Spain and there was knock on the door while Luna was sitting brazenly in the middle of the cabin. I literally threw a coat over her as the door opened and a steward came in, telling us it was time to vacate the cabin. Luckily Luna remained quiet and still during this time, as always the perfectly behaved doggy, probably shocked barkless at suddenly being plunged into darkness!

Luna (top), the house transformed (below)

All was peaceful back in Spain and work progressed on the house. A friend from England made a patio outside the back door out of flat river stones and Andy tiled the remaining rooms, putting the occasional blue star among the traditional copper coloured tiles. Meanwhile another wwoofer and I collected rich red ochre earth from the hills above Casa Alma, strained it with a kitchen sieve and used these natural pigments to paint the inside walls. By now we had built a two seated compost toilet, which after a year of decomposing produced a dry, non-smelly product which we would spread around the fruit trees.

Romany and John had bought a couple of terraces just opposite my house, where they built a circular straw bale house and created a beautiful half-wild garden, full of fruit trees, flowers and the occasional patch of vegetables. Romany and I were constantly in and out of each others' houses sharing tools, meditations, inspiration and food. John was less sociable but always a lovely presence as he worked the land and walked the hills collecting bits of firewood with their dog Leo.

The land nourished my spirit and I wrote many poems inspired by nature and this environment of clear blue light, vivid white mountains, crystal streams and wild flowers. There were also the strange lenticular clouds which hung in the sky looking like space ships, and the coloured wings of para gliders who floated serenely above us.

Unfortunately, living in that small hippy hamlet, I didn't have much contact with the local Spanish community. I wanted to integrate more and felt drawn to their warm character and the sound of the language but most of the inhabitants of the hamlet were English speaking. I was learning Spanish with books and tapes but it was a struggle as I got very little opportunity to practice. I only went to town to shop and never chose to hang out in bars. So when Veronica, my only Spanish woman friend, visited one day and suggested we run a weekend retreat for Spanish women I was delighted. Perhaps my dream for Casa Alma as a centre for retreats and healing was going to come to fruition.

'If you find the women,' I responded excitedly, 'I'll prepare the house and buy in the food.'

Eight women arrived from around the Órgiva and Granada area. Some looked nervous, as no one knew what to expect—including me!

We began in a circle, sharing what we wanted from the weekend. Next we did some yoga and visualization and then I led the women to my sacred spot, a natural hollow in a circle of rocks on the hills above my house. It was a misty day and as we climbed the hill, past the little spring which is the hamlet's supply of drinking water, the earth shone in a grey green haze of sage and rosemary.

'Let's walk around in silence for half and hour and see if we are drawn to anything we would like to pick up from nature, a gift we will bring back to the house for a ceremony we will do this evening,' I told them, struggling with my Spanish.

Back in the *tinao* we made a spiral labyrinth of stones, herbs, feathers, seeds, branches and clay. It seemed as if we had shared a long journey as we placed our finds in the snaky spiral. Making it in silence became a powerful ritual which linked us beyond language. We were totally in the present.

In the evening we lit the *tinao* fire and decorated our labyrinth with red votive candles, which created a warm generous glow of rose. This time Veronica took the lead. 'First we will each write down on a piece of paper those aspects of our lives and ourselves which we would most like to let go of,' she said. 'Then we will walk the spiral individually while the rest of us chant. When we are in the centre we will make a resolution of the positive aspects we would like to bring into our lives.'

As the night descended, we held hands in a circle and chanted, '*Tierra mi cuerpo, agua mi sangre, aire mi aliento y fuego mi espiritu*'—earth my body, water my blood, air my breath and fire my spirit—while each of us walked slowly and meditatively to the centre and back again.

When we had all walked the spiral, one by one we threw our pieces of paper on the fire and as each of us did so the others cheered. Next each of us chose a little bell to represent her wishes for the future, which we hung on the twigs of an olive branch we had prepared earlier to represent the tree of our dreams.

The following day we shared our feelings about what it is to be a woman today, our cyclical nature, our relationship with our bodies and the earth, our intuitions hopes and aspirations. Many women received inspiration and guidance. In the afternoon we drew pictures or made models in clay representing what we had discovered.

'We will finish the day with another chant in a circle and a big communal hug,' I said, exhausted from my first weekend of speaking only Spanish. I had stumbled along, not quite able to keep up, but reading the emotional intensity of the sharings, noticing the way the women's faces transformed over the weekend and how nobody wanted to leave on Sunday.

'We will hold another group in a couple of months,' said Veronica enthusiastically. But, although I continued running a few yoga classes and groups on developing intuition with my foreign women friends, another Spanish weekend never did happen.

By March all the trees had been pruned and compost from the toilet had been spread around as many of them as it would cover. A vibrant pale green began to lighten the fields, enlivened by dots of blue borage and blood red poppies. The willow showed a mist of silvery green buds while oranges and lemons still glowed in the orchards, spreading warmth against the violet cold of the mountains. Snow melt was rushing through the *acequias* and it was time to start clearing the water channels again to water the land.

The deeds of the house entitled me to an hour and a half of watering time on a Sunday afternoon, when I could open the metal gates of the communal *acequia*. This doesn't sound like much but it was enough, as the water would come gushing onto my land like a living creature. Then my wwooFers and I would rush around with our *azadas*—the all-purpose garden tools like large bladed hoes with short handles—clearing any blockages of debris, and directing it's path with dams of stone and mud, channelling it to fill the smaller furrows which fed every vegetable bed and tree.

It always felt exciting seeing this precious flow feeding the land and I realised how precarious the water supply is. The snow on the high Sierra acts as a reservoir, which as it melts provides the summer flow to the rivers which in turn feed the *acequias*. If climate change leads to rain falling in place of snow the *acequias* will dry up and the Alpujarras will become a desert.

The Wise Woman of the Woods, 2005

To My Mother

You look so frail—broken—
A sudden dowagers hump making me tower over you
Your incongruous black hair falling over your shoulders
Like a strange aged doll
At last I am the stronger
But the child in me is quaking—still wanting your love
Still silently begging you to hear and see me
Before it's too late
Yet you speak to your husband
As if it was he not I who is leaving tomorrow
While I, who am fifty wait for a sign of love
Knowing this could be our last time together
With so much unsaid never to be said
As you, always stoical always needing to pretend
At five and a half stone say 'It's OK—I'll mend'
And your voice shakes as I say goodbye
Choked with ghosts and dying hopes of closeness
Knowing that it is only I who will whisper *I love you*
As we embrace before I drive away
Weeping

The casita, before (top) and after (below)

One evening in spring of the following year, as I sat quietly on the *tinao*, watching the sun fading into apricot gold over the mountains and contemplating planting the summer vegetables, my mobile rang. It was my brother Robbie, 'Harold has gone into hospital and is really ill,' he said. Our father had been partially bed ridden for several years and was quite prepared to die. He used to jokingly say, 'I'm past my sell by date.' So I wasn't too surprised to hear the news.

'I'll come back right away,' I said, gazing at the mountains, which looked so unchanged and peaceful as my mouth went dry.

When I arrived in London my stepmother invited me to stay in their flat for a few days and visit Harold in hospital while she went to Cornwall for a break.

'It's so good to see you,' I said as I took Harold's dry skeletal hand in that impersonal hospital ward.

'And you,' he replied faintly, still looking beautiful but gaunt and faded in his blue plaid dressing gown. 'How's Spain?'

'It's always interesting,' I replied. I told him about my land and how the olive harvest had gone that year. I told him how I was having the mule shed converted into a *casita* and was transforming the previous owner's rubbish area into a beautiful garden of raised beds made with dry stone walls. I told him I wasn't lonely because of my wonderful friend Romany next door, and her habit of asking for spiritual guidance on the smallest things, such as what to buy when she entered a shop, how she was always 'tuning in' and saying 'Let's see if I get a message.'

Harold laughed quietly. He had always been an eccentric himself and loved to hear about others. I told him of the difficulty of getting anything done in a country where the response of people you're dealing with is usually, '*Que vuelva mañana!*'—come back tomorrow, but that the up side of this is the warmth and colour of the Spanish character and their enjoyment of life, how they walk around arm in arm and have no qualms about sitting in cafés during the day, spending hours over a family meal in a restaurant at the weekend, and are happy to stay up until the early hours of the morning socialising, often with their children running around the table.

This reminded Harold of his brief time in Madrid back in the 1930s, before the civil war, working as a messenger boy for a film studio. 'They pronounced it "Madree",' he whispered hoarsely, his skin looking like old parchment. 'I loved my time in Madree.'

'What a shame you haven't been able to visit my place,' I said, looking sadly at his struggling body. He hadn't been strong enough to travel for many years.

'Yes, I would have liked to have seen your new home . . .' he seemed to be fading with the effort to talk. 'But tell me more about the people you live with.'

'Well there's Annette, a friend of Romany's who appeared at my house one day with a plastic pyramid on her head, as if it was the most natural thing in the world. "Oh Annette, you've got a pyramid on your head!" I said, stating the obvious.

'"That's right," she replied. "It helps the energies. I've given one to Romany too!" And sure enough Romany walked in a bit later with a pyramid on her head, followed by her son-in-law looking totally bemused.' Harold laughed but I knew he was really too weak to keep up with such stories, so I told him about the poems I'd written, inspired by the land and life in the Alpujarras, and of the CD I'd recently made of them. 'Perhaps you can hear those instead of coming to visit.' I felt my heart contracting.

After that first visit he seemed to be declining fast and we hardly spoke. Those few days were a gift for me, being able to sit at his bedside holding hands. I felt we were sharing a love way beyond words, and that's all that mattered. He died a few weeks later.

My mother was also in her final illness that summer, but unlike Harold she was not ready for death. I so much wanted to resolve our lack of communication before she died and had a fantasy that on her death bed all would be healed. But as she was dying I was hardly allowed to see her. My stepfather Ivan wanted to have her to himself. When I was finally invited to visit her in the hospital near their home in Wales, they both practically ignored me while I sat in the corner.

The following day I was able to be alone with her briefly and we made desultory conversation. I had already spoken to her doctor privately and he said that he'd told her she didn't have long to live. Yet, when she asked me what the doctor had said and I replied that she was very seriously ill, she said, 'Oh dear,' and looked disorientated, as if suddenly realising she was on her death bed. 'Poor Ivan.'

On my way out I had a strong feeling that I might not see her again and needed to speak my heart. I raced back inside. Although it was quite a small hospital the corridors suddenly seemed like a labyrinth. It felt like they were closing in on me. I found it difficult to breathe and felt nauseous from the familiar smell which held so many bad memories for me. I took a deep breath to calm myself before coming back to her bedside. 'I just needed to tell you I love you,' I said with my heart beating wildly. Then the child in me quavered and asked, 'Do you love me too?' She looked at me with a cool blue gaze and was only able to say, 'I think so.' It was a sword in my heart which bled as I drove back to Glastonbury weeping.

A few weeks after my mother's funeral I went to my friend Emma's birthday party on the beach at Charmouth, near Lyme Regis. She was the one who had kidnapped her daughter and gone to America. All had turned out well in the end and she had in been able to keep Lily and return to the UK. We had kept up our friendship over the years, despite both of us moving home several times. Today was her sixtieth birthday and half a dozen of us were sitting sharing cake on the pebbly beach. After we had eaten I found myself talking with a woman I didn't know about death and psychic phenomena. I told her both my parents had died recently, within three months of each other, although they had separated when I was three. She went all quiet and inward looking.

'I am a medium and I'm getting your mother here with us now.' She closed her eyes and went very still. 'She would like to communicate with you,' she said. 'I can see her here right in front of us.' I looked ahead but could see nothing. 'Do you wish to speak with her?'

'Yes, I would,' I murmured, remembering that deathbed scene.

'Here she is,' the psychic smiled. 'She is so pleased to be able to speak to you.' I felt goose bumps all over my arms.

'She is saying she is so sorry for how she was with you in her lifetime. She didn't know how to love then. Now she can see how afraid and limited she was. She is handing you a pink rose and asking for your forgiveness.'

I started weeping. 'I forgive you,' I whispered, feeling a warm glow of love encircling my body.

'She is saying she is very happy now, happy to have been able to tell you she loves you,' said the medium smiling. 'Now she is fading.'

'Thank her for coming, and thank you for bringing her,' I said gazing beyond the pebbly beach toward at the calm grey sea.

That night I had memories of my adolescence. In the light of knowing my mother from spirit I felt I could understand myself better.

I'm thirteen and at last we've got rid of my stepfather Terence. He's gone off with my mother's best friend Eva. Finally I can breathe. Those straying eyes and steam engines have gone and Harold has bought us a real house of our own. I paint my room yellow, and my mother buys blue Picasso print curtains. At last things are going to be good.

But two days later another man has moved in! I don't know him and when I see him kissing my mum a dagger of pain shoots through me. Who is this sudden invading stranger living with us? But I can't speak. I can't tell my mother I don't want him here. Instead I become completely mute at home and start smoking dope at school.

My two brothers are living in a different world, studying at grammar schools. Now I've stopped being a good girl and become a terrible teenager. By sixteen I'm hitch-hiking around London fearlessly on my own in mini skirts, or meeting friends in Soho jazz clubs. I love music and we start going to the Roundhouse to hear psychedelic sounds with light shows, and to art school dances to meet young men.

The men eye me up flirtatiously. It's the only time I feel appreciated and seen. My mother has never given me a feeling of self worth or told me I'm pretty. Inside I feel empty. I lap up the attention and find myself going to bed with an artist who wants me.

I fall in love with him but he's older and only phones to draw me or have sex. He's obviously not interested in me. I'm so hurt that soon I'm sleeping around with any guy I fancy. I don't consciously know that I'm looking for the love and attention my mother never gave me. I just need to feel wanted.

I love the excitement of the wild parties, jazz clubs and CND marches, where we feel like a community fighting for world peace. My mother doesn't know what to do with me, and Harold bemusedly asks his friends if it's normal for young girls to be promiscuous these days! I've started stealing dresses from shops in the West End, because I can't ask my mother for clothes money. We're not able to communicate about even the smallest things.

At my mother's funeral I met my Swedish uncle, Lasse, and later he visited me in Spain. We had a lovely connection and I felt as if we had always known one another. So I was happy when the following summer he invited me to Sweden to celebrate his eightieth birthday. He met me at the airport just outside Gothenburg and drove me to his and my aunt's summer house on a small rocky island called Tjörn. He was as emotionally warm as my mother had been cool and he and my aunt welcomed me into their traditional wooden summer house.

The day after I arrived, the rest of the family came, some of them staying with us and others in hotels and guest houses. My uncle and aunt drove us to a beach where I met my four cousins, their wives and children. Soon we were all sitting in an outdoor hot tub on a plinth of grey rock overlooking the sea. I looked around at this new family, some of whom reflected my own looks, with the same dark hair and bright blue Swedish eyes. I had only met my cousins briefly, long ago on childhood holidays. Now they were all in their forties, wealthy handsome Swedes, world class sailors with yachts, good jobs and beautiful children who ranged from five to fifteen. It was an extraordinary feeling sitting in that bubbling hot tub looking around and feeling that I was part of an extended family with shared genes but such different lives.

That evening we dressed in our best clothes and drove to a coastal restaurant. There, tables had been prepared with flowers, candles and ornate name places. Lasse and his wife had thought of everything and I was so touched to see they had made sure everything I ate was gluten free, as I had recently discovered I am coeliac. About fifty friends and family members greeted Lasse as he entered and I had to blink away tears when his friends made speeches praising his fine qualities and life achievements, not the least of which was producing such a beautiful family.

The day after, as I lay on my bed in the summer house surrounded by a picturesque garden, a distant lake and fir trees, I had a strong waking dream. I met a part of myself which I called the Wise Woman of the Woods. She came to me out of the forest onto the seashore of Tjörn, dressed in traditional Scandinavian costume, with huge blue eyes.

'You can heal your lack of children by letting nature and the animal kingdom be your family,' she said comfortingly. 'You have a special link with the ethereal world, the world which forms nature, and this invisible world can be a great source of nourishment for you.'

I remembered my time in Harold's cottage in Wales, when I had felt so happy and connected to the natural world, to the point where I heard the music of the fairies. I realised that this trip to Sweden was not only about connecting with my family but also about connecting with my Swedish roots. As a baby I had been uprooted from nature, from my home in the lakes and woods, and had been brought up in the alien environment of a noisy city. The trauma of moving country and living in London with a damaged stepfather made me cut off my roots and disengage from my body.

I didn't want to live in the disturbed world of noise and psychic disharmony, so I withdrew my life energy and became a frozen child.

The Wise Woman seemed to be saying I should have been brought up here, in the good clean air, in the woods where bilberries and mushrooms grow amidst the firs, rocks and mosses. I should have been with both of my parents, living near Gothenburg, a city of beauty and culture. This wise woman of my reveries was an unacknowledged part of myself, unafraid of being alone. She was not afraid because she had never been separated from nature, her true home.

A Waterfall and Psychic Surgery, 2006–2008

Door of Life

As the warm autumn sun caresses my skin
Thoughts break free their cords within
And for a moment
I am held in the vast arms of stillness
And as dark clouds build castles
Over the mountains
And whispering winds rise and sing
Patterns of mind swirl and fall
Like sheaves of leaves quivering
And here comes the rain
Healing the thirsty earth
And setting the sparrows twittering
And I have left my husband and home
To live in this spaciousness alone
This special Self
Which has been quietly
Watching and waiting
While I stood at the door of Life
Not realizing
It was always open

Occasionally I visited my Spanish home briefly in summer, when I was teaching workshops at a local retreat centre called Cortijo Romero. One year I stayed on after the work was over and asked my dear friend Zia to come and spend a holiday with me there. For her this was a break from living in a council flat in Hackney, which despite all her loving care was so far from the sort of environment which she longed for.

By the time she arrived it was fiercely hot, in the upper thirties centigrade. We had to get up early to go for even a short walk, and most of the time we spent lounging on the *tinao*, which was north facing and cool, or floating on a lilo in Romany and John's hand made swimming pool next door. The two of us had long conversations about life and love. She was wary of any sort of drugs, although we agreed they could open doors of perception which can change and broaden our experience of life forever. In fact she thought she may have lived a former life in the sixties—she was twenty years younger than me—in which she had died of an overdose. I too was wary of mind altering drugs now and I'd had little more than an occasional puff of marijuana since the beginning of the seventies, so I understood how she felt. 'How amazing it would be, 'I said laughingly, 'if we had known each other in the sixties in another life and that's why we feel so close to one another now.'

We both loved the balmy Mediterranean nights when the jasmine which grew by the door wafted an erotic scent through the house, while the cicadas sang their high pitched song and a loud chorus of frogs croaked outside. But the heat of daytime was enervating. One sultry day we decided to go up to the hills, where it would be cooler. 'I'll phone Javier,' I said as we ate fruit salad for breakfast. 'He's one of my few Spanish friends. He lives up in Bubion. It's one of three beautiful white villages high up in the mountains. It'll be cooler up there and he knows the way to some fantastic waterfalls.'

'What's he like?' Zia asked.

'He's gorgeous, both physically and in character. Unfortunately he's got a partner at the moment! He's an alternative vet and he's also writing a spiritual book.'

'Sounds interesting,' she said eating a spoonful of yoghurt.

I had met the lovely Javier when Luna was ill. He had prescribed her some homoeopathy, as he used orthodox drugs as little as possible. He was such a sensitive soul that he even found it hard to give a dog an injection because he so hated to inflict pain. When Luna had her first rabies shot, I helped him hold her still as she struggled and yelped, and he looked almost as terrified as her.

The three villages are clusters of flat roofed houses, originally huddled together for safety, all whitewashed, often with geranium filled balconies overlooking the narrow cobbled streets. The streets and passageways thread around the houses and are crossed with flowing *acequia* channels which bubble their way through the villages. You can see coach loads of Spanish tourists arriving excitedly from Madrid, but the villages stay unspoilt, with traditional family shops selling the vibrantly coloured cotton rugs, which hang outside emitting softness and warmth.

We met Javier at his house and, after a short drive, clambered up the steep rocky slopes until we saw the waterfalls high above us cascading down the hills. Underneath them was a flat rocky spot where we changed our clothes

'Here you can go under the water,' said Javier, pointing towards the torrent which fell from fifty feet above us. He ran under and we watched his lithe dark body dancing through the swirling torrent. He came out shivering and laughing. 'You want to go?' He touched my shoulder with icy fingers. I held my breath and ran through the shimmering sheet until I was in the dry heart of the waterfall. It was like a watery cave where I could watch the fierce liquid cascading in front of me, creating a rainbow wall of droplets and bubbles. The sound was a huge symphony of energy and I felt like some tiny animal sheltering there with water streaming all around and the brilliant sun shining through the torrent.

I came out and Zia took her turn. Always beautiful, she looked like a nymph as she danced through the shimmering sheet of water. I lay on a rock, feeling it warming my back as the sun warmed my belly. Javier asked Zia if she would like to climb some rocks with him, and I noticed him taking her hand tenderly to help her up a sharp incline.

'I take you to my house for food now,' said Javier linking arms with us both as we walked towards the car. We ate a simple supper of maize bread,

Me outside the Casa Alma

goats' cheese, olives and tomatoes, feeling the intimacy of people who have shared a peak experience.

'Would you like to come down and share a full moon celebration with us on Thursday?' I asked him in my hesitant Spanish before we drove back down the hills.

'I am always happy to see you,' he replied in his courteous English and gave us both big hugs.

Romany and John's terraces were now a profusion of flowers, tomatoes, egg plants and courgettes. Their circular straw bale house was plastered, white-washed and decorated with painted climbing flowers. Wooden steps carved with Mayan designs led up to a flat roof, perfect for dancing and celebrations. We mounted the steps in single file, carrying glasses of peach juice, dishes of colourful vegetables and rice. Luna didn't want to be left behind, so I carried her up the steep steps and she curled herself down close to me, my constant familiar. From the roof we had wide views overlooking the riverbed, the nearby hills and the distant mountains. The sun was just setting and a curtain of balmy dusk began to fall, bringing with it the warm night scent of summer jasmine.

Javier appeared with his partner Nieves, who looked a bit overdressed and uncomfortable, not used to being with a group of unusual foreigners on a circular rooftop in a darkening sky. But soon we were all relaxed, eating and drinking as we watched the stars waking and a full moon rising, dusting the distant hills with an eerie glow. We lay on a heap of pillows and blankets, intimate and sated. The roof looked romantic, with a rosy light cast from the red skinned candles the Spanish use to celebrate their dead.

'Let's sing our song now,' I whispered to Zia.

'Not just yet—when the moon's a bit higher,' Zia replied, gazing upwards as the great silver orb rose slowly.

That afternoon we had practised a two part Spanish song, *Levantate y mira las montañas*—Rise up and look at the mountains. Written by a Chilean revolutionary, the song exhorts the oppressed masses to rise up and come into their power. We had learned it in the Avalonian Free State Choir several years before, little knowing that one day we would be singing it to the mountains on a rooftop in southern Spain.

We stood up together holding hands and sang into the soft moonlit night. The song felt like an ancient pledge or prayer, as we harmonised in the darkness. The caressing air seemed to collect our voices and charge them with the power and courage to transform our world. Afterwards I felt filled with a liquid hope as we sank quietly back into the cushions.

'Come on folks lets dance,' said Romany, ever energetic and enthusiastic. I struggled out of my exhaustion. Though my body was spent my soul was

Romany and John's roundhouse

flying. I joined Romany and Zia dancing silently to the accompaniment of moonshine, croaking frogs and singing cicadas. We all wore long dresses, and mine was white. As we danced into the darkness I felt we were like doves, spreading peace and stardust into the dark night.

Soon I returned to England and stayed there helping Patrick with our courses until October. Patrick then travelled back with me and we arrived in time to harvest the almonds and figs, savour the juicy pomegranates and taste the last of the summer vegetables. There was also a winter's supply of squash and onions to dry on the roof. The house felt welcoming, light, warm and dry after a long hot summer, with geckos sleeping lazily on the walls. I enjoyed having Patrick stay for a month, sharing my Spanish life and helping me with the autumn work. It was such a comfort to have his easy company, but by the time he left the inevitable November rains and winds had started whipping around the house and I felt bereft again.

Winters seemed to be getting colder and colder. By January we had temperatures of minus five in the early mornings and I was collecting wood with my wwooFers up on the hills in thick snow. One night, when I had no wwooFers staying with me and I had to get up at three in the morning wearing a woolly hat and bed socks to re-light the wood burner, I began to have my doubts about the sanity of choosing such a primitive home.

I started to feel weak and ill. Pains around my gall bladder and liver, which I had had over the years, were becoming stronger and more frequent and would make me literally roll around in agony despite taking strong pain killers. I thought about going back to England, where at least we had central heating, but I didn't want to give up on my Spanish dream, and by this time Patrick had decided he thrived on months alone. He has a strong bachelor sub personality

It was a freezing night and I was alone. I'd had fierce pains in the afternoon and now my heart was skipping around all over the place. I was scared and my hands were shaking as I went into the icy kitchen to make myself a warming Yogi tea. What was the matter with my heart? I felt as if I was suffocating and could hardly breathe. I tried to calm myself and meditate on my breath. Observe your thoughts, I said to myself, this is the time you really have to use your spiritual practice. I called upon my unseen guides, but it was no good, I could feel no presence.

I felt as if I could die alone and not one of my family would know. I didn't even have a number of a doctor or ambulance and anyway I would never have been able to explain where I lived in Spanish. It was hard enough in English! I knew Romany and John would have their phone off and there was no way I could walk the hundred yards to their place. I doubted my other neighbours would have their phones on in the middle of the night either.

I'd better make a will, I thought irrationally, scrabbling about in the dim light for a pen and paper. If I died without a will, under Spanish law the house wouldn't automatically go to Patrick. What a nightmare, I thought, ineffectually scribbling away in the cold dim bedroom.

Something inside me broke that night. My dream house in Spain no longer felt like a safe haven. It was an intimation that I would need to move on. I felt the terrible desolation of knowing that I would probably have to start again, after all the work and energy I had put into my first true home.

The following day I took myself to the hospital. There I was given an ECG and they put me on a pacing machine to measure my heartbeat in motion, but they could find nothing untoward with my heart. I told them about my fierce liver pains and they suggested a whole body scan. A nurse put me in a totally enclosed metal tube, and I felt terrified. My one phobia is being trapped in small spaces, a result of getting shut in a chicken shed when I was little. Why did I always seem to end up having to go through these traumatic experiences alone?

The machine slowly sucked me in. There was some bland ambient music playing in the background as I went into that caterpillar of steel. Please help me, guides and angels, I prayed, surely I have suffered enough in this lifetime. Maybe they're going to tell me I'm riddled with cancer and will die soon. Or even worse, another long drawn out illness.

As my prayer finished, the Beatles' 'All You Need is Love' started playing loudly inside my metal capsule! It was my signature tune, that same song which had first woken me up to everything which has been important to me throughout my life. And here it was being played for me as if in answer to my prayers. I'd never heard the Beatles played in Spain, let alone this, my very special song. I breathed deeply and felt my shoulders relax.

'We haven't found anything serious,' said the German doctor gently, as I sat in his surgery after the scan. 'But we can see that you have a lot of TB scarring all through your abdomen. This could be causing you a lot of pain. Many of your organs are adhesed together.'

'So what can I do about the pain?' I asked.

'The only thing to do is to have the adhesions operated on, but this could make even more of a mess. I suggest we leave it and see how you get on for the next few months.'

Given this inconclusive diagnosis, when a friend suggested I go to a psychic surgeon I decided I had nothing to lose. The pain was getting worse and I was often writhing in agony.

I set off with my good friend Lisa and her husband Peter one cool March morning. After driving around the outskirts of Malaga for hours and having a puncture, we finally managed to find the small satellite town and the ordinary looking suburban house where the psychic surgeon lived. The walls of the little sitting room where we waited were covered with pictures of Christ and the saints, along with written testimonials of miracle cures. The room was hot and full of patients chatting away in the impossible Andalucian dialect. Every now and then a middle aged man would appear from the treatment room in a surgeon's green outfit carrying a large bowl which he would empty into the toilet, and then beckon the next in line. This was Rogerio, the psychic surgeon. Finally after a couple of hours waiting he called us in.

We all went in together and found Rogerio creating a circle of salt around a treatment couch in the centre of the room. Next to the couch was a tray of frightening looking scalpels, cotton wool pads, and thin rubber gloves. He asked one of us to go first and lie on the couch. I lay there feeling like a lamb going to slaughter. He asked me what were my symptoms. Lisa translated as I told him I had had these acute physical pains around my liver area.

'OK, we'll do the operation now,' he said, lifting up the scalpel.

I put up my hand in horror.

'Are you going to use that scalpel on her without any anaesthetic or anything?' asked Lisa, pale with terror.

'*Por supuesto,*' he said—Of course. '*Pero no te molesto,*'—I won't hurt you, he added, taking my hand and smiling into my eyes.

I fell into a timeless moment in which I confronted my terror. I told myself that I had always believed in a spiritual reality superseding the physical and this was my ultimate test. I had to believe I wouldn't feel the pain of being cut open. After all we'd been sitting outside that room for two hours and hadn't heard any screams of agony. Also I knew I just couldn't cope with the pain any more, or the dubious prospect of a conventional operation which would lead to more scarring. Feeling as if I was jumping off a cliff and only God knew if I would land safely or die, I said '*Sí.*'

I closed my eyes on Lisa's disbelieving face, and felt Rogerio drawing a line across my abdomen. It tickled a bit but there was no pain. Then I felt his hand go into my body and had a sense of things being rearranged inside me. I briefly opened my eyes and looked down to see half his hand submerged in me and some blood running down my stomach. I looked over at Lisa and Peter as they stood near the wall. Lisa looked grey with her hand over her mouth and both of them were frozen-eyed with astonishment.

After a few minutes Rogerio took his hand out and threw some nasty looking purple lumps of flesh into the plastic bowl on the floor. He rubbed my now closed up stomach with some surgical spirit. I looked down with disbelief and could see a pink line where he had 'cut', and some small blood stains on my cream trousers. He gently sat me up, dazed. 'There was a big mess in there,' he said through Lisa's translation, 'But it's better now. *Mucho mejor*.'

Peter also had some psychic surgery and I watched as blood spurted out of his body and hit the wall! Lisa and I got hysterical giggles watching it and ended up helplessly sitting on the floor trying not to laugh. It was just too surreal. We travelled home speechless. My insides felt tender but I had no pain. We had been given a glimpse of another dimension where normal laws don't hold true any more and miracles can happen.

The following day we sat around my patio in suspended animation trying to analyse what had happened. My insides felt tender but I was free of pain for the first time in weeks.

'Quantum physics is *proving* that matter isn't solid, that we're composed of 95 per cent space, and that consciousness can affect matter,' I tried to reassure myself and the others as we sat on the patio drinking delicious fresh orange juice. 'I think that healer must speed up matter with his own consciousness, so it's no longer solid, and then he operates.'

'I don't understand.' Peter sighed wearily. He had been withdrawn and uncommunicative since yesterday, trying to come to terms with the impossible.

'I think it's like water, which can be ice or steam, depending on which frequency it's vibrating on,' I said, trying to explain it to myself at the same time. 'It's the same stuff of H_2O but appears completely different. So if a healer can speed up the vibration of our skin I suppose he can put his hand through it and operate.' Peter looked unconvinced. 'Quantum physics is proving all this stuff that the mystics knew centuries ago,' I repeated, 'that consciousness can change our physical reality. There have even been experiments where people have altered the shape of their DNA with the power of thought.'

Peter looked away. He'd experienced a miracle but still didn't want to believe it, and I understood why.

Several months later I recounted my terror of the scalpel to the friend who had been cured of her cancer by this healer. 'Oh, she said, 'I should have told you, he doesn't actually cut your skin with the scalpel. He uses it to psychically cut through, but then he really does put his hand inside your body and operate.'

''Thanks,' I replied. 'It would have been a lot easier if I'd known that!'

After the psychic surgery, a mature New Zealand wwoofer arrived. She was a landscape gardener by profession, taking a year's sabbatical. I told her I had been unwell and needed to convalesce down on the coast.

'I'd love to be alone in the house and have some space,' she said happily. 'I've been with people non stop for ages.'

Within days I had found a place to stay in the coastal town of La Herradura. 'What a mad situation,' I said to her, laughing to disguise my feelings of distress. 'I'm leaving the house I bought to be warm in winter, in order to be warm in winter! I suppose I just have to trust in the wisdom of the universe,' I added, swallowing down the increasingly bitter realisation that I would have to find somewhere else to live in winter.

La Herradura lies around a beautiful horseshoe shaped bay, with a coastal road following the contour of the beach, bordered by palms full of bright busy parrots. Although it earns most of its income from tourists it still has the feel of the friendly little town which twenty years before had been a fishing village, where all the families know one another and are part of a community.

While I was there I had time to think and reassess my life. What do I really want? I asked myself. I wanted to feel at home in my house, not to be cold in winter, and to have a loving partner to share my life in Spain. Did that mean I had to completely give up my house, as it seemed impossible to make it really comfortable, and did it mean I needed to separate from Patrick and find someone else? Was the community of friends I had created in Spain enough for me and what about work now that renovating the house was almost finished? Although the Spanish women's retreat had gone well, I realised that the house wasn't really suitable for residential retreats. My women's groups and classes weren't flourishing either as the women in the area were so busy with land and children. There were no simple answers, so I tried to relax and enjoy the coast.

I was pleased to go home to Casa Alma in early April. The weather was warm and sunny. The swallows had hatched their chicks and were teaching them to fly around the *tinao*. The orange blossom was beginning to waft its scent of femininity to my back door. I started planting my summer vegetables and getting the house and land ready for leaving in May. Another of the greatest dilemmas and sadness about my life in Spain was that May and September are among the best months in the Alpujarras, yet the timetable of our courses in England demanded that I leave in May and not come back till the end of September. On our permaculture courses I teach a spiritual and emotional approach to the coming ecological crisis, exploring how we can learn to live harmoniously together and give up our addiction to the consumerism which is destroying the planet. On every course I offer an evening healing circle. This is a profound experience for some participants, as they're able to feel the subtle healing energies for themselves, and so take on the reality of spiritual realms. I assure them that spiritual practices such as meditation and prayer can affect our bodies and our outer reality, and thus help transform our planet. As Gandhi said, 'We must be the change we wish to see in the world,' and this is why working on ourselves is so important.

We often have students on our courses who want to buy land and live more communally, sharing resources, living sustainably and growing their own food. Increasingly it seems this may be the way we are going to survive the coming earth changes which will inevitably hit us as climate chaos increases, oil prices rise and economies collapse.

'Then why are you thinking of leaving your place in Spain?' asked Therese, a participant on our course in June of that year. 'You said it's so beautiful, and you can live reasonably sustainably in that small community of friends.'

'It's physically hard work living there, especially as a woman alone. It would be different if Patrick could live there with me to help with the heavy jobs. I'm just not strong enough to cope with looking after all the land and that New Age peasant lifestyle.' I thought of the stress I had suffered the previous winter. 'And I don't always want to have to live with wwoofers,' I added. Although it had been inspiring to share my life with younger people it had often been exhausting too. 'Now I'm older I feel the need for more comfort, and there are also emotional problems, living in a small community like that.'

'And what are they?' Therese was curious.

'Perhaps we have all become too individualistic, and still have too many choices at the moment,' I pondered. 'We all want it our own way and aren't psychologically ready to really share. I think that until we're forced by necessity to share, like in the past, when neighbours had to pull together to survive, we probably won't do it very well.' I thought of all the disputes which constantly divided our hamlet, many about the Dragon Festival. But I also remembered how much I had been supported and helped when I arrived. 'Don't get me wrong. In our hamlet we do help each other out and share a lot, but it isn't an intentional community, just a group of random people who've ended up in the same place. Considering that, we do pretty well.'

'What about money? Don't you think it's because most of us can't afford land and houses here in the UK that we can't get communities together?'

'Yes, I think that's part of the truth,' I replied. 'It's one of the reasons I and many others have bought in Spain. Externally it always seems to come down to money, yet I do believe if the time is right and the intention is clear, the money thing can be overcome. I visited a flourishing spiritual community in Italy called Ananda Assisi, based on the teachings of Yogananda. They had to work in faith for the first few years with virtually no money but eventually, through loans and donations, the most beautiful retreat centre was built. It works as a community because everyone has something in common, a dedication to a particular spiritual path.' I remembered the feeling of love which pervaded the community.

'A common goal does seem to make communities work,' Therese agreed. 'You can see that from the monasteries of the past. Like you said, most of the communities that have worked have been old fashioned ones, where people either needed each other to survive or have some spiritual belief which helps when things get difficult.'

'Patrick and I visited a community on the Isle of Erraid a long time ago,' I told her, remembering one of the sweetest times of our relationship. 'It's a tiny island off the west coast of Scotland, a branch of the Findhorn community. They live as sustainably as possible and run workshops, have paying guests, and make crafts for a small income. They all tune into spirit before eating, having meetings or trying to make decisions. This really makes the place work. They're consciously bringing spirit into matter in their everyday lives. It felt as if they were being guided to do all the mundane tasks of life for the highest good.'

'What do you mean by the highest good?' she asked.

'Well, I mean that when we're tuned into our spirit, or our essential nature, we'll do what's best not just for ourselves but for everyone and for the planet. You know that feeling, when you're really tuned in and everything works well and seems special?' As I spoke, I felt the familiar spiritual heat rising up my spine.

'Yes, I think I know what you mean,' she sighed. 'So how come you and Patrick didn't go and live on Erraid as it seemed to be what you wanted?'

'We might have if the climate had been better,' I answered sadly. 'But neither of us can take the damp and cold, so here I am in my sixties still without a home where I can be truly comfortable.

The quest to find and create the home of my dreams had been such a deep longing all my life, and in Casa Alma I had achieved much of that dream. I loved the house, the land and the surrounding landscape, but now I could no longer support a lifestyle where I had to carry my own drinking water and live with unreliable solar electricity, where the only form of heating was logs and where the roof would often leak when the hard rains came. So when I returned to Spain in October I didn't go back to Casa Alma. I felt both bereft and relieved. It was the end of an era.

An Echo of the Past, 2009

Soul Eyes

You take my past
And throw it to the winds like so much dust
And you take my patterns of mind
Unwinding them to find threads which are true
And then it is you who breathes life back into me
With sunshine and sweet water, gifts of vivid colour
From your burnt sienna skirts of earth
You who show me secret soul eyes
In shifting skies above the mountains
Conceal your wounds in black clad widows
Chained barking dogs like prisoners
And scorched parched lands
Where weary hands have worked the ochre earth though time
You who take my past and throw it to the winds like so much dust
Show me people with the warmth of sun in their blood
The pulse of flamenco in their veins and fierce strong spirits of fire
Here amidst your harsh wild beauty you meet me in sweet mystery
Revealing your heart in the gift of glittering mountains
The darkness of shadows
Paths of starlight

I rented out Casa Alma and found a pretty little house to rent just outside Órgiva. It was part of a small complex of modern *casitas* called Jaramuza, with lovely shared gardens and a swimming pool, lying amongst the oldest olive groves in the district. The people I lived amongst now were much more mainstream than the hippies of the hamlet and the riverbed dropouts who had been my neighbours before.

Now I had more time on my hands I could treat myself to more days out. Granada was the place to go for a complete contrast to the peasant land of the Alpujarras and Lisa was the person to go there with because she's got that cosmopolitan side to her. In her working life she's a tour guide.

It would soon be Christmas, so we decided to go and look around for some small presents. First we walked through the souk, a Moroccan market of steep narrow lanes packed with shops and tea houses, smelling of exotic perfumes and incense. It reminded me of the souk of Istanbul, my first taste of the East way back in the sixties, especially when pushy vendors stood outside their shops and tried to entice us in. Once inside it was like being in Aladdin's cave, a treasure trove of ceramics, mirrored wall hangings, pointed Arabian slippers and marquetry. I found a beautiful miniature Backgammon set to give to Patrick. Outside again we looked at floaty oriental clothes and sequinned belly dancing costumes which took me back to Arab-Egyptian dancing at my first dance camp in Glastonbury.

Afterwards we walked up to the old part of town, the Albaycín. I became breathless climbing the steep narrow streets, so we stopped to rest. We peeped through a wrought iron gate into a *carmen,* an enclosed patio garden with a central fountain tinkling delicately in the sun. I gazed at the miniature orange and lemon trees, the geraniums and herbs in pots, and felt the magic of this ancient city. After a while we walked on, catching vignettes of the fabulous Alhambra palace beyond the red tiled roofs of the town.

'This looks like a good place to have a tea,' Lisa said, and we entered an enticing *tetería,* a little world of dusky latticework screens, coloured mosaic lamps, velour curtains, and hookahs. After tea we went on upwards to the view point of Plaza San Nicolás, perched high on the hills. Now we could see the Alhambra in all its glory, like a red fortress guarding the city, with the mysterious snow capped mountains in the distance. As we drove homewards I felt renewed by her beauty.

Since I was no longer struggling so much with the physical aspects of life I had more energy to devote to what I consider my true calling, to pass on some of the wisdom I've learnt throughout my life. So I started a new series of women's self development groups.

One of the most consistent elements of what I taught was how to get in touch with our own inner wisdom or essential core Self. We would sit around on cushions in my sitting room, where the sun streamed in, while I led the group in visualisations, meditations and sharings. One of my favourite visualisations was one taken from psychosynthesis, a form of spiritual psychology. We would imagine ourselves climbing up a mountain to meet a wise person within, an aspect of ourselves who we could question for support and guidance. This was often really helpful and the women usually returned from the visualization inspired with new strength and insights. As we shared our stories, joys and tears, I would remind the participants that by becoming conscious of our shadows, the repressed hidden parts of ourselves, we can become emotionally whole and healthy.

'It's about learning to listen to ourselves and what our body sense has to tell us,' I told them. 'The body doesn't lie and once we learn how to interpret its messages we are well on the way to healing. We all have to learn to hear and comfort the child within us, ask her what would make her feel better and what she needs, like a good mother would with her own daughter.'

It was through this group that I met Monica, a German woman my age who was also wintering in Spain for her health. She immediately felt like a soul sister and one day, sitting outside my casita eating lunch together, we shared our life stories.

'So I never saw Johann after we left India, or heard from him after that last letter,' I told her, still feeling a jumpiness in my solar plexus when I spoke of that time. 'We never really said goodbye and it feels unfinished. I'd love to know what happened to him. I've been trying to find him on line for the last two years, searching reunion.com and other sites, but with no luck.'

'You said he came from near Frankfurt?' she looked genuinely interested.

'And that you still have the address of his parents?'

'Yes, it's a place called Buchschlag. Have you heard of it?' I felt my belly contracting.

'Yes, it's very near where I live, do you want me to see if they still live there?' she asked enthusiastically. 'I'm going back to Germany in a couple of weeks. They might still be there and then you could find out where Johann is.'

'You could try,' I said half heartedly, not believing anything would come of it.

'I'll look in a phone book when I get back.'

'That would be great,' I replied, thinking that his parents would be dead by now, which is why I hadn't even thought of contacting their address.

A few months later I got an e-mail. It was from Johann, the first communication I had had for thirty-eight years and I found my heart racing! Would this be the healing resolution I had always longed for?

> I have just been given your e-mail by my mother. She got it from a friend of yours who phoned her. So much distance has passed since those Formentera and India days. How are you? I am living in the most beautiful place in California, I have had a good life running an organic farm here. I have a wife and two grown-up children who are doing well, but the last year has been hard as I was diagnosed with pancreatic cancer last March, given three months to live, and have been on intensive Chinese medicine and acupuncture regime since then. Now nine months later I am still here, feeling positive but living a much more sedentary life than before, but appreciate every moment.

I wrote back immediately.

> I'm so pleased to hear from you after all this time, I always wondered what happened to you after we separated. I am so sorry about your illness, and understand how hard it is. I was ill for many years after our journey and never was able to have children after that

miscarriage. I also took the path of complementary medicine, and have regained much of my health, and am now living half my life in Spain, as the climate suits me better, and half with my husband in the UK.

No reply. I suppose he didn't want to hear my story. He was very ill, had his own struggles and perhaps it made him feel guilty, which was not my intention. But it hurt. An acknowledgement would have helped. But I didn't even know if he'd received that e-mail

That Christmas I sent him another one: 'I hope you had a good Xmas, and you are doing well with your healing. I wonder if you got my last e-mail?'

'Thank you, I had a good but quiet Christmas with my family,' he replied. There was no mention of my previous e-mail, or any intimation of his first open-hearted communication.

In March I received an e-mail with a picture of Johann and his wife in Venice, with no attached words. Perhaps he was too ill to write by then, or perhaps it was a message from his wife telling me to keep away. But I decided to reply anyway.

'Thank you for the photo,' I wrote, 'I hope you are not suffering too much with your illness. I just wanted to tell you that you were the first great love of my life.'

I received an e-mail from his wife a couple of months later, 'To whom it may concern: I found your address on Johann's e-mail account and I know you were one of his friends. He died on May 12th of adrenal cancer. I thought you might like to know.'

I had been hoping for a loving completion, but I was not overly upset by the lack of it. After all, it was all a long time ago.

Although Romany and John were no longer next door neighbours I saw them often. They were still living in their round house when John became ill with leukaemia. It was a shock to see him growing weaker, as he had been the kind of man who could walk for miles or work on the land all day right through his seventies. It was hard to witness his frustration at not being out there in their extensive garden which was his greatest joy. Despite a life of physical fitness he was one of the few people who had really been able to empathize with my physical challenges. He was always compassionate and concerned, asking me how I was and if I needed any help carrying gas bottles and such like. He was a rare gem of a man.

In the last months of his life I visited him often as he lay in the roundhouse. Their bed looked like a canopied ship, with its turquoise mosquito netting floating above him and the ceiling billowing with the different coloured fabrics Romany had attached to it. He had no privacy, as the house consisted of a single open-plan space. The 'bedroom' was in one segment of the circle, the next comprised a zany mosaic bath area, then a pretty tiled kitchen, and a cosy sitting area with a wood burner completed the circle. Miscellaneous wwoofers and people in need of healing drifted in and out of the house looking for Romany and saying hello to John on their way. I have no idea if this was a comfort or a disturbance for him, a bit of both, I imagine.

The day before he died I sat on the side of his bed holding his hand, while Romany sat on the other side stroking his hair. He was so uncomfortable in his body, tossing and turning and murmuring that he was ready to go. 'We love you so much,' we both told him. 'You can go now.' My cheeks were wet with tears.

Early next morning Romany phoned me. 'He died peacefully last night,' she said. 'It was a sacred moment. I really experienced his spirit leave his body and felt a huge sense of release and peace.' It was a Thursday in late May and as Romany pointed out, it just happened to be Ascension day.

However John had converted to the Muslim faith a few weeks before, when he heard that being a Muslim meant he could be buried in the earth without a coffin. He felt a great affinity with the Koran and had read it many times, before becoming involved with the Sufi tradition and more recently Subud, both of which have roots in Islam. But his main reason for converting was ecological. 'It would be such a waste of wood,' he said, 'putting a new coffin in there to rot.' He had always collected firewood as he walked along the riverbed on his way home from town, and he'd collected abandoned pallets and made a little shack out of them. He loved to go to the dumps to pick up and recycle other people's waste. Ideally he would have liked to be buried on his land, but he certainly didn't want to be put in a new coffin and it didn't seem that you could get recycled or cardboard ones in Andalucía.

In Spain there is a tradition of burying the dead quickly and under Muslim law it had to be done within twenty-four hours, and the next day was a Friday, the Muslim day of prayer, which is considered the best day for a burial. This urgency to bury the dead is at odds with the *Tibetan Book of the Dead*, which teaches that the body should be left peacefully for at least three days while the soul is doing its difficult and final journey towards the light.

Lisa collected me and we drove up the riverbed to their house. Mists rose like breath from the valley and the rising sun tinted the mountains amber. We found John, his face beautiful and serene, all tension of illness gone and his features relaxed and peaceful. His body was covered in a white sheet strewn with spring flowers which friends had left as they visited. Bright yellow posies decorated the entire bed and garlanded his soft white hair.

Romany, Lisa and I decided to go up on the roof to tune into his spirit and be with him on his soul journey. We sat there in the centre of the painted mandala, which many of us had worked on over several months. We spoke to him in spirit, wishing him well and singing in praise of his life. Romany seemed relieved. 'I'm so glad he's free of suffering,' she said, 'And he's here with us. I can feel him.' She had no doubts about John's life going on after death and simply saw it as a transition.

At the same time, John's son, daughter in law and grand daughter, ardent Catholics, were sitting by his bedside solemnly saying their prayers for him. It was an equally beautiful way of showing respect and grief. Meanwhile, on a rocky hillside, a group of young Muslim men were chanting verses from the Koran while they dug his grave on their holy day. John would have loved this. Even in death he was a peacemaker, creating union between the religions.

The Muslims had only just acquired their burial ground and he was the first to be buried there. It was right beside the Christian cemetery and I'd never been inside a Spanish one before. They are quite different to those in the UK, protected by white walls and guarded by tall cypress trees. Coffins are placed above ground in oblong structures, each one in a niche, one on top of the other like huge concrete pigeon holes. At the front is a marble façade bearing inscriptions and sometimes a little picture of the departed. Little shelves jut out in front of each tomb, where vases of plastic flowers perch liberally alongside the traditional red-skinned candles which burn for several days. But John wanted none of this.

Considering the short notice, a surprisingly large group of us gathered to celebrate John's life and mourn his parting. We processed up to the open grave amidst Muslim prayers and Celtic chants. His body, wrapped in a simple white sheet, was laid deep within the recently dug burial hole. The grave diggers placed heavy slates directly on his shrouded body, which was hard for some of us to watch. Lisa and I walked away crying, but at the same time I could feel him smiling his compassionate smile, saying, 'Don't worry. I'm fine now. All is well.'

The following morning I had to leave for England. I had a passage booked on the Santander ferry which would get me there in time for the first permaculture course of the summer. 'What perfect timing,' Romany said. 'It's another win-win situation!' She had originally planned to travel back with me and Luna, and everything was booked, but with John dying she had thought she wouldn't be able to make it. 'He's always been the most considerate man,' she said, laughing through her tears. 'Now I can go to my brother's golden wedding celebration!'

We left together in my little Daihatsu, chanting mantras for John all the way to Madrid.

Life and Death, 2009–2010

A Buddhist Monastery

At the monastery
I turned the prayer wheel
Walking slowly
Feeling the strength
Of a thousand prayers
Behind me
Remembering my father now dead
Telling me
To keep the prayer wheels turning

At the monastery
I felt my Tibetan self again
And remembered
Vast spaciousness within
Like the wide blue Andalucian skies
Like the silent snow capped mountains
Like the whispering quivering pines
When the cluttered mind stills.

The following winter I was back in my rented home in Jaramuza and Patrick came to stay for a few weeks over Christmas. Christmas has often been a difficult time for me as, being a family season, it highlights my childlessness. Even now it still hurts, as my friends proudly show me pictures of their grandchildren and I try to accept what has been my destiny.

This year I received something that really helped. Paul, one of our former permaculture students with whom Patrick and I had both felt a strong connection, always sends out a circular e-mail at this time of year. Sometimes we have hardly replied, but this time we wrote back to him with a fairly detailed e-mail. In it I wrote, 'I have been quite itinerant since leaving my own house and do suffer from lack of family, which hasn't been easy. But I think, on a soul level, I am learning detachment, to make everyone family, and to live in the moment and be grateful for what I have.' Paul replied:

> I think we are all somehow parents to all children. Kahlil Gibran writes about this in his book *The Prophet,* which you probably know, and of how 'Our children are not our children. They come through us but not from us, they are with us yet they belong not to us.' We of course influence and teach our children to some extent, but that influence and teaching comes to us as parents through our encounters and experiences with other folk. So some of what I share with my children comes from you both, and may I say that what you have shared through me are some of the most positive, powerful and important things I know. So to me, you are also parents of my children and, through all the years, of countless other people's children as well. You could in effect be parents of many of those you have directly encountered, and what you have shared goes on through the generations.
>
> I have found in my own experience that sometimes even relatively short relationships and personal encounters can be the most profound and important in one's life. Whether you have known it or not, you both are such people in my life, and therefore in the lives of my/our children. Thank you.

On reading this I burst into tears. This is what I had been telling myself for years but to have an outside voice, and one I really respected, bear witness, gave me a feeling of validation which I have never been able to give myself.

We were invited for Christmas dinner with some friends high up on the hills. On Christmas morning we woke to a continuous curtain of rain so thick we couldn't see the familiar landscape.

The phone rang. It was a friend who had been invited to the same dinner, ringing to wish us a happy Christmas because she wouldn't be seeing us that day. She and her partner lived in a more remote area of the hills, at the end of a zigzag dirt road with sheer drops of a hundred metres to the river below. She sounded upset. 'This crazy weather! We can hardly get out with the track being so slippery and we dare not brave the road. We've heard that some of it has fallen away and it's becoming impassable.' Patrick and I dressed in our waterproofs, ran to the car and had no trouble driving up the tarmac road for our Christmas party. We settled down to our nut roast around a glowing log fire, cheerily ignoring the increasing force of rain and wind outside.

We drove back down into the valley through the wild night with headlights dipped. When we woke up the next day it was still raining relentlessly. The hills looked like smoky ghosts. Neighbours had invited us to a musical gathering that afternoon and although we all moaned about the weather none of us was too concerned, as heavy rain is part of an Alpujarran winter. But it went on raining. The *acequias* were filling with runoff water and flooding onto the tracks, making them increasingly impassable, and we started feeling worried. At least at Jaramuza we were within walking distance of the food shops in town, we reassured ourselves.

In the morning we were woken at dawn by the roar of the Rio Chico, a small tributary which was dry most of the year and rarely more than a gentle trickle. I felt disaster in the air as we got up early to walk down to the river. We found the ford which was our nearest access to the main road completely washed away. Along with it had gone part of an orange orchard, leaving a bare cliff of earth beside a void where yesterday several trees had grown. The river was like a wild beast, frothing with mud and carrying uprooted trees and debris from the town. My heart contracted as I watched it carelessly fling broken branches and the carcass of a dog towards the banks.

We were hardly back at the *casita* when Lisa rushed round. 'Have you heard about the riverbed?' she asked. Between us 'the riverbed' could only mean the stretch in front of Casa Alma, where many travellers lived in their vans and buses. 'It's been washed away in the floods!'

'What do you mean washed away?'

'There were really fierce floods on Christmas Eve and lots of the travellers' trucks have been swept downstream and wrecked. The access track's completely gone. At least no-one's drowned, thank God.'

There must have been many narrow escapes that night but none more scary than what happened to our friend Nicole. She lived in a caravan on her patch of land on the edge of the riverbed. She woke up to the sound of gushing water. She didn't take it too seriously but thought she should just check on her children who were in a yurt across the yard. As she opened the door of her caravan water streamed in. It was waist deep outside! She found herself wading through a fierce torrent in the dark towards the yurt. Inside her two little girls were fast asleep, floating on their mattresses in a sea of water! She was struggling to rescue them when her nearest neighbour appeared to help, and together they managed to float the girls to higher ground on their mattresses! At dawn, Neil and another neighbour, went down with ropes and rescued goats who where stranded there. Neil had lived in the area for years and had seen floods before, so he knew there would be animals in danger.

Nicole lost everything—caravan, yurt and all her possessions. It was a terrible shock for her and that little community. Her girls could have drowned so easily. Afterwards everyone came together to help. As well as her low-lying land she owned a ruin high up above the hamlet, and the neighbours helped her to renovate it so that she and her girls could live there.

Many travellers lost their homes. The whole landscape was devastated, littered with capsized cars and trucks and uprooted trees in the mud. The river had changed course and completely taken out the road which gave access to the hamlet. I was so relieved that I wasn't still living there, as it was now a twenty minute walk to the nearest parking place and with my weakness I wouldn't have managed to carry heavy shopping that distance. Although I was one of the fortunate ones who hadn't actually lost my home, I wouldn't be able to live there again and it hardly boded well for selling the place.

In Órgiva the gossip was all of the floods and how it had affected the locals' land and their livelihoods. Old folk remembered nothing like it in their lifetime and word got around that these were the worst floods in Spain for over a century. Global warming was creating extreme weather patterns, and it was said that the jet stream, an air current which usually affects Scotland, had come farther south and was hitting us in southern Spain.

As if to compensate for the destruction of the floods, there was never such a beautiful spring after all that rain. Towards the end of January the delicate pink and white almond blossom began to appear, intimating the coming season, although it was really still winter and often cold.

Lisa and I took our annual trip up the Sierra de la Contraviesa to look at the vistas of almond orchards. The dark barked almonds have such a frilly feminine pink and white blossom it reminds me of girls petticoats and party frocks. We strolled along the hillsides and lost ourselves in the pink stars of flowers and fallen petal confetti until we felt satiated by beauty and had to get back to earth with some tapas at the hotel in Torvizcón.

In March the weather warmed up and I went walking with Luna through the pale green fields, where the bright yellow oxalis flowers opened their petals to the sun. Poppies were blood red splashes against the grass and snowmelt rushed through the acequias. But I felt a sense of ending. The river authorities had no intention of rebuilding the track to Casa Alma. My friends in the hamlet were now walking a kilometre to their cars, carrying shopping and gas bottles in wheelbarrows or by mule.

Over the years I had grown ever closer to Luna. Now she was old and becoming increasingly delicate with a cancerous tumour on her little black nose. I still took her out for short walks, but soon she would only walk a few metres and then turn back sadly and wait outside the back door for me to return. It reminded me of myself and all those times when I had been too weak to walk more than a few metres. I felt like weeping as I watched her deteriorate. The tumour was inoperable and I knew it was just a matter of time before she would die. I made her special food and spent long hours holding and stroking her. When her legs finally gave way and she stopped eating I silently begged her to die naturally. It would be so much easier. But I didn't want her to suffer unnecessarily so I booked the vet.

The last night of her life I held her soft little body on my bed and silently wished her goodbye and told her how much I loved her. We gazed into each others eyes for several minutes as a profound love flowed like balm between us. In the morning Lisa came round to support me. Holding Luna while the vet gave her the last injection was one of the most difficult things I have ever done. I felt the visceral severing of separation squeeze my heart.

It was time to head for the hills for spiritual solace.

The stupa at Osel Ling

Shortly before I came to live in Spain I read a book about a Tibetan lama
who had been reincarnated as a Spanish boy. When he knew his death was
approaching, the great Lama Yeshe told his followers that he would be re-
born in the West. Some time later one of his Spanish students gave birth to
an exceptional child at her home in Spain. Following Tibetan tradition, the
boy was tested to prove whether he really was the reincarnation of Lama
Yeshe. Amongst other tests, he was presented with a large range of objects,
including those which had belonged to the deceased lama, and asked to
choose from them. He chose the ones which had belonged to Lama Yeshe
and the Dalai Lama proclaimed him to be the true reincarnation and
named Lama Osel.

Almond blossom and the Sierra Nevada

I was so impressed by the story that I even wrote a short story of my own about Lama Osel. I'd always felt an uncanny familiarity with all things Tibetan and I believe I lived there in a past life. Little did I realize then that before long I would be able to sit on the verandah of my own home and see the stupa of his monastery, Osel Ling. It was just visible from the *tinao* of Casa Alma, a white speck on the distant tawny hills, foothills of the towering Sierra Nevada.

Now I drove up the curling roads towards the monastery, through the farmland around Órgiva, where citrus, almonds and olives grow, up to the higher altitudes where chestnuts, apples and cherries flourish, and above them the pines. Finally I reached the arid track which leads to Osel Ling. It has precipitous drops on one side, with wide vistas of the rocky hills towards the sea, and I could just make out the faded silvery scar of Morocco beyond. On the other side, the smell and taste of fine cold air flowed down from the snow capped peaks above.

As soon as I arrived on the monastery's land I felt a sense of peace beyond the grief I was suffering. The whole area resonated with my soul and reminded me of my Tibetan self, who seemed much stronger than the fragile me of today.

I stopped by the prayer wheel, a huge copper cylinder filled with thousands of prayers, and gently turned it. As I did so, I walked around it and found myself chanting, '*Om mane padme hum,*' the most sacred Tibetan mantra—Hail to the jewel in the heart of the lotus. I walked slowly, stepping mindfully, as I blessed Luna and imagined her now in another realm. It felt as if I was walking beyond time as I went more deeply inwards with each turn. My noisy thoughts dropped away and I began to feel my mind clear like the azure dome of sky above me. I prayed for Luna to be at peace, and I prayed for my parents. I prayed for release from my own suffering and for the release from suffering of all sentient beings.

I felt Luna's presence telling me to be happy, just as she was happy, free and wagging her tail again! It was such a relief to feel her happiness. When the vet had injected her she'd squealed, and I'd felt terrible that this had been her last experience of life on earth.

I also felt the presence of Harold. When I'd had problems he used to say jokingly, 'Don't forget to keep the prayer wheels turning,' although he knew nothing of Tibetan Buddhism.

From the prayer wheel I followed a stony path to the stupa. Strings of Tibetan prayer flags in white, blue, yellow, green and red were tied up there fluttering gently in the breeze, scattering sacred mantras over the vast mountains. I gazed at the perfect white monument, designed with sacred geometry to represent the elements of earth, fire, air and water, and to embody the idea of the infinite spirit. I paced slowly around it clockwise feeling the cool air caress my face. The stupa contains the remains of the enlightened Lama Yeshe and thousands of prayers which the monks have placed there. It is said that by circling it you can receive many blessings from the energy within.

Nearer the monastery building is a stone painted with the Dalai Lama's famous saying, 'My religion is kindness'. I sat beneath it and thought of how the Buddhists believe that the mind is truly in the heart, and how learning to love unconditionally is the most important thing in life. I remembered how Luna had been such a teacher of unconditional love, bringing out love in everyone she met, even people who didn't really like dogs!

Sitting there, meditating in the fine thin air amidst those spacious hills, with the white cloaked mountains in the distance, I felt at peace. I remembered my dream of being initiated as a Tibetan monk, and the serenity of that monastic lifestyle, so different from the emotional roller coaster of my present life. I longed to sustain that sky-like consciousness. I reminded myself that I need to keep remembering to dip into my core Self where peace is always present.

I remembered a time I visited Assisi and felt the presence of Saint Francis as I stood by the cave where he used to meditate. I felt his voice saying: 'Pray with your feet, so that every step you take will bless the earth.' I had the image of this life being like a dance where we are both the dancer and the ones being danced by the Divine. The art of life is being able to simultaneously hold these two polarities.

I climbed the steep stony path to a bench which overlooks a pool where a huge statue of the Green Tara, goddess of compassion, has been placed. I gazed into her vibrant blue eyes, which appeared to mirror my own. She seemed to be saying:

My eyes are yours. I am always with you for we are One. Look through these eyes and never believe that you are alone, that you are not whole. Through your Being you will continue to spread love and compassion. It is your work, your purpose, and no small task to embody love and live in your heart. By the end of this life you will understand why you chose this path, why in this lifetime you have experienced illness and childlessness and have repeatedly needed to search for a home. You needed to consciously bring spirit into matter through healing your body and through finding out that your true Home is within. It is the hidden gift of your suffering. Your Path is to bring the light of awareness into everyday life for the healing of yourself and the planet.

I gazed at the distant mountains with a deep sense of blessing and serenity. I felt a wide spaciousness within, as my mind became still and dissolved into the vast arc of sky above.